HANDICAPPING

FOR BETTOR OR WORSE

HANDICAPPING
FOR BETTOR OR WORSE

A Fresh Perspective to Betting the Races

John Lindley

ECLIPSE
PRESS

Lexington, Kentucky

Library of Congress Control Number: 2003114574

ISBN 1-58150-105-6

Printed in the United States
First Edition: April 2004

Distributed to the trade by
National Book Network
4720-A Boston Way, Lanham, MD 20706
1.800.462.6420

A Division of
Blood-Horse Publications
Publishers Since 1916

Contents

Introduction

"Does it ever end?" Lonnie says aloud to no one in particular after being snapped at the wire. "I've lost so many photos they ought to bury me a nose short of the finish line after I die." While he is not too happy with the result of the previous race, he immediately walks right over to a television screen to see the odds of a different race. Does he analyze why he lost again, other than more bad luck? Probably not. Like most bettors, he will most likely handicap the next race using the identical approach, for "bettor" or worse! Why?

First, Lonnie, like most regular players, has had success here and there, so his method has merit. In fact, when most players win, they attribute it to their handicapping and betting approach. When they lose, they find something else to blame, such as bad racing luck.

Second, in the past several years the amount of handicapping information available to players has exploded — from *Daily Racing Form*'s Beyer speed figures to Sartin pace calculations to Ragozin/Thoro-Graph sheet figures. There are workout reports, trip/bias reports, breeding/training statistics, and race replays available on demand. Not only is the amount of information vast, but it also is available in many forms. Due to full card simulcasting, consider that the number of potential races available for a player to handicap has also exploded. This results in many players spending most of their time trying to use all that information and then hurrying to get their bets down. Who has time to analyze what just happened?

In addition to evaluating large amounts of information, the player must establish value, not only for individual horses, but also for many exotic wagers the player considers betting. Thus, the player's ability to choose what information to use, determine which races to bet, and figure out how to bet those races usually is key to whether the player is successful over time.

When I first attended the races, I wanted to learn more about handicapping and betting in order to win. However, my goals changed a few years later when I began selling selections (via a tip sheet). For me to be successful in selling selections, my selections had to win, and they had to win more often than those of my competitors.

Another result of being in the business of making and selling selections is that it forced me to handicap live races and many simulcast races every day. I had to come up with winning selections for every type of race, from two-year-olds sprinting two furlongs to older horses running marathon routes on the turf. To do this successfully, I had to look at all areas of handicapping and figure out what worked and what didn't. I didn't have the option of skipping a race or concentrating on a certain area of handicapping.

After a few years of selling selections, I started conducting handicapping seminars/classes. Given all the questions participants asked, I needed to be educated on all aspects of handicapping and anything related to horse racing.

I also decided to get involved in owning horses via claiming. Making decisions on claiming horses is similar to making decisions on betting them. While I haven't claimed hundreds of horses, I have claimed at least one or two a year for the past fifteen years or so. Owning and racing horses have given me a different perspective on many areas related to handicapping. For example, learning how trainers and jockeys view horse racing or what happens to the horse between its races can result in a better understanding of horse racing overall and, thus, a better ability to select winners.

After reading the first several chapters of this book, you might think "not another book that discusses speed figures, trouble, biases, Lasix, etc." It is true that most players are using the same handicapping techniques they did twenty years ago. That doesn't mean that new methods won't be offered in the future or that everything about handicapping Thoroughbreds is known. This book will focus on the most successful strategies that players use, while also discussing the advantages and drawbacks of each.

This book is based on the assumption that its readers already know how to read the *Daily Racing Form*'s past performances and are somewhat familiar with the most common elements of handicapping, such as speed figures, pace, trouble, biases, etc. Beginners may also find this book useful because it discusses many important basic elements of handicapping.

So it is my hope that after reading this book you will achieve the following:

1. Better understand the key factors involved in picking and betting a horse and some contributing factors that either are not normally considered or are misunderstood.

2. Understand the strengths and weaknesses of each of these handicapping factors.

3. Understand how to leverage the strength of any one handicapping factor by analyzing it in the context of other factors.

4. Gain some insights into value and betting strategies.

When handicapping, every player has a particular factor he emphasizes. Some players concentrate on and enjoy analyzing speed figures (see Chapter 1) or are skilled at watching races both live and on replay for valuable information (Chapter 2). Others excel at evaluating horses in the paddock or post parade (Chapter 3). Some players concentrate on backstretch decisions: jockeys, race strategy, and claiming (Chapter 4). Trying to become an "expert" in every area of handicapping is not realistic. Concentrating on a few areas while being aware of the others is how most successful players approach horse racing.

The first part of this book covers handicapping information currently available, such as speed figures and trip/trouble information, and also explores areas such as medication, the condition book, claiming, etc. Part II advises on how to approach value and wagering. Part III discusses a few areas of horse racing/handicapping that many players either misunderstand or approach with common misjudgments. One last note, following the format of most other handicapping books, I will be using examples of specific horses in specific situations. Most of these horses ran at

Emerald Downs, and a few of them were raced by my partnership. I use horses raced by my partnership because I feel confident discussing exactly what was happening to the horse while it was in training and racing.

John Lindley
Bellevue, Washington, October 2003

PART I

Making Better Use of Existing Information

In the past twenty years authors such as Andrew Beyer, James Quinn, Tom Brohamer, and Len Ragozin have written some excellent handicapping books. Many are geared toward evaluating a horse's last race or last several races to predict how it will next perform. In most cases the authors discuss evaluating speed figures along with other factors, such as form-cycle, trip, pace (early speed), bias, medication, and equipment.

These popular staples of handicapping are not new and not the only methods successful players may be using. The difference between successful and unsuccessful players most likely is a function of how the individual player applies the large amount of information available plus how that player uses a betting strategy that addresses "value." Before the 1980s, obtaining the above information wasn't as easy as it is now. These days the information is easily available and the first section of this book offers suggestions on how to evaluate and understand much of that information.

Speed Figures:
Straightforward yet Complex

Speed figures are one of the most important tools a handicapper can have. They are used to compare horses that
raced on different days and/or at different distances and to
evaluate the horse's form cycle. Speed figures are calculated after
each race and take into account several factors, including, at the
very least, the effect of the track surface on the race's final (or
fractional) time.

As most players are probably aware, a track surface can change
from day to day and sometimes within a day. This, of course,
affects the final times of the races run on that track. If the surface
is fast, resulting in fast times, those final times are more a reflec-
tion of the track surface than of the relative abilities of the horses running that day. Conversely, if the track surface is slow, the
slower final times are a result of the track surface and not the ability of the horses running that day.

The moisture in a track's surface has the greatest impact on its
speed. Even in dry, "fast-track" periods, weather (heat and wind)
affects the evaporation rate of water placed on the track. The surface becomes faster or slower, depending on how fast the water
evaporates. This varies from day to day and sometimes from race
to race. Other factors such as track maintenance may also affect
the speed of the surface.

The speed of the track surface is normally calculated by comparing that day's final times to historical averages (pars). The dif-

ferences are used to determine a variant, which is integral to calculating an accurate speed figure. If you are not familiar with pars or variants, see Appendix A at the back of this book.

Should You Use Speed Figures?

The use of speed figures exploded in the 1970s after Andy Beyer wrote about their importance in *Picking Winners*. Since then, speed figures have become available from many sources. Because most everyone has access to some sort of speed figure (such as the Beyer speed figures in the *Daily Racing Form*), many believe they offer handicappers no advantage. But, ironically, that exact explosion has made speed figure usage as advantageous as it was before speed figures became popular.

For example, compare the explosion in speed figure usage to the increase in proper play and card counting in blackjack after several books were published on those subjects. At first the casinos ran pretty scared about card counters. They soon realized, though, their fear was unwarranted. Though many people read the books, they really didn't become proficient in the method. They lacked the necessary discipline and work ethic (any mistakes will eliminate the edge) needed to win at blackjack. They fell into the category of the old saying, "a little knowledge is dangerous."

Using speed figures is very similar. Most players really don't understand how the numbers are derived and how to use them properly. While using speed figures is not an absolute requirement to be a successful player, having accurate figures and properly applying them will give you an advantage.

Which Speed Figures Should You Use?

There are two key steps to using speed figures. The first is to arrive accurately at a speed figure for each race and each horse. The second is to evaluate a horse's previous speed figure or series of speed figures to determine what that horse is most likely to run in its next outing.

Today's most popular speed figures are of three types: Beyer speed figures, sheet figures, and pace figures. All are explained in detail in some of the more popular handicapping books (see the bibliography in the back of this book).

Even recognized experts still debate the use of speed figures. Just after the *Daily Racing Form* started printing Beyer speed figures as part of its past performances in 1993, Andy Beyer's fourth and most recent book, *Beyer on Speed,* was published. Beyer devoted several pages to discussing Ragozin's sheet figures and Brohamer/Sartin pace calculations and the drawbacks of using them exclusively. Beyer also recognized some of the insights that Len Ragozin brought to handicapping. When Ragozin published *The Odds Must Be Crazy* in 1997, he offered a fairly strong defense of his figures, in response to Beyer, while at the same time criticizing Beyer's figures. While Beyer and Ragozin have significantly different perspectives of speed figures and their use, there is room for both of their views.

Most players concentrate on using one type of speed figure, and a single method to evaluate that speed figure. They don't pay too much attention to other types of speed figures. However, being aware of the different types of speed figures that other players (your competition) are using can help you in several ways.

First, you may recognize why certain horses are drawing play. You almost certainly have looked at the betting of any one race and asked, "Why is the number four horse getting play?" The answer may be that a certain speed figure or method has pointed out that horse, and the players who use that figure or method are lining up in droves to bet on it. Maybe the horse has a big Beyer advantage, maybe the horse has a pace advantage, or maybe it has a nice "sheet" line pointing toward improvement.

Also, knowing how other players are thinking and/or knowing what other players are looking at can help you determine where the money will be bet, thus helping you in determining value. For example, you might look at a race and think to yourself, The Beyer players are going to bet the three, the pace players are going to be betting the six, and the sheet players will key on the seven. If you can look at a race and see where other players may be concentrating their betting, you will be better able to predict which horses may be overbet/underbet in advance of the race, thus using that expectation in planning your wagers (discussed in Chapter 5).

Second, by being aware of and understanding each type of

speed figure and/or method, you will be able to improve your overall handicapping even if you don't use that type of speed figure/method. Each speed figure/method is based on some fundamental "truths" in handicapping. Being aware of those "truths" can only help you, even if you don't use that particular method. At the same time, any one of those methods, if followed exclusively, may lead players astray in any given race because each has drawbacks that may not be well known.

This chapter deals with the pros and cons of the three most popular types of speed figures. Understanding their strengths and drawbacks can be very useful in your handicapping, especially if you know how those speed figures are derived, what they include, and what they don't include. You can gain even more of an advantage by doing your own speed figures, a process that is discussed later in this chapter.

What works best for you can only be determined by your interest and available time. I have a strong background in math, so doing speed figures comes naturally to me. If calculating your own speed figures is out of the question, let's make sure you understand the commercial numbers you are using.

Beyer Figures

Most everyone with basic handicapping knowledge is familiar with the Beyer speed figures and how to locate them in the *Daily Racing Form*. However, I've found that many people don't know how these figures are derived or what they include.

Beyer Associates compiles the speed figures that are in the *Daily Racing Form*. The company employs several people who calculate the daily variant for those tracks they cover. The *Daily Racing Form* then purchases and publishes those figures.

Beyer speed figures are fairly straightforward. They are a measure of a horse's final time in a race and are calculated by adjusting a horse's final time for the speed of the track surface and for the lengths by which it was beaten (if any). The horse's final time is converted into a number that makes it easy to compare horses that raced on different days over different distances.

The winner receives the top speed figure, and all the other competitors' speed figures are calculated based on a lengths-beaten chart, which assigns a specific number to each length (or partial length) a horse was beaten by, then subtracts that from the winning horse's speed figure. The actual number subtracted for each length beaten varies, depending on the distance of the race. The scale of the Beyer speed figures spreads from 0 to the 130s, though there is no limit. The higher the number earned, the better the horse's effort. Instead of saying a horse was beaten three lengths at six and a half furlongs on a day when the track was three-fifths of a second fast (the track variant) and the winner's time was 1:16⅗, the Beyer figure will condense all that information and assign a figure of 85.

While the Beyer figures are accurate for the most part, it is important to consider what they do not include. Many factors can affect a horse's final time: the early fractions of a race, the trouble or loss of ground during a race, and, on occasion, a track bias that may favor a certain type of horse, such as front runners or horses that race on a certain part of the track, such as along the rail. Beyer speed figures are not adjusted for any of these or other common variables. They also do not take class levels into consideration.

In his books Beyer suggests handicappers look at each speed figure in the context of "how it was earned."

For example, was the speed figure earned as a result of a perfect trip, a lonely lead, or a wet track? If so, that speed figure can be discounted if a similar condition is not likely when the horse races next. If the speed figure was earned despite a rough trip or by contesting a fast pace or against a bias, Beyer suggests you upgrade those speed figures. By establishing how each horse earned its speed figure, you can better compare the recent efforts of each horse.

In addition to understanding the circumstances surrounding any particular horse's Beyer speed figures, you should also understand how speed figures from very long or short distances don't translate well to mid-range races, how speed figures vary from track to track, and how speed figures can sometimes be inaccurate.

Distance

Beyer states that speed figures earned in a sprint (a one-turn race) don't translate well to a route (a two-turn race) and vice versa. In each case Beyer says the horse may earn similar speed figures when going from a sprint to a route (or from a route to a sprint), but there is no direct expectation that a horse will be able to repeat sprint figures in routes.

In my experience, good speed figures earned in short sprint races, such as five furlongs, don't imply that the horse will earn similar speed figures at normal sprint races such as six and a half furlongs. A good speed figure earned in a short sprint is probably more of a result of the horse being able to "go all out" for the entire distance. In a longer sprint that effort wouldn't be sustainable.

In addition, it is also my experience that the speed figures earned by horses in the longer route races, such as a mile and one-eighth or longer, don't translate well to speed figures earned by those same horses in the normal route races. The breeding industry in the United States breeds horses for speed, not distance. Many horses that route successfully at one mile or a mile and one-sixteenth may find that a mile and one-eighth or longer is too far.

On the flip side, the few horses that are bred more for distance earn average speed figures at one mile to a mile and one-sixteenth and can earn better figures in the longer races.

Tracks

Beyer says that, ideally, a speed figure of 80 earned at Santa Anita would be the same as a speed figure of 80 earned at Hoosier Park. While in general this is true, experience has taught me that horses at certain tracks may be earning higher Beyer speed figures that are inflated (or undervalued) in relation to other tracks.

The circuit I follow (West Coast) includes Emerald Downs near Seattle and northern California tracks. Figure 1.1 is for Cash'n Prizes, a horse that raced for the partnership with which I am involved. After winning his last three starts at Emerald Downs, Cash'n Prizes shipped to Golden Gate Fields. The Beyer speed figures published in the *Daily Racing Form* for his two starts at Golden Gate (70 and 75) were significantly higher than his Emerald Downs figures (61, 62, and 64). The speed figures I calculated myself didn't reflect the same large improvement. In fact, my figures from his efforts at Emerald Downs didn't vary much from my figures for his efforts at Golden Gate. I found it hard to believe that Cash'n Prizes' Beyer speed figures suddenly improved fourteen points from his last start at Emerald Downs (61) to his first start at Golden Gate (75).

Figure 1.1

'n Prizes

ned from Turf Club North for $8,000, Glatt Ron Trainer 1997(as of 2/15): (-)														
–4GG gd 1⅟₁₆	:22⁴ :46² 1:10⁴1:43²	Clm 10000	**70**	3	1¹	1¹	1¹	3²	35¾	Gonzalez R M	LB117 b	2.20	80– 15	*CherokeeCal*119ⁿᵏ GrandpHillis117⁵½ CshnPrizes117ⁿᵒ	Set pace rail, wknd 6
–3GG fst 1	:22³ :45⁴ 1:10²1:36³	Clm 8500(8.5–7.5)	**75**	1	12½	1²	1²	2ʰᵈ	2¹	Gonzalez R M	LB117 b	2.90	86– 16	TacticalAlert117¹ CashnPrizes117¹½ *CherokeeCi*122¹½	Set pace rail, wknd 9

viously trained by Glatt Mark

–2EmDsly 1	:23¹ :46³ 1:11⁴1:40²	Clm 6250(6.25–5)	**61**	5	12½	1²	1²	1⁴	1²	Belvoir V T	LB122 b	*1.10	- -	Cash'n Prizes122² Chirrup116½ Delicate Balance120½	Driving 6
–6EmDfst 1	:23¹ :47 1:11⁴1:39	Clm 6250(6.25–5)	**62**	2	1⁴	1²	12²₂	1³	12½	Belvoir V T	LB122 b	*1.30	- -	*Cash'n Prizes*122²½ Delicate Balance120½ Chirrup114¹4½	Led throughout 5
–2EmDsly 1⅟₁₆	:23³ :48 1:13³1:48²	Ⓢ Clm 6250(6.25–5)	**64**	5	1³	12½	1²	1³	1¹	Belvoir V T	LB121 b	2.90	- -	*Cash'n Prizes*121¹ Foot Race120½ Delicate Balance120⁶	Led throughout 6

Experience has shown me that when a horse ships from Emerald Downs to a northern California track, its Beyer speed figures tend to increase, most likely because the speed figures calculated for Emerald Downs are a bit low.

You may want to evaluate these types of patterns in the tracks you follow most closely to ascertain the validity of certain Beyer speed figures. Also, horses shipped from another track might not repeat their previous speed figures because track surfaces differ, such as sand-based tracks versus dirt-based tracks. A horse's body type, conformation, or shape of foot may be better suited to one type of track surface over another.

Inaccuracies

When using the *Daily Racing Form*'s Beyer speed figures, you may notice some other inaccuracies. The individuals calculating the Beyer speed figures sometimes break up the daily variants (for example, use one variant for the first few races and then a different variant for the rest of the races on any given day), which could result in some discrepancies, or they may make separate figures for an "odd" race (more on those later in this chapter). This may be good, as the track surface can change speed during the day, so if the figure maker breaks up the variant, the resulting speed figures will be more accurate. But it does leave room for human error, and you should be aware of these potential inaccuracies when using Beyer speed figures.

For example, Figure 1.2 shows two horses, Wild Blackberries and Bishop Wins, both of whom ran at Emerald Downs on the same day, over the same distance. The raw final time for Bishop

Wins was :59 flat; the Beyer speed figure assigned was 57. Wild Blackberries ran her five furlongs in :59⅗, three-fifths of a second slower than Bishop Wins ran his five furlongs, yet the Beyer speed figure assigned was 60.

Wild Blackberries

Figure 1.2

21Jun01–2EmDfst	5f	:22¹ :46¹	:59³	⑤Md 16000	**60** 7 1	2hd 2hd 1hd 1hd	Mitchell G V	LB117	1.50 79– 18	*WildBlackberries*117hd ShastLke119² BogusPln1171¾ Stiff drive, preva

Bishop Wins

21Jun01–3EmDfst	5f	:22³ :46²	:59	Md 25000	**57** 6 3	2¹½ 2½ 1¹ 12¾	Russell B R	B118 b	2.00 82– 18	Bishop Wins1182¾ Tough Jazz118no Stamper119hd Prompted, drew cl

I don't know why Wild Blackberries' win was assigned a Beyer speed figure of 60 and Bishop Wins' race was assigned a 57 despite Bishop Wins' race being run faster. The races were within twenty-five minutes of each other, and there was no change in the weather or anything else that might have affected the speed of the track surface.

There are many times when you might come across similar Beyer figures that do not make sense; be aware that there can be miscalculations. Beyer Associates reviews its figures monthly and will make adjustments if necessary.

Fancy High first received an 81 for his effort on November 25, 2001. When Fancy High appeared after his December 15, 2001, race, the speed figure for November 25 race had been adjusted to a 74 (Figure 1.3).

Fancy High

Figure 1.3

25Nov01–7GG gd 6f	:21² :43⁴ :56¹¹:08⁴ 3+ Clm 16000(16–14)	**81** 1 10	53½ 35½ 45½ 37½	Baze R A	LB117 fb	*2.10 86– 12	El Diago117⁶ Court Shenanigans1171½ FancyHigh1171½ Off slow, svd grn
27Oct01–6BM fst 6f	:22 :44³ :56³1:09 3+ Clm 20000(20–18)	**86** 7 1	2¹½ 2² 1hd 2²	Baze R A	LB117 b	3.60 94– 08	*LytleCreek*119² FncyHigh117² ByshoreBoulvrd1173½ Prssd pace 2w, wkn
25Nov01–7GG gd 6f	:21² :43⁴ :56¹¹:08⁴ 3+ Clm 16000(16–14)	**74** 1 10	53½ 35½ 45½ 37½	Baze R A	LB117 fb	*2.10 86– 12	El Diago117⁶ Court Shenanigans1171½ FancyHigh1171½ Off slow, svd grn
27Oct01–6BM fst 6f	:22 :44³ :56³1:09 3+ Clm 20000(20–18)	**86** 7 1	2¹½ 2² 1hd 2²	Baze R A	LB117 b	3.60 94– 08	*LytleCreek*119² FncyHigh117² ByshoreBoulvrd1173½ Prssd pace 2w, wkn

Also be aware that speed figures for turf races are difficult to calculate because of the limited number run at any track on any given day. This makes it difficult to come up with an accurate variant. In addition, Beyer speed figures earned on the dirt may not translate well to the turf and vice versa.

One last note: the above discussions (distance, tracks, discrepancies) may apply to all types of speed figures, not just Beyer's.

Summary

Overall, Beyer speed figures are a great handicapping tool. When I am traveling to an unfamiliar track or when I am scanning races at tracks I normally don't follow, I first look at the Beyer speed figures in each horse's past performances to see if anything catches my eye. If I find any horses that appear to have an advantage based on those speed figures, I will look at the race more closely. Finding a horse that has tactical speed and competitive Beyer speed figures is a quick way to come up with a play, especially if the odds are reasonable.

The key to using Beyer speed figures is to evaluate how they were earned. While the Beyer speed figures are fairly accurate, you need to keep track of some of the many factors that influence each figure to use them to their fullest extent.

Sheet Figures and Pattern Analysis

"Sheet figures" are also popular among handicappers who use speed figures. Jerry Brown's Thoro-Graph figures and Len Ragozin's sheet figures are similarly derived and used, though each claims his is better. I treat them as equal and refer to both of them as either "the sheets" or "sheet figures." These figures have some commonalities with Beyer speed figures and also some significant differences, which will be discussed in the next few pages.

Sheet figures use a scale opposite of Beyer speed figures — the lower the number the better the result. The best or lowest sheet figures range from 0 to -3 with most sheet figures ranging from 40 to 0. Like the Beyer speed figures, the sheet figures reflect final times adjusted for the speed of the track surface and lengths beaten (if any). The sheet figures are also adjusted for a horse's loss of ground, the weight carried (jockey and saddle), the effect of wind, and any other observations deemed important. Sheet figures try to measure a horse's total effort.

Both Ragozin and Brown have independent contractors watching horses run at most racetracks they cover. These observers keep track of things such as loss of ground and wind changes, and they time the races from when the gates open, rather than when the horses cross the beam at the initial distance marker. They also clock some horses, picked at random, to address the potential inaccuracy of the race chart's running lines. This can give the observers an advantage when analyzing final times to determine a variant, for example, when there are timer malfunctions or when the gates for turf races are not placed in the same location for similar distances (many tracks move the "rails" in or out to protect the surface, which may result in a different gate placement for the same distance), or when the result charts published by Equibase contain inaccuracies. (Equibase is the company that collects the data from which the past performances of the *Daily Racing Form* are derived.)

While the winning horse in any given race will earn the top Beyer speed figure for that race, the winning horse in the race may not earn the "top" (lowest) sheet figure. In other words, a horse that raced wide and/or carried more weight could earn a better sheet figure than the winner, who may have carried light weight and/or had a ground-saving trip.

So what do the sheet figures not include? As of this writing, in their calculations of sheet figures neither Ragozin nor Brown appears to consider the pace (early fractions of the race) and its possible effect on the horse's final placing.[1] Track biases are also not included in sheet figures.

Sheet users give three general reasons why early fractions and track bias aren't considered. First, they say including both would lead to more problems than they'd be worth because of the difficulty quantifying them. Each horse in a race is affected differently by any given pace scenario, and track biases are subjective and even more difficult to translate into a speed figure.

Second, sheet users say they would be able to "read through," or ignore, an exceptionally good or bad effort caused by either an extreme pace or track bias because they look at a horse's overall sheet figure pattern.

Finally, sheet users think that if other players don't use sheet figures because of the omission of early fractions or track bias, those who do use the sheets will be better off because fewer players will be betting "sheet" horses, thus resulting in better odds.

Handicappers at smaller tracks may never have heard of the sheets, as they are more popular at the larger tracks. In fact, at Emerald Downs I know of only one person who is using the sheets. Whether you are familiar with the sheets or not, you have

---

[1]Thoro-Graph, while not using early fractions or possible bias in calculating Thoro-Graph figures, will mark or note a bad rail or a fast/slow pace on a horse's sheet.

probably heard some sheet terms for racing patterns, such as the "bounce." And again, even if you are not aware of the sheets, you should be aware that players who do use them are betting a significant amount of money at those larger tracks.

Sheet-Pattern Analysis

Both Beyer speed figures and sheet figures are measures of previous races. Beyer figures are a measure of a horse's final time adjusted for the speed of the surface and lengths beaten (if any). Sheet figures measure a horse's total effort, as they incorporate weight, ground loss, and the effect of wind (from which precise mathematical adjustments can be assigned). Again, both are just measures of previous races. Just because a horse earned a big Beyer speed figure or a low sheet figure in its last race doesn't mean that it will repeat the performance in its next race. Using either type of figure to predict the future is your job. So how do you go about that with sheet figures?

As described in the previous section, Beyer suggests evaluating each Beyer speed figure in the context of "how it was earned" — and then comparing the horses running in the race to see which one is fastest. Both Brown and Ragozin go much further in the use of their sheet figures. They publish graphs on sheets of paper, from which the name "sheets" is derived.

Sheet makers provide the sheets (with the figures) and each handicapper (customer) is supposed to use his own handicapping skills (in pattern analysis), but some don't want to or don't have the time for the analysis, so they purchase an analysis in addition.

The sheet figures for a horse's races are commonly called "lines" and go back as far as three years. You look at a horse's "line" and use established "patterns" to evaluate what type of sheet figure that horse may run. In other words, you compare a horse with itself and see where it is going from a conditioning (form cycle) point of view. Will the horse's form be likely to improve, repeat, or regress from its recent races? Based on that analysis, you predict the sheet figure it may run. You look at each horse in this way and then compare them based on their expected sheet figures.

For example, the sheet makers suggest looking for horses that have an improving or a recently improved (but not too much improved) sheet figure without having reached its "top," the highest sheet figure the horse has earned. Sheet makers also emphasize looking for value.

Some common patterns that originated with the sheet makers are "bounce" or "react," "pair-ups," and "0-2-X." These are only a few of the possible patterns, and they are fairly simple examples. Sheet pattern analysis can become complicated, and it may take years of experience to become an "expert."

Bouncing or reacting is probably the most easily recognizable sheet pattern. The pattern suggests that if a horse comes off a huge or much-improved race, it is more likely to regress or not repeat that effort in its next start. Not all horses will bounce off a "top"; some may even improve. But a horse's chances of bouncing are directly related to its previous sheet figures and the amount of rest it has had between starts. Also, the chances for bouncing are different for horses of different age groups, for sprinters versus routers, for females versus males, and for turf performers versus dirt performers

For example, Royal Bengal Tiger ran big on March 15, 2003, after being away from the races for more than nine months. He came back quickly (fifteen days later) and was bet down to 1-2 off his March 15 effort. His effort (a third) in his March 30 race was a classic bounce (Figure 1.4).

Royal Bengal Tiger

Figure 1.4

30Mar03– 8OP	fst	5½f	:22³	:47¹	:59² 1:05⁴	Md Sp Wt 31k		61	2	1	3¹	42¾	3ⁿᵏ	3²	Marquez C H Jr	L116	*.50	85– 17 ElusiveFigure121ʰᵈ BartsPage121² RoylBenglTiger1161½	Not enough la
15Mar03– 8OP	fst	6f	:21³	:44⁴	:57¹ 1:10¹	Md Sp Wt 30k		86	11	3	3³	4²	3⁴	42¼	Murphy B G	L116	8.20	87– 15 Mr Rocket116² Wish and Try123ʰᵈ Saint Waki116ⁿᵒ	Not enough la
25May02– 3LS	fst	5f	:22³	:46³	:59²	Md Sp Wt 27k		58	6	4	3²	3²	2²	23½	Meche D J	118	4.20	86– 20 RoylMmbo1183½ RoylBnglTgr118² KcknKontry118²	Bid 1/8, no match la

WORKS: Sep11 AP 4f fst :49² B *8/31*

Alleged Whisper is another good example of a "bounce." On July 20 at Belmont she earned a Thoro-Graph figure of an 8, this after running figures of between 12 and 17 in all her previous races. Sheet users would predict a bounce off that 8, which was also a lifetime top. She did bounce and received a 15 in her next start when running at Saratoga on August 21 (Figure 1.5, with Thoro-Graph figures listed to the left of her past performances).

Pair-up is another common sheet figure pattern. If a horse has two similar efforts, it is said to pair-up its sheet figures. This pat-

Figure 1.5

TG Alleged Whisper

ure																			
15	21Aug03-7Sar	fm	1	Ⓣ :243 :483 1:124 1:363	3↑ⒻⓈAlw 46000N2x	**66**	7	32	42	31	76¾	98½	Santos J A	L115	4.90	80- 10	ExchangeBay119½ BeebeLake1191¾ BoundOnBi119hd	Chased 3 wide, tired	9
8	20Jly03-7Bel	fm	1	Ⓣ :231 :46 1:103 1:351	3↑ⒻⓈAlw 46000N2x	**82**	9	57½	710	41¾	22	24¼	Santos J A	L115	6.40	80- 16	*DynmicLis*1204¼ AllegdWhispr115¾ CountingVisions1204	Gamely for place	10
15	25Jun03-7Bel	fst	1	:223 :452 1:103 1:363	3↑ⒻⓈAlw 46000N2x	**62**	1	411	513	47½	58	46	Santos J A	L114	7.30	77- 17	HotGoldenJet1141 Broughshn1172 BuckMountin1203	Inside trip, no rally	6
12	11Jun03-6Bel	fst	7f	:222 :452 1:10 1:23	3↑ⒻⓈAlw 45000N2x	**67**	2	7	53	42½	36½	36¼	Coa E M	L118	8.70	79- 17	StSmnth1184¾ *KrkrmCrsdr*1201½ AllgdWhspr118hd	Chased outside, no bid	8
13	15May03-9Bel	fst	6½f	:221 :452 1:111 1:182	3↑ⒻⓈAlw 43000N1x	**65**	1	4	84¾	45	33	1nk	Santos J A	L115	10.60	81- 12	AllegedWhisper115nk ShesSwthrt117hd *Cologny*1153½	Inside move, in time	11
	Previously trained by Moquett Ronald E																		
17	17Apr03-4Kee	sly	7f	:224 :471 1:131 1:271	ⒻClm 30000	**50**	9	3	52	32	69	711	Velasquez C	L118 f	13.20	57- 22	JoyousAppl1202 GoldnDyjur1181¾ WstrnHonor1162	Stalked,5w,weakened	12
12	30Mar03-6TP	fst	6f	:222 :461 :584 1:122	3↑ⒻMd 30000(30-20)	**58**	2	6	65	67½	43½	1½	Lumpkins J	L115 f	3.70	80- 17	Alleged Whisper115½ Lady Viking1151¼ A Diller a Dollar1186	Finished fast	10

tern suggests that the horse will have a good chance to "go forward" (improve) in its next race. Again, this is in relation to a horse's overall sheet figures or line.

The 0-2-X pattern is also common. The 0 is a recent top sheet figure, or best effort; the 2 is a race close to the top; and the X is the bounce or poor effort. In general, a horse can be expected to put in a good race after this pattern.

Molta Vita is a good example of a "0-2-X" pattern. When she ran at Churchill Downs on July 4, she earned a Thoro-Graph figure of a 3, which was a lifetime top. In her next start on July 26 at Saratoga, she earned a 4 (in the 0-2-X pattern, the next start after the top doesn't have to be exactly two points from the top, just close). Sheet users would see these two races as fitting an 0-2-X pattern and then predict a bounce or poor effort in her next start on August 23. In that start on August 23, she did bounce to an 8. Finally, to complete the pattern, sheet users would expect her to put in a good effort in her next race, which was on September 18 at Belmont, a race she did win at 4-1 (Figure 1.6).

Figure 1.6

G Molto Vita

re																			
	18Sep03-8Bel	fst	6f	:223 :454 :58 1:102	3↑ⒻAlw 51000N3x	**94**	3	3	2½	2hd	11½	1nk	Santos J A	L118	4.10	87- 12	Molto Vita118nk Tina Bull1203¾ City Sister1201½	Clear, gamely, held on	5
8	23Aug03-7Sar	fst	6f	:22 :45 :564 1:093	ⒻVctoryRide76k	**79**	4	4	52½	62¾	65½	66¼	Santos J A	L116	6.00	88- 07	CountryRomnc116½ ShsZlous114¾ EbonyBrz1222½	Stumbled start, chased	9
4	26Jly03-9Sar	fst	7f	:223 :451 1:081 1:204	ⒻTest-G1	**92**	3	5	1½	1hd	47½	57¾	Coa E M	L116	37.25	95- 08	Lady Tak1224½ Bird Town1221½ *House Party*1221¾	Stumbled start, tired	7
3	4Jly03-4CD	fst	7f	:223 :45 1:092 1:221	ⒻAlw 67980NC	**94**	1	1	23	21	12½	14¾	Velasquez C	L120	2.50	91- 10	Molto Vita1204¾ Souris1181¾ Belle of Perintown1185¼	4w,driving,clear	4
8	30May03-8CD	fst	7f	:223 :453 1:11 1:234	3↑ⒻAlw 42200N1x	**81**	5	2	51¼	72	2hd	12½	Velasquez C	L114	6.50	83- 16	*MoltoVita*1142½ Chirimoya111nk ChanceDance114nk	Bmp start,split,drv,5w	8
8	17May03-2CD	sly	1	:222 :46 1:121 1:39	3↑ⒻAlw 37325N1x	**78**	7	21	21½	21	21½	21¾	Velasquez C	L114	2.30	70- 24	GloriousGrace1171¾ *MoltoVita*1142 KeyApproval117hd	Pressed,4w,2ndbest	7
9	30Apr03-8CD	fst	7f	:221 :444 1:10 1:23	ⒻAlw 33460N1x	**75**	10	2	31½	44½	42½	45	Desormeaux K J	L119	12.90	82- 13	*Spoken Fur*121nk Meet Me At Midnite1173½ *Stellar*1151¼	5w trip,empty late	11
5	11Apr03-5Kee	gd	6f	:212 :452 :573 1:101	ⒻAlw 54000N1x	**58**	11	6	41	33	66¼	615½	Day P	L118	7.40	72- 14	Crow Jane1185 Halory Leigh1163¾ Dance Hall Girl1202½	6w trip,flatten out	11
9	2Mar03-6FG	fst	6f	:221 :461 :584 1:113	ⒻMd Sp Wt 26k	**74**	1	4	11	11	1hd	11½	Day P	L119	*1.00	82- 18	Molto Vita1191½ Majestic Smoke1194½ Rouquine119no	Ridden out	7

While both Ragozin and Brown suggest using *their* pattern analysis in conjunction with *their* sheet figures, their insights on a horse's form cycles can be valuable to players who do not use their sheet figures, because in general a horse's performance will follow these types of patterns (keep in mind that there is a lot more to reading a horse's line than the above patterns, which are only a few of the possibilities). Many players will apply sheet patterns when using the Beyer speed figures. You might hear or read that "this horse bounced off his big Beyer of 91 last time" or "this horse paired up on his Beyer last time and is ready to move forward." On the surface there may be nothing wrong with applying sheet patterns to Beyer speed figures (or other speed figures), but remember that *each figure is measuring different things* — Beyer speed figures are only a measure of a horse's final time adjusted for the speed of the track surface, whereas sheet figures try to measure a horse's total performance. Neither includes many other factors that can affect either a horse's final time or a horse's total performance.

Disadvantages of Sheet Figures and Pattern Analysis

One disadvantage of regularly using the Ragozin/Thoro-Graph figures is their expense (about $30 per day; and if you use them, you must win enough to cover their costs). But the biggest disadvantage in evaluating patterns such as bounces, pair-ups, etc., using sheet figures (or Beyer speed figures) is that these figures are not all-inclusive of a horse's performance. Beyer has emphasized (in his books) that his (Beyer) speed figures are not all-inclusive of a horse's performance. But both Ragozin and Brown are very confident that their figures are a complete measure of a horse's total performance. They believe their sheet figures are the most comprehensive information available regarding a horse's previous performances. Obviously, many sheet users realize other factors affect a horse's previous performance, but they view those factors as having minimal impact.

For example, let's say you have a horse that has run the figures shown in Table 1-1 for her last four races:

Table 1-1.

Race	Beyer Speed Figure	Sheet Speed Figure
November 12	69	23
October 25	79	16
October 3	72	22
September 12	71	21

Players using either Beyer speed figures or sheet figures may say the horse bounced off her good race on October 25 in her next start on November 12. But, in reality, since neither figure includes every factor that affected the horse's final performance, bouncing may have had nothing to do with the lower figure earned in her last start. For example, perhaps she is a front runner, and in her two starts, September 12 and October 3, she battled for the lead but tired a bit late. In her start on October 25, maybe she was able to get clear early while setting slow early fractions. Then in her most recent race, on November 12, she again battled for the lead and tired. In this case she didn't bounce at all. Instead, her total performance was a result of the pace rather than a bounce. While this is a simple and obvious example, similar scenarios occur frequently.

Other factors also impact a horse's performance. For example, in adjusting for ground loss, horses that race on or near the lead don't go wide very often, and horses that come from behind are pretty much always wide. The sheet figures will, in a way, give a horse credit for having no early speed because it was wide, when, in fact, it is always wide. The same problem exists with horses that don't break quickly or always tend to break slowly.

Many sheet users are cognizant of these drawbacks, and their handicapping success is testament to their ability to analyze patterns and apply theories.

I had an interesting exchange on both Thoro-Graph's web site (thorograph.com) and Ragozin's web site (thesheets.com) about some horses my partnership had been running that illustrates the drawback of not having complete information. Comparing the two sheet makers' (through their bulletin boards) analysis of the horses' patterns with my firsthand knowledge of the horses gives a little more detail about some of the disadvantages of using any speed figure in analyzing form cycles.

The Novelist

Figure 1.7

One of the horses we discussed is The Novelist, whom my partners and I claimed in May 2000. Figure 1.7 shows his *Daily Racing*

Form past performances prior to his January 10, 2001, race, with the Thoro-Graph figures added to the left of each race (for The Novelist's entire sheet, please see Appendix B).

Posting to Thoro-Graph's bulletin board, I asked what other participants thought of The Novelist's line prior to his January 10, 2001, race. Here are their comments: "Right off the bat when you look at this sheet you notice that this horse has had problems physically racing only for a four-month stretch as a three-year-old and four-year-old. Also, while he developed from age three through age four in terms of improving his tops, the top efforts did affect him. As a five-year-old this year, The Novelist has run in many more races, but he did not get back to his four-year-old top until that first race in California, his ninth race that year. Twelve was the best he could do prior to the 6. The 6 was a four-point new top, and one has to think it will knock him out for a long while. Note that trainer M Glatt is good with first timers in his barn, and he did get a number out of this horse (referring to the 6 on October 14). He may improve some today, but the line is negative, and there are horses with much stronger lines in the race."

These comments seem to make sense when you look at the horse's past performances. However, the Thoro-Graph bulletin board posts made two comments about The Novelist that really had nothing to do with his "line." The first is about his racing for only four-month stretches as a three- and four-year-old. Emerald Downs is open for only five months a year, and there really isn't another track in the Northwest where local owners can run a horse like The Novelist. Many locally owned horses will run for only four or five months during any given year, even when the horse has no physical problems.

Second, the comment that trainer Mark Glatt (Thoro-Graph also very actively promotes and sells trainer statistics) has done well when starting a horse for the first time wasn't quite right because the horse was not a first-time starter for Mark. He trains with his father, Ron, who had entered the horse under his own name in its previous races.

Also, I, as one of the owners, was aware of many other factors that came into play. Here is some specific information about each of the races shown in Figure 1.7:

October 14, 2000 (Figure 1.8) — Thoro-Graph figure 6. My notes: He had a perfect trip, sitting fourth off a three-horse speed duel and did earn one of his better lifetime speed figures.

Figure 1.8

Oct00– 2B M fst 6f   :22⁴ :45⁴ :57³1:10 3↑ Clm 8000(8-7)   86 5 3   42¼ 1¹ 1⁵ 16½ Gonzalez R M   LB 117 b   3.80 89– 15 TheNovelist1176½ StreetsofLrdo117³ Puddls1173½   Ranged 4w, ridden out 5
Previously trained by Glatt Ron

November 10, 2000 (Figure 1.9) — Thoro-Graph figure 12. My notes: To me, in regard to pace and final figures, he ran a race similar to his effort on October 14. The sheet figure had him bouncing to a 12. I did have his final speed figure a bit slower than his effort on October 14, but he contested a much faster half-mile fraction in this race, offsetting the decrease in his final figures (the raw half-mile fraction was a *full second* quicker).

Figure 1.9

Nov00– 7B M fst 6f   :22¹ :44⁴ :57¹1:10 3↑ Alw 32560n1x   80 4 5   32½ 3² 4³ 5³   Radke K   LB 119 b   10.50 86– 14 Unshackled116¾ Hobar119¾ Seayabyebye119¹½   2w turn, even late 8

November 24, 2000 (Figure 1.10) — Thoro-Graph figure 10. My notes: While his sheet figure varied somewhat from his first two starts in California (6 to 12 to 10), I had him running speed figures (pace and final time) similar to his two preceding races.

Figure 1.10

24Nov00– 7G G fst 6f   :22 :44⁴ :56⁴1:09 3↑ Alw 32000n1x   78 10 8   63½ 2½ 21½ 43¾ Schvaneveldt C P LB 119 fb 33.40 91– 10 Kinetic Bend118¾ Seayabyebye119¹ Play Well T C116²   Bid 3w, flttnd out 10

December 24, 2000 (Figure 1.11) — Thoro-Graph figure 14. My notes: So what happened? The sheet implied that the "6" earned on October 14 would knock him out for a while, and maybe they were using this race as proof (remember, they said his overall pattern was negative). But, in reality, on December 24 the horse was stuck inside for the entire race. While not obviously blocked, he just never really had room. Also, he hates running while inside of horses; he becomes intimidated.

Figure 1.11

24Dec00– 7G G fst 6f   :22 :45² :57⁴1:10³ 3↑ Clm 20000(20-18)   67 1 7   63¾ 7⁵ 7⁶ 6⁶   Radke K   LB 117 fb 7.40 81– 16 Woking117hd Nabber1171¼ C Merrill Run1172½   Svd grnd to no avail 8

When the race for January 10, 2001, came along, I expected a good effort because he drew an outside post (Figure 1.12 on following page). The Thoro-Graph analysis had an opposite expectation based on his pattern.

Figure 1.12

10Jan01-3GG	sly	6f	:212	:432	:553	1:084	4↑ Clm 16000(16-14)	**81**	5	3	21½	2½	2hd	23	Gonzalez R M	**LB**117 fb	10.30	91-11	Be the Bunny1173 TheNovelist117no *MintRoyale*116no	Pressed, bid, he

After the race, in which he ran second after forcing some rocket fractions, Thoro-Graph's bulletin board said "he ran well but overall his line was negative." I disagreed because I had found the horse to run much the same race (based on pace and speed figures) as in each of his starts in California except the December 24 start, and he continued to run similar races until April 15, 2001. The Novelist's efforts (at least to me) were fairly consistent; his "line" was consistent rather than negative. Below are The Novelist's past performances through his April 15, 2001, race with his Thoro-Graph figures (Figure 1.13).

Figure 1.13

TG The Novelist

TG Figure																					
10	15Apr01-5BM	fst	6f	:222	:45	:571	1:094	4↑ Alw 12500s	**74**	3	6	65¼	43½	43	55¼	Alvarado F T	**LB**119 fb	2.60	87-12	BetheBunny1221½ DependbleWill117¾ Thisonsforrni1171	2w turn, r
6	31Mar01-3GG	fst	6f	:22	:443	:564	1:091	4↑ Clm 25000(25-22.5)	**88**	5	4	33	32	3nk	1hd	Alvarado F T	**LB**117 fb	6.40	92-12	TheNovelist117hd *BthBunny*1191½ FlyingDnoumnt1171½	Bid 3w, dug
8	28Feb01-6GG	fst	6f	:214	:443	:57	1:094	4↑ Alw 35360N1X	**78**	5	6	65¼	64¾	62¾	51½	Alvarado F T	**LB**119 fb	19.90	88-17	Airiasaffair1181 Subpoena118hd Jaklin's Last Kin118no	3w turn,
9	11Feb01-8GG	wf	6f	:214	:443	:563	1:091	4↑ Clm 25000(25-22.5)	**81**	1	7	75¾	54½	53½	32¼	Gonzalez R M	**LB**117 fb	12.80	90-09	Brodrick117nk AmericanShine1192 TheNovelist1171½	Steadied nea
8	21Jan01-3GG	fst	6f	:213	:434	:552	1:08	4↑ Clm 22500(25-22.5)	**83**	4	4	33	23	24	36¼	Gonzalez R M	**LB**115 fb	16.20	92-09	Orvald1126 First Stringer119nk The Novelist115¾	Stlkd 3w
12	10Jan01-3GG	sly	6f	:212	:432	:553	1:084	4↑ Clm 16000(16-14)	**81**	5	3	21½	2½	2hd	23	Gonzalez R M	**LB**117 fb	10.30	91-11	Be the Bunny1173 TheNovelist117no *MintRoyale*116no	Pressed, bid,
14	24Dec00-7GG	fst	6f	:22	:452	:574	1:103	3↑ Clm 20000(20-18)	**67**	1	7	63¾	75	76	66	Radke K	**LB**117 fb	7.40	81-16	Woking117hd Nabber1171½ C Merrill Run1172½	Svd grnd to r
10	24Nov00-7GG	fst	6f	:22	:444	:564	1:09	3↑ Alw 32000N1X	**78**	10	8	63½	2½	21½	43¾	Schvaneveldt C P	**LB**119 fb	33.40	91-10	Kinetic Bend118¾ Seayabyebye1191 Play Well T C1162	Bid 3w, flt
12	10Nov00-7BM	fst	6f	:221	:444	:571	1:10	3↑ Alw 32560N1X	**80**	4	5	32½	32	43	53	Radke K	**LB**119 b	10.50	86-14	Unshackled116¾ *Hobar*119¾ Seayabyebye1191½	2w turn, ev
6	14Oct00-2BM	fst	6f	:224	:454	:573	1:10	3↑ Clm 8000(8-7)	**86**	5	3	42¼	11	15	16½	Gonzalez R M	**LB**117 b	3.80	89-15	TheNovelist1176½ StreetsofLrdo1173 Puddls1173½	Ranged 4w, ridd

Previously trained by Glatt Ron

In defense of Thoro-Graph, The Novelist did not win the January 10 race, and I don't know whom Thoro-Graph ended up liking in the race as I was asking only about the pattern of one horse. It is possible Thoro-Graph preferred the line of the winner, Be the Bunny. Also, the track was sloppy, a condition that can significantly affect a horse's performance and throw a wrench into the analysis. While this is just one of hundreds of horses whose patterns are evaluated daily by sheet users, it illustrates that many more factors can be involved in a horse's performance than those reflected in sheet figures (or Beyer speed figures). Plus, it shows the potential drawbacks of sheet users trying to fit an individual horse into general theories and in analyzing a horse's line with figures that are not really complete (because they don't include early fractions or other factors).

Advantages of Sheet Pattern Analysis

Overall, the sheet makers' insights to a horse's form cycle are valuable and cannot be ignored. Some horses do bounce, some will follow a 0-2-X pattern, and most require rest between races to sustain good efforts, as emphasized by sheet makers. No one can correctly evaluate every horse's pattern all the time — you only need to be right enough of the time at the right price to make a profit.

Despite some of the drawbacks of using sheet figures, sheet users commonly do three things that I believe make them successful. First, since they look at a horse's overall line, they don't place as much emphasis on a horse's last race. As long as this broader approach continues, sheet players will have an advantage.

Second, sheet users emphasize looking for value, sometimes keying more than one horse in a race if the odds are high. In a strange way, their method of analyzing patterns by looking at a horse's overall line results in uncovering horses that the public tends to ignore. The public has a tendency to emphasize a horse's last race, while the sheet users tend to emphasize a horse's past performances as a whole. Because of this, sheet users are able to find excellent value (in terms of odds) on many horses that are likely to run well.

Finally, sheet users see the time off between races as an important factor. They believe that the bigger the effort, the more time between starts is needed in order for horses to repeat those big efforts. Most other handicappers don't consider time off as being that important. This is the one insight the sheet makers have developed that I find most useful. Horses have much different requirements when recovering from exercise (races or workouts) than do humans. It is natural for human athletes to be able to repeat top efforts day after day, sometimes on the same day. In contrast, the Thoroughbred's physiological makeup cannot stand up to daily racing. But what is more important is the ability to predict which horses can repeat big efforts and which horses cannot.

When I first started attending the races, if I saw that a horse earned a big speed figure and then returned within seven to fourteen days, I saw no reason it couldn't repeat that effort. The days off didn't matter too much to me; in fact, I had read in many books that coming back within seven to fourteen days was a good thing. Also, I was playing soccer frequently, and it would take me only a day or two to recover from a game, so I thought, "Why should it be different for horses?" However, I have found over the years that while some horses were able to repeat those big efforts, many didn't and lost while being well bet.

Patterns promoted by the sheet makers can be very helpful in predicting when a horse will be able to repeat a big effort. In general, a horse that has a short time to recover from a big effort is not as likely to repeat that effort as a horse that has had a longer time between races to recover. The bigger the effort, the more time a horse may require to recover. Also, as an owner, I have learned that most horses will benefit from a decent amount of time between races, especially between good efforts. There have been many times when a horse I owned came off a big race, and our trainer told me that the horse was doing great, kicking and playing two or three days after a race. Our trainer suggested that we should run him back within a couple of weeks. I have found that almost always when we did this, the horse fooled us; the horse might run well (and sometimes win[2]) but not be able to repeat that same big effort when run back quickly.

Both Ragozin and Brown actively advise clients on horses to purchase or claim. They may recommend that a client either claim or buy privately a horse that has an excellent "line" and a ton of room to improve. Also, some trainers (whom you might become aware of when you read interviews with them) use the sheets in deciding on placement or claiming horses.

Summary

Unlike calculating your own version of something similar to Beyer speed figures, calculating your own version of sheet figures is fairly involved and unrealistic for most people. If you can afford them, if you like using them, and if you understand their drawbacks, they are valuable, and many players who currently use Ragozin's sheets or Thoro-Graph figures do so successfully.

In summary, while Beyer speed figures have been popular for some time, using and analyzing sheet figures has increased in popularity over the past several years, in large part due to the publication of Ragozin's book, *The Odds Must Be Crazy*, and the

---

[2]One comment about "bouncing or reacting": A horse can bounce or react and still win the race. Many players will look at how the horse finished to determine if a horse bounced, but speed figures tell the story regarding a bounce, not the finish position of the horse.

Internet. Many players either use sheet figures directly or apply many of the insights to a horse's form cycle that sheet makers have developed over the years.

Similar to using Beyer speed figures, being aware of what a sheet figure includes and doesn't include can help in using them more effectively. Even if you are not using sheet figures, understanding the underlying theories behind pattern analysis can also help you in your overall handicapping.

Pace Figures

Another popular type of speed figure is a pace figure (a figure for the early fractions of a race), which is used in conjunction with a final speed figure.

In many cases a horse's pace and final figures are related. For example, if a horse is on or near the lead in a race with a slow early pace, its final speed figure will probably be good. If the early fractions are slow, those horses near the lead early will have more energy for the finish. A slow early pace lessens the chances of those horses that are farther behind.

Conversely, if the same horse is on or near the lead in a race with a very fast early pace, its final figure will probably not be as good. The faster the early part of a race, the less energy horses on or near that early fraction will have for the finish. A fast early pace can benefit horses that race farther back early.

To the extreme, rocket early fractions or very slow early fractions can lead to absurd final times. A very slow early pace can lead to a very fast final time. A very fast early pace can lead to a slow final time as all horses, even those coming from behind in the race, may be affected by the fast pace and stagger in the stretch.

Entire books have been written on early fractions; some offering very simple methods of determining which horse will be on or near the lead and others touting very elaborate methods of establishing pace figures. Pace figures can be fairly simple, similar to Quirin's speed points (discussed in *Winning at the Races*, by William Quirin), or more complicated, like Sartin's pace model (discussed in *Modern Pace Handicapping*, by Tom Brohamer).

No one type of pace figure ranks above all others. The Sartin method of breaking down times to feet per second and analyzing energy distribution, turn times, and track profiles is probably the most complicated. Many players employ a pace figure similar to what Andy Beyer suggests in *Beyer on Speed*, where you adjust the raw fractions with a variant and convert the fraction to a number that allows for comparison with races of different distances.

Unlike Beyer speed figures and sheet figures, pace figures are not readily available, although some businesses do sell them. Most people have to calculate their own, which may be the biggest disadvantage.

Advantages of Using Pace Figures

Accurate pace figures provide some big advantages (as do final speed figures). You may be able to determine what is commonly called the "race shape." Race shape varies from slow-slow (early pace slower than par, final time slower than par) to fast-fast (early pace faster than par, final time faster than par) and all the types of races in between. You can establish race shape by using the actual pace and final speed figures compared to the pars for that type of horse. Once you establish the race shape for any given race, you can improve your ability to evaluate the efforts of the competitors. For example, if you are using pace figures similar to the way Beyer figures are calculated and you come across a sprint race where the par figure is 80-80 (the first speed figure is for the half-mile and the second speed figure is for the final time), and the actual figures are 90-80, you note that the half-mile is above par and the final figure at par, which results in a race shape of "fast-average."

If you are using pace figures, you will easily be able to find pace "standouts." These horses have been setting or pressing much quicker early fractions in their recent races than their upcoming rivals. They may not stand out to others who are looking only at their final speed figures or the raw, unadjusted fractional times.

In addition, you will be able to avoid favorites that have weak pace figures. These types of horses look good from the standpoint of a final speed figure, but their pace figure points out a potential weakness. If you expect the pace to be faster than the pace in those horses' recent races, they will have to expend too much energy to keep up early and, thus, have less energy available for the finish.

Conversely, you will be able to avoid horses that come from far behind early and benefited from a faster-than-normal pace in their previous start. Or you will be able to upgrade those that finished well when coming from behind in a race with a slow pace.

Another advantage is you'll be able to spot a horse that might be on the upswing. When you see a horse's most recent pace figure increase but its final speed figure remain the same, you may be able to project improvement in its final speed figure in its next race, while other handicappers may not be aware of the potential improvement.

Challenges of Doing Pace Figures

The first difficulty is getting an accurate pace figure for each race. Rather than offering a specific method to calculate a pace figure, I will refer you to the books already mentioned (such as *Beyer On Speed, Winning at the Races,* or *Modern Pace Handicapping*). However, if you currently are using a pace figure or want to start using a pace figure, the next few paragraphs may help.

You must always consider the placement of the gate for races of varying distances. For almost all races the starting gate is placed somewhere behind the actual marking pole of the distance of the race (Figure 1.14). The distance between the gate and marker, where the clock starts, is commonly called the run-up and can vary between a few yards and a good distance. The official timer

Figure 1.14

1 Mile Track

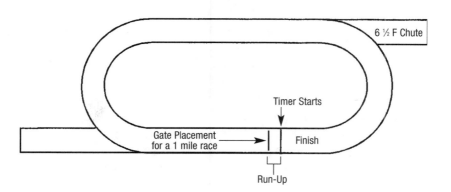

Gate Placement for a 1 mile race · Timer Starts · Finish · Run-Up · 6 ½ F Chute

starts when a horse breaks the light beam at the distance marker and not when the gates open.

Thoroughbreds do not reach top speed until approximately one hundred to two hundred yards after breaking from the starting gate. This wouldn't be a big deal if the starting gate were placed at the same distance behind the distance marker for all races. But because of the design of racetracks, the starting gate is placed at varying distances behind the marker, depending on the individual track's configuration.

For races that start close to the turn, the starting gate is placed farther behind the distance marker to give the riders more time to get position before the turn, which can make the turn a bit safer for everyone. Also, for races that start near the end of a chute (i.e., seven-furlong races at mile tracks), the gate may be placed right near the distance marker because that chute may not have much extra room.

This placement will affect raw times of the early fractions. Since Thoroughbreds don't reach top speed in their first few strides, a race with the gate placed close to the distance marker may have fairly slow early raw fractions compared to a race in which the gate is placed farther back. The shorter the run-up before the timer begins, the slower the early fraction.

The early fractions will also be affected by the amount of turn included in that fraction. The more time on a turn that is incorporated in the fraction, the slower the fraction because horses run more slowly through turns. Finally, how close the gate is to the turn can affect fractions in different ways. The riders, aware of a short run to the turn, may hustle their mounts more at the start than they would for a race starting farther away.

Trying to visualize the effect of gate placement and the effect of the turn on early fractions at each different race distance can make your head spin. Not only that, tracks throughout the country are of different circumferences with different turns and/or different configurations: tight turns and a long stretch/backstretch or wide turns and a shorter stretch/backstretch. Because of these various track configurations, there are no good general fractional par times that players can use that would be accurate at all tracks. If you are interested in doing your own pace figures, you will need accurate *fractional* par times that will take into account the specifics of each track you are playing.

Even if you don't use pace figures in your handicapping, it is important to be aware of gate placement and its effect on raw early fractions.

Summary

Pace figures can range from the simple to the very complicated. I don't use elaborate pace figures. I prefer a simple pace figure for the half-mile fraction in sprints and the half-mile plus the three-quarter-mile fraction in routes. My goal is to have good pace figures without spending too much time calculating them. Then I can better evaluate a horse's previous performances and also evaluate whether there is a horse that has an advantage. In addition, pace figures help determine how any one race might shape up.

The main disadvantage to using pace figures is actually calculating them. Just like calculating a speed figure for the final time, it isn't easy to calculate a pace figure for the fractional times. The next section discusses some of the challenges in calculating your own speed figures for both the final time and for the early fractions of a race. But if you are able to calculate an accurate pace figure, you will be able to gain a valuable advantage. That advantage can be significant and will be maintained as long as pace figures are not generally available.

Doing Your Own Speed Figures

Instead of using Beyer speed figures or sheet figures, you can calculate your own speed figures. Many players were eager to do their own figures in the 1970s and '80s, but since the inclusion of Beyer speed figures in the *Daily Racing Form* and the increased popularity of the sheet figures, most players now rely solely on commercial figures. For most players, having one of those types of speed figures to use in their handicapping is probably better than not using any figures at all.

However, if you can calculate a more accurate speed figure, you will have a bigger advantage because you will be basing your handicapping and betting on better information. This section offers some advice on doing your own speed figures.

One key to calculating any speed figure is coming up with an accurate variant. If you have done your own speed figures in the past or are currently doing your own speed figures, you know how hard it can be to derive an accurate variant at your home track. It is even tougher to come up with an accurate variant for several tracks each day. Remember, commercial producers of speed figures, such as Beyer Associates, Thoro-Graph, and Ragozin's sheets, are attempting to derive an accurate variant for tracks their figure makers may have never visited. If you watch races live at the track, on TVG, or at a simulcast outlet, have a good feel for the horses running each day, and note any changes that can affect the speed of the track surface, you can't help but have an advantage when calculating a variant and thus will have more accurate speed figures.

While calculating your own speed figures is not easy, you will know how each figure was calculated. You will know when you are confident of the figures or when you are not as confident (such as on days when doing the variant was difficult). This includes trying to do variants on days when the track is wet, on very windy days, or on days when the weather is changing during the card (such as a day when it starts raining mid-card). Again, players who are not at that track may not be aware of these changes, and you will have an advantage when doing the variant and using your own speed figures.

Disadvantages in Doing Your Own Speed Figures

Doing your own speed figures offers several challenges. These include the daily race mix and changes in the speed of the track surface throughout any given day. Again, if you are not familiar with pars or variants, see Appendix A at the back of this book.

It is fairly easy to come up with a quick variant by using only races with no restrictions, such as open, older-horse claiming races, which are the best type of races for determining a variant. You would ignore the rest of the races that day and then hope that the resulting variant is a good representation of the track surface speed. However, because of a mishmash of races, erratic results, changing weather, or track maintenance, calculating a variant using pars on some days can border on the impossible.

For example, during midweek, most tracks run only eight or nine live races. Even if there are no major weather changes or changing track conditions, it is unlikely that many of the races on that given day will be for open, older claiming horses. In fact, most of the races will be restricted either by age (two- or three-year-olds), condition (non-winners of two races lifetime or non-winners of a race this year, etc.), state-bred (restricted to horses foaled in that state), or any other type of race in which the quality of the field can vary greatly. On days like this, your par times may not be a good representation of the fields and will make calculating an accurate variant difficult.

Sometimes you are faced with an indescribable mess of races. The eight-race card at Santa Anita on December 28, 2001, was the type of card that makes calculating a variant difficult:

Race #1: Maiden special weight for two-year-old fillies, 1 mile.
Race #2: Three-year olds and up, allowance non-winners of $3,000 three times other than maiden, claiming, or starter, or that have never won four races or claiming price of $100,000, 1⅟₁₆ miles.
Race #3: Three-year-old fillies, claiming price $16,000, 6½furlongs.
Race #4: Two-year-old fillies, bred in California, stakes, 7 furlongs.
Race #5: Fillies and mares, three years old and up, claiming $62,500, 6½ furlongs on the turf.
Race #6: Maiden two-year-olds, claiming $32,000, 6 furlongs.
Race #7: Two-year-olds, bred in California, stakes, 7 furlongs.
Race #8: Maiden two-year-olds, claiming price, $40,000, 1⅟₁₆ miles.

In addition, some days there is no consistency in the final times despite the presence of several "good" quality open races, a situation that makes calculating an accurate variant difficult. Some days there may be only one route race, again making it difficult to calculate an accurate variant for that route. Many players will combine sprints (one-turn races) with routes (two-turn races) to help determine a variant for the day. This method can be okay at times but does not take the wind into account; wind may affect the final time of one-turn races compared to two-turn races.

Another challenge of doing your own speed figures is a changing track surface. In most cases the speed of the surface will change when it starts to rain or when the track starts out wet but dries during the day. On other days the speed of the surface may change for less obvious reasons. Knowledge of your home track can help greatly in determining a variant.

For example, Emerald Downs is a sand-based surface that needs to be watered constantly during the racing season. If the track isn't watered, the surface will quickly become very loose. Imagine you are on a beach; when you are walking near the water, the sand is hard and compact, and when you are walking away from the water, the sand is loose and gives easily.

Let's say it is a warm Friday in July and the first race is at 6 p.m. with the sun shining. The track is watered prior to every race, but the sun will evaporate the water quickly and the track will be a bit loose. The final times will reflect that loose surface. After the sun goes down, the surface may be faster for the final race or two than for the earlier races, even if there is no apparent change in the weather. This is a result of the track's being "tighter" or faster because the water is not evaporating as quickly later in the evening. Under those conditions, I will be forced to break up my variant (make a separate variant for those last couple of races) just because of the effect unique to Emerald Downs.

Anyone who is not aware of this effect will have less accurate figures. For example, whoever is doing the variant to calculate the Beyer speed figures for Emerald Downs may not be familiar with the nuances of the track. In addition, that person would have to know whether the sun was shining that day. If you used those last couple of races along with the earlier races in calculating the daily variant, you would have a less accurate variant and, thus, less accurate figures.

While this is just one example, this principle applies to every track because each is different. Maybe it is a timer that malfunctions often. Maybe it is wind that changes during the day or something unusual, such as a bad spill, that delays the next race and means that water trucks are not able to get on the track between races, effectively changing the track speed for one race. The list is endless.

Adjusting Your Figures for Lengths Beaten
The *Daily Racing Form* provides the fractional times of the leader during a race and the final time of the winner. However, some

adjustment must be made for horses that lost. Additionally, if you are calculating your own pace figures, you must adjust those figures for the horses that were not on the lead.

Anyone using any type of speed figure applies some sort of lengths-beaten chart to adjust those figures. Most players use the running lines in the *Daily Racing Form*'s past performances and a lengths-beaten chart. For the most part this is okay, but be aware of some things when looking at the running lines of any horse and also when adjusting a horse's final figure for lengths beaten.

First, the running lines. While it's a fair assumption that the running lines of any given horse are fairly accurate, on occasion they are not as accurate as you might believe. It can be difficult for Equibase's chart caller to get exactly right the position of each horse in a large field at each call. Many times I have noticed small errors; other times, serious errors. For instance, the chart for the 2001 Kentucky Derby was revised twice by Equibase, once a few days after the Derby and again two to three weeks later. If Equibase can't get the chart of the Kentucky Derby accurate on the first or second try, how accurate do you think the chart is for the second race at Lone Star Park? While, in general, Equibase does a good job, the company has different employees at each track and some are better than others. They also may have a different view of exactly how long a length is.

Second, regarding a lengths-beaten chart, what is the value of a length? It first was commonly assumed that a length was worth a fifth of a second. This assumption made things easy since most published times are in fifths of a second (some tracks now publish times in hundredths of a second, but most are still in fifths). It was a nice assumption, but it is not true, as many books have pointed out. In general, the longer the race the less "value" a length has.

But more importantly, the "value" of a length depends on the point at which it is measured. The horses "covered" a length quicker in the first quarter-mile compared to the last quarter-mile. For example, if the first quarter-mile of a race was run in :22, the horses are moving pretty fast compared to later in the race, when the last quarter-mile was run in :25. As a side note, a common assumption in races on dirt tracks is that closers are "finishing strongly" in the stretch, when in most cases the closers are also slowing down, just not as much as those near or on the lead.

The key is being aware that the value of a length is different, based on *when* it is measured. If the final time of a one-mile race is 1:40, the horses are traveling slower at the finish than in a different race in which one mile was run in 1:35. Using the same lengths-beaten chart to adjust the figures for both races will lead to some inaccuracies. While this isn't a big deal because the adjustments may be minor, it is important to be aware of the value of a length when adjusting a horse's speed figure.

Projecting Speed Figures

While doing your own speed figures can have advantages, you may encounter situations in which calculating a variant becomes very challenging. For instance, the par figure for the individual race you are evaluating might not be a good representation of the field. If you know the horses well, you can predict a speed figure (based on a horse's previous speed figures). This is commonly called "projecting."

To project, you look at horses that ran well in their previous races, then look at their speed figures, and then use those speed figures to project what they will run in the race you are handicapping.

For example, let's say your par figure for a $4,000 open claiming race is 70. However, the horses that finished close to each other in the first three placings in today's $4,000 race have speed figures of about 65 in their past few races. You then may want to "project" that the horses ran a 65 and base your variant off your projected figure rather than the par time of 70.

If you believe in your speed figures and use them to make your selections, why not use them to project the final figure? Projecting rather than using par figures can become tricky, and the accuracy of the variant produced is a result of skill and knowledge of the local horses and local track characteristics. If you are skillful at projecting figures, your variant will be even more accurate. The main drawback of projecting is that if you are wrong about your variant, not only are the figures for that day wrong but future figures may be wrong, too.

Using Your Own Speed Figures

When doing their own variant, handicappers will always come across a race here and there that doesn't fit the variant they arrived at for the day. The race either comes up very fast or very slow when compared to the figures previously earned by the horses in that race.

The main question is what to do with the odd race. Should you say, "they ran what they ran" and assign a speed figure you know probably isn't accurate? Or are you better off not to assign the race a speed figure rather than guessing at one and judge the horses out of their previous races? Or should you assign a speed figure (using a separate variant) for that race based on what you think the horses should have run, assuming that something strange happened such as a timer malfunction, change in the track maintenance, etc.? The answer isn't easy. Whatever you decide, the key is to know what you did for that odd race and to be a little leery of the horses returning out of that race. Others using the commercial figures won't be aware of those "problem" races.

One note: If you are doing your own speed figures and have a race in which the horses earned fast speed figures and if the first couple of horses have run poorly in their next start, it is easy to assume that the original speed figure is wrong. But be aware that your original figure still may be good. What if each of those first few horses had a legitimate excuse? For instance, you find out later that one popped up on the vet's list as "bled," another suffered a minor injury, a third may have bounced. For more on this see the "key race" concept in Chapter 9. You must be able to trust the speed figures you are using to have the confidence to bet, and at the same time you must constantly try to verify them or make adjustments when necessary. It is a tricky balancing act.

In summary, doing your own speed figures can help you realize a significant advantage over others, either those who use the commercial speed figures or those who don't use speed figures at all. Doing your own speed figures isn't easy, but if you can overcome the challenges involved, the advantages are large.

Other Advantages of Speed Figures

Another advantage of using any speed figure is that you can see through a horse's running line and class level, thus concentrating your efforts on other important factors.

Running Lines

Running lines are useful in determining a horse's best running style, but trying to read too much into them is dangerous because they are not related to a fixed par time.

For example, a common comment you might hear at the track is "Horse Y has been running well but has lost lengths in the stretch in each of its last three starts when the real running begins." My question is this: Does it really matter if a horse gained or lost lengths in the stretch?

Let's say Horse Y had a running line of:

$$4^3 \ 4^2 \ 3^2 \ 3^4$$

It appears Horse Y lost two lengths in the stretch. Below is the running line of the winner:

$$2^1 \ 1^1 \ 1^1 \ 1^3$$

If you "removed" the winner's running line from the race, Horse Y's running line would now look like this:

$$3^2 \ 3^1 \ 2^1 \ 2^1$$

The reality is that most players will look at a horse's running line at each call to determine how it ran. However, those running lines are in relation to the performance of other horses in the race, not a fixed par value. *This is an important distinction.* If you are using Beyer speed figures and the horse ran an 80, the horse ran an 80. It doesn't matter if the horse gained or lost lengths in the stretch. It doesn't matter if the horse won the race or was well beaten. The speed figure is what the horse earned and is what you will use in your handicapping. An 80 earned while gaining lengths in the stretch is not better than an 80 earned while losing lengths in the stretch.

Another problem with looking at running lines is that they can lead some players into emphasizing the last part of the race. For example, in a six-furlong race you are given a call that includes position and lengths behind the leader, if any, after two furlongs (quarter-mile), four furlongs (half-mile), the stretch call, five furlongs (five-eighths of a mile), and, of course, the finish at six furlongs (three-quarters of a mile). It is human nature (consciously or subconsciously) to put equal value on all those calls even though the first two calls are a quarter-mile apart and the last two calls are only an eighth of a mile apart, because the stretch call is between the half-mile (four furlongs) call and the finish (six furlongs).

Since the stretch call is listed, it implies, and some players subconsciously believe, that the halfway point of the race is the half-mile (four-furlong) call and the last half of the race is shown in the stretch and finish calls. In fact, at the four-furlong call, a six-furlong race is two-thirds over, not halfway. The effect of this when looking at running lines can mislead players into concentrating as equally on those last two calls as on the first two calls when in reality they are not equal.

Figure 1.15

e the Bunny

lar02-5GG	fst	6f	:21^{4}	:44^{4}	:57^{1}	1:10^{2}	4↑ Clm 6250	**74**	6	1	2^{1}	2^{1}	2^{2}	$4^{3¼}$	Russell B R	**LB**117 fb	8.50	82- 17	A J Flyer117^{hd} Sami's Tango117^{3} *Proud Louie*122no	Pressed pace, wknd 7
eb02-4GG	fst	6f	:22	:45^{1}	:57^{4}	1:10^{1}	4↑ Clm 8000(8-7)	**67**	8	1	2^{hd}	2^{hd}	$4^{¾}$	$7^{5½}$	Russell B R	**LB**117 fb	4.90	80- 13	*Fog City Willy*117^{2} Natural Style112^{1} E Coupon117^{1}	Dueled 2w, gave out 9
eb02-8GG	sly	6f	:21^{2}	:44	:56^{2}	1:09^{4}	4↑ Clm 8000(8-7)	**81**	3	3	2^{hd}	$2^{½}$	2^{1}	$2^{1¼}$	Russell B R	**LB**117 fb	5.60	87- 11	Proud Louie122^{1¼} Be theBunny117^{½} NaturalStyle112^{2}	Dueled, outfinished 7
an02-3GG	gd	6f	:22^{2}	:45^{4}	:58^{1}	1:11^{1}	4↑ Clm 8000(8-7)	**81**	5	2	$1^{2½}$	2^{hd}	3^{1}	4^{1}	Delgadillo A	**LB**117 fb	12.60	80- 21	*ProudLouie*119^{hd} FlyingDenouemnt119^{hd} *NturlStyl*112^{¾}	Met bid, stayed on 8
ec01-2GG	sly	6f	:21^{4}	:45	:57^{2}	1:10^{1}	3↑ Clm 10000(10-9)	**76**	7	2	2^{hd}	$2^{½}$	3^{2}	3^{4}	Delgadillo A	**LB**117 fb	4.50	83- 19	ThNovlist117^{2½} FlyingDnoumnt117^{1½} BthBunny117^{1½}	Dueled, outfinished 9
ec01-7GG	fst	6f	:22	:44^{4}	:57	1:09^{3}	3↑ Clm 8000(8-7)	**75**	5	2	$1^{1½}$	1^{1}	3^{1}	4^{4}	Delgadillo A	**LB**117 fb	8.00	86- 14	*Proud Louie*117no Barrybrown117^{2½} IAmtheRuhler117^{1½}	Pace inside, wknd 7
lov01-4GG	my	6f	:22	:45^{3}	:58^{3}	1:11	3↑ Clm 10500(12.5-10.5)	**61**	7	1	$3^{½}$	$3^{½}$	6^{3}	$6^{9½}$	Delgadillo A	**LB**116 fb	8.80e	73- 13	*FirstStringer*119^{1½} EveningNews117^{1} DvesMoment117^{1}	Dueled 3w, empty 9
lov01-1GG	fst	6f	:21^{3}	:44^{4}	:57^{2}	1:10^{2}	3↑ Clm 12500(12.5-10.5)	**76**	3	3	$4^{1¾}$	$4^{1¾}$	$5^{2¾}$	$5^{3¼}$	Delgadillo A	**LB**117 fb	15.10	83- 14	*First Stringer*117^{½} FlyingDenouement117^{hd} Orvald117^{hd}	Shifted 4w, evenly 6

Previously trained by Arterburn Lonnie

Figure 1.16 — with stretch calls removed

e the Bunny

lar02-5GG	fst	6f	:21^{4}	:44^{4}	:57^{1}	1:10^{2}	4↑ Clm 6250	**74**	6	1	2^{1}	2^{1}	$4^{3¼}$	Russell B R	**LB**117 fb	8.50	82- 17	A J Flyer117^{hd} Sami's Tango117^{3} *Proud Louie*122no	Pressed pace, wknd 7
Feb02-4GG	fst	6f	:22	:45^{1}	:57^{4}	1:10^{1}	4↑ Clm 8000(8-7)	**67**	8	1	2^{hd}	2^{hd}	$7^{5½}$	Russell B R	**LB**117 fb	4.90	80- 13	*Fog City Willy*117^{2} Natural Style112^{1} E Coupon117^{1}	Dueled 2w, gave out 9
Feb02-8GG	sly	6f	:21^{2}	:44	:56^{2}	1:09^{4}	4↑ Clm 8000(8-7)	**81**	3	3	2^{hd}	$2^{½}$	$2^{1¼}$	Russell B R	**LB**117 fb	5.60	87- 11	Proud Louie122^{1¼} Be theBunny117^{½} NaturalStyle112^{2}	Dueled, outfinished 7
Jan02-3GG	gd	6f	:22^{2}	:45^{4}	:58^{1}	1:11^{1}	4↑ Clm 8000(8-7)	**81**	5	2	$1^{2½}$	2^{hd}	4^{1}	Delgadillo A	**LB**117 fb	12.60	80- 21	*ProudLouie*119^{hd} FlyingDenouemnt119^{hd} *NturlStyl*112^{¾}	Met bid, stayed on 8
Dec01-2GG	sly	6f	:21^{4}	:45	:57^{2}	1:10^{1}	3↑ Clm 10000(10-9)	**76**	7	2	2^{hd}	$2^{½}$	3^{4}	Delgadillo A	**LB**117 fb	4.50	83- 19	ThNovlist117^{2½} FlyingDnoumnt117^{1½} BthBunny117^{1½}	Dueled, outfinished 9
Dec01-7GG	fst	6f	:22	:44^{4}	:57	1:09^{3}	3↑ Clm 8000(8-7)	**75**	5	2	$1^{1½}$	1^{1}	4^{4}	Delgadillo A	**LB**117 fb	8.00	86- 14	*Proud Louie*117no Barrybrown117^{2½} IAmtheRuhler117^{1½}	Pace inside, wknd 7
Nov01-4GG	my	6f	:22	:45^{3}	:58^{3}	1:11	3↑ Clm 10500(12.5-10.5)	**61**	7	1	$3^{½}$	$3^{½}$	$6^{9½}$	Delgadillo A	**LB**116 fb	8.80e	73- 13	*FirstStringer*119^{1½} EveningNews117^{1} DvesMoment117^{1}	Dueled 3w, empty 9
Nov01-1GG	fst	6f	:21^{3}	:44^{4}	:57^{2}	1:10^{2}	3↑ Clm 12500(12.5-10.5)	**76**	3	3	$4^{1¾}$	$4^{1¾}$	$5^{3¼}$	Delgadillo A	**LB**117 fb	15.10	83- 14	*First Stringer*117^{½} FlyingDenouement117^{hd} Orvald117^{hd}	Shifted 4w, evenly 6

Previously trained by Arterburn Lonnie

Figure 1.15 shows the standard past performances of Be the Bunny prior to a race he was entered in on April 6, 2002.

You are looking first at the standard past performances and then an altered past performances, showing equally spaced running lines. To have an equally spaced running line for six-furlong sprints, you would have a running line with only the quarter-mile and half-mile calls and the finish. These calls would each be a quarter-mile apart. Figure 1.16 shows Be the Bunny's past performances with the stretch call removed so as to have equally spaced calls.

Again, this effect in the running line doesn't mean as much to you if you are using some sort of speed figure.

Class Levels

Another advantage to having accurate speed figures is that you don't have to worry much about the class level in which the figure was earned. If a horse earned a final Beyer speed figure of 80 while running for a claiming price of $10,000, it is the same as if it earned an 80 when running for a claiming price of $25,000. Class levels can be very confusing and/or misleading because a higher claiming price or class level doesn't necessarily mean a better quality field. Using speed figures eliminates this confusion.

Players who don't use speed figures in their handicapping are left to make up things based on a horse's running line and class level. They will try to fill holes with generalizations because they can't accurately compare efforts by horses that did not race against each other in their previous starts. If you come across a person who touts you on a horse because it "gained lengths in the stretch against $20,000 claimers and is in for $16,000 claiming," don't walk away — run.

Summary

What type of speed figure is best? Obviously, players prefer all sorts. I prefer to use a combination of speed figures, one for the early fractional times (pace figure) and another for the final time. The speed figures I use are similar to Beyer's and are adjusted only for the speed of the track surface. Sheet figures try to measure a horse's total effort (they include factors such as weight carried and ground lost), but that doesn't mean they are more effective. I lean toward evaluating, as Andy Beyer suggests, how my speed figures are earned. I want a speed figure that is accurate while also being easy to calculate. To me, including factors in a speed figure such as weight carried, ground loss, etc., while ignoring other factors such as early fractions and track bias lessens the overall value of that speed figure. The weight carried will affect each horse differently, and similar trips affect horses differently as well.

Within reason, I keep track of as many factors as possible that I feel affect a horse's effort, and I will use those factors to evaluate each horse, in addition to looking at its speed figures. You may be familiar already with such factors as a horse's trip or trouble encountered during a race. Chapter 2 discusses some of the factors with which you might be less familiar. Also, many players will view pace as part of a horse's overall trip and not use a combination of figures (pace and final figures).

If you are using any type of speed figure, be aware that all speed figures have limitations or flaws. Be flexible; don't handicap every race the same by "framing" the race in terms of the speed figures. Obviously, speed figures don't provide the only answer in many races. If you either are or become an "expert" in speed figures, you will need to "diversify" in other areas of handicapping. I have seen too many players use speed figures as the main and only factor in every race. Those players chalk up their wins to the use of speed figures, and when their selection loses, they attribute it to some other event, such as a bad ride, etc. While having accurate speed figures is a powerful handicapping tool, in many races the more important factors (which may help in determining a winner) are not speed figures. The next few chapters will explore some of those more common factors players use to evaluate a horse's previous race(s) or speed figures.

What is the future for speed figures and sheet figures users? Hopefully, at some point, there will be a final time taken and published for each horse in a race, not just the winner. I find it amazing that a final time is still currently published for only the winner. If Secretariat owns the fastest final time for the Kentucky Derby, does second-place Sham belong in the record books for the second-, third-, fourth-, or fifth-fastest Derby ever? Since he didn't win, there is no published time for him, and thus no place for him in the record books. Also, the addition of an exact final time for each horse would eliminate the need for a lengths-beaten chart and the inaccuracies involved in those charts.

Watching the Races to Maximum Advantage

Whether or not you use speed figures when handicapping, be aware of several factors that can affect a horse's performance, particularly trip trouble and track bias. Also keep in mind that a horse's performance can be influenced by equipment, medication, and workouts (Chapter 3), as well as the condition book, strategy, and claiming (Chapter 4).

The Race
Watching for Trouble Spots

Trip handicapping — watching every race for trouble or the lack thereof — requires that you keep an eye on the entire field, which many players find difficult because they prefer to watch only their betting interests. Most casual observers can see obvious trouble, such as horses that break slowly, race wide, or are blocked leaving the turn. Many times, this obvious trouble will attract a lot of attention, and those horses will be overbet in their next couple of races.

The bigger advantage in trip handicapping comes from observing the less obvious. I try to key on certain spots during the race to see if anything subtler is happening, and then if I notice something, I make a note to watch the replays.

The first trouble spot is the gate. I usually make a note if a horse is reluctant to load. If the assistant starters have to make several attempts, the horse has probably become distracted and will run poorly. If so, the loss can be excused when evaluating that horse's past performance next time out.

If a horse acts up or rears once in the gate, its chances of running well decrease and its chances of injury increase. Horses can lose interest in racing or injure themselves by banging a head or nose on the gate, scraping a leg, etc. In addition, some horses will break through the starting gate prior to the start, need to be retrieved, and have to be reloaded. Other times horses will become fractious and have to be backed out, examined by the state veterinarian, and either reloaded or scratched.

I will completely ignore a bad race if a horse runs poorly after acting up significantly or breaking through the gate. In addition, certain horses are always bad in the gate. In those cases I have to factor in potential gate trouble before betting on those horses.

If you are watching from the grandstand, you can easily see which horses break slowly, stumble, or hop from the gate. What is usually not obvious is the crowding and bumping, which can cost a horse valuable position and force the rider to change tactics. Crowding and bumping may also alter the makeup of the race and even completely eliminate some horses from contention because they won't be able to recover quickly enough. Again, this can be very hard to see from the grandstand, especially with a large field, so take the time to watch the head-on replay. The head-on view will show more clearly horses swerving in/out, breaking in the air, getting squeezed back, etc., and you can note any such occurrences for future reference.

Also, because the quickest way around the track is along the rail, riders are constantly trying to move closer to the inside. Horses that draw inside post positions are more susceptible to being crowded, bumped, and blocked at the start and again when approaching or running on the turn.

After the start I always note the race's first quarter-mile fraction. If the first fraction seems faster than normal, I know those horses near the early lead are probably going to be at a disadvantage later. I note which horses stayed in the race longer than the other early speed horses and watch to see if a rider asks his horse for a lot after other horses have passed them. If the first fraction seems slower than normal, I know that those horses far behind probably won't have much of a chance, but I will look for the horses that do try to get into contention or that make up significant ground late. Afterward, calculating a pace figure will help clarify whether these fractions were really slower or faster than normal.

When considering trip trouble, handicappers sometimes overemphasize a horse's being blocked inside of a turn. On the turn some horses will be wide while others will be on the inside. I would rather have my horse stuck on the inside, saving ground and waiting for room, than clear and wide. The horse stuck on the inside, even though it may be forced to wait for room, is actually getting a pretty good trip, saving both ground and energy. Don't put too much emphasis on horses that have to wait for room leaving the turn. If they finish well or win, it isn't likely they would have won by more or run much better had they been clear. There are exceptions, but remember that saving ground on the turns is a big advantage over racing wide.

It makes sense that front runners/pressers that are wide on the turn are having a tougher "go" than horses racing inside or horses coming from behind (who are almost always forced to go wide). This disadvantage is magnified if the pace is hot or if a horse, while running in a route, is parked wide on or near the lead on both turns, especially the first turn. If a front runner is breaking from post seven in a one-mile race (on a mile track) and that horse breaks a length slowly and moves up while three wide on the first turn to force the pace, that horse has already had a pretty tough time after the first quarter-mile. The horse will have to be much the best to overcome what at first glance isn't that bad a trip (1 slow, 3 wide).

Contrast this with the deep closer that breaks slowly out of the gate and races wide. Since this type of horse has no early speed anyway and usually goes wide, a slower-than-average start and wide trip probably won't affect its final performance while it probably would eliminate a front runner. This is a case when similar trips for different horses mean different things, depending on the horse's style (front runner or come from behind).

On the other hand, sometimes horses racing on the outside have a different advantage: not being intimidated by being stuck on the rail. Horses that are along the rail, or between runners, can be intimidated and may not be able to relax, while a horse running along the outside won't have those worries.

In addition to watching for trouble, you might notice which riders are aggressively asking their mounts to run, which ones are just sitting, which ones have taken a good hold on their mounts or, to the extreme, which riders are strangling their horses to keep them from moving too soon.

For example, you might see a rider take a good hold of a horse that usually shows tactical speed, thus taking the horse farther back than is its style. If that horse runs poorly, you now probably know why. Or, you may notice a rider that is all over a horse right from the start, constantly asking the horse to run. Some horses need to be ridden this way; other times it might be a bad sign. When a rider begins hustling the horse early in the race, it could indicate the horse isn't interested in running.

Our partnership raced a decent, trying $5,000 claimer that would sit five or six lengths behind early if the pace was average and seven to eight lengths behind the leaders if the pace was fast. He pretty much always made a run leaving the turn. Sometimes he would get to the wire in time.

One day at Emerald Downs he was entered with several viable contenders. When the gates opened, our horse broke well, and after about a sixteenth of a mile he was sitting about three lengths off the lead, much closer than normal. Even though I knew his style was to come from a little farther behind, I also knew that he had been feeling good that day (he was an older gelding that earlier in his career had had good tactical speed). But since he was sharp that day, I thought he had just pulled the rider up close. I watched the rider and didn't see him doing anything that would imply he was hustling or asking our horse early.

As they reached the midway point on the turn, our horse was moving right up to the leaders, and I said out loud, "I'm putting my binoculars down," implying that the race was over and I needed to get down to the winner's circle. The horse was already on the leaders and about to pass them, and since he appeared to be going strongly, I didn't think he would be beaten. I didn't really put my binoculars down, and as they left the turn, I noticed our horse wasn't going by the leaders as he should have. He stayed even with them for a while and then tired in the last sixteenth and ended up sixth.

At first I didn't understand his race; he should have finished strongly and won. I thought something had happened to him (some injury, breathing problem, or whatever). But when I watched the head-on replay, I noticed that right out of the gate the rider tapped him a couple of times with the whip (I couldn't see this from the grandstand). Of course, this was the reason that he ended up so close to the leaders early in the race and probably the reason he had nothing left entering the stretch. He had been asked to do something contrary to his style, the style that gives him the ability to run his best race. I expected him to run back to his previous efforts in his next outing, which he did with a proper ride.

Watching How a Horse Wins

Some players generally assume that if a horse wins big or wins without being hit by the whip, it could have run faster if asked. Many handicapping books have rightfully mentioned that, in most cases, this is a fallacy. But there are times when horses do win with "some in reserve." On occasion, you may have seen a horse win by a long head, but you know that although the margin was close, the horse was never in danger of being beaten. This type of horse is worth noting.

Younger horses commonly pull themselves up once they reach the front. The first time they reach the lead they don't know what to do, so they slow down and wait for other horses or just stop running at full speed. As horses get older and learn about racing, some still pull themselves up after reaching the lead because they are looking for competition. If you notice this, you can make a note and possibly realize that this horse may not have been "all out" at the end of the race.

Keeping an eye on a horse's ears while it runs can give you a clue as to whether it was all out in the race. A horse that moves its ears back and forth *could* be looking around at other things, or a horse pricking its ears after reaching the lead *could* have lost concentration. These horses may have been able to run faster had they stayed focused.

In another instance in which a horse may have won with some in reserve, you may see the rider "wait" before really asking the horse for its run. Knowing there's a ton of horse underneath, the jockey isn't worried about winning big. The rider will let the horse do just enough to win. Similar to horses that pull themselves up after getting the lead, this type of horse could have won by more. You won't see this type of horse every day, but when you do, it is worth noting for the next time it runs.

Watching How a Horse Runs

When I started going to the racetrack, I heard the terms "bad action" or "changing leads," but I didn't understand what people were talking about. I couldn't tell if the horses were on the correct lead or if they had a bad stride. Once I started watching replays, especially head-on views, though, I found it pretty easy to spot horses with bad action or that don't change leads. Keeping track of these types of horses can be very useful in your handicapping.

Determining if a horse has a fluid stride (good action) isn't easy, but when I watch the head-on replay and compare horses, the ones with the awkward stride (bad action) will stand out. With a normal stride, the horse's front feet hit the ground, come straight back toward the horse's belly, and then go straight forward while extending for the next stride. The most common types of bad action are "paddling" and "winging." A horse that paddles or wings is usually offset in the knee or his feet point outward or inward, causing his lower foreleg(s) to make circular motions in (paddling) or out (winging).

Horses with noticeably bad action can run big races but are less likely to repeat the effort because of the toll it takes on their bodies. When I encounter a horse that I know has bad action and that horse is being dropped suspiciously in claiming price, I often conclude that the stress caused by the poor action has caught up with the horse, and it is probably damaged goods.

C.J.'s Dancer was entered in his first start, a $10,000 claiming race, off of some nice works (Figure 2.1). When he won easily by four lengths in a fast 1:09⅗, I didn't understand why he had been entered for only $10,000 until I watched the head-on replay. His left front leg paddled so badly that it was clear that this horse wouldn't stand up to much racing. Between the pressure placed on his leg during a race and his leg hitting the ground at such a bad angle, I didn't think he had much of a future. Even though

Figure 2.1

C. J.'s Dancer
Own: South Jetty Stables

Dk. b or b. g. 6 (May)	
Sire: Petersburg (Danzig) $1,500	
Dam: Satin Morn (Prince O'Morn)	
Br: Lila M Furukawa (Wash)	
Tr: Kenney Daniel(0 0 0 0 .00) :(86 9 .10)	

Life	3 1 0 0	$4,045	71	D.Fst	3 1 0 0	$4,045
2000	3 1 0 0	$4,045	71	Wet(362)	0 0 0 0	$0
1999	0 M 0 0	$0	–	Turf(274)	0 0 0 0	$0
Bel	0 0 0 0	$0	–	Dst(313)	0 0 0 0	$0

4Jly00– 5E mDfst	6f	:221 :45³ :58²1:111		Clm 6250N2L		– 8 6 1ʰᵈ – – –	Landeros J¹⁰	LB111	*1.10	– 10 BnnrofLght121½ FortunsSoldr121¹ AlsknGmblr118½	Pulled up, vanned o
8Jun00– 8E mDfst	6f	:22 :45¹ :57³1:10⁴		Clm 14000(16–14)N2x		56 5 2 3½ 21½ 45 5¹⁰	Perez M A	LB116	*1.50	76– 18 PlayWellTC118½ CherokeeStr1186½ Muscovy117ⁿᵏ	Came in, no respons
19May00– 1E mDfst	6f	:22 :444 :56⁴1:09²	⑤Md c-10000			71 3 2 1½ 1ʰᵈ 11¼ 14¼	Perez M A	LB121	6.20	93– 11 C. J.'s Dancer1214½ Dr. Evil121³½ Sly Schemes121¾	Dueled, kicked awa

Claimed from Bridges, Bill D. and O'Connor, Bill for $10,000, Harris Ben Trainer 2000(as of 5/19): (-)

he ran huge in his first race, the chances of the horse running that well again with that type of stride were slim, and he didn't in only two other starts.

After watching many races, you will be able to spot other types of bad action. When you see a horse with bad action run well in a race, I am not saying to throw the horse out next time it runs. But consider that these horses are more susceptible to injury and/or not being able to repeat good efforts. In addition, this information can be important if you are looking to purchase horses via claiming.

Another thing to look for during a race and on the replays is whether a horse changes leads at the proper time, if at all. When horses run, the front leg that hits the ground first is the lead. More stress (weight) is placed on the lead leg, so it fatigues more quickly. As it tires, a horse will naturally change leads.

Imagine that you are running while carrying a five-pound weight in one hand. After carrying the weight in your left hand for a while, your left arm begins to tire, so you shift the weight to your right hand. You pass the weight back and forth to give each arm a rest while you are running. The extra weight is similar to the extra weight a horse's lead leg experiences during a race.

When horses are entering a turn (because races in the United States are run counterclockwise, all turns are to the left), if they are not already on their left lead, they will change to the left out of necessity to handle the turn. If they stay on their right lead during the turn, they may bolt or lug out because making a left-hand turn on their right lead is difficult.

By the time most horses exit the turn and get to the top of the stretch, they will change off their left lead, which has borne the brunt of the stress during the turn, onto their right. Other times the rider will have to do something to get a horse to change leads; occasionally, a horse may never change leads.

There are a couple of reasons that horses will not change leads when entering or coming out of the turn. One of the most common is because of physical problems in one of their legs. If a horse has a problem in its right front leg, putting more pressure on that leg causes pain and the horse will avoid changing leads onto it. Sometimes you will see a horse change leads several times during the stretch run, another possible sign of leg problems because the horse is trying to avoid pain. If I notice a horse didn't change leads in one race, I will expect the rider to prompt the horse to change leads the next time and possibly improve. Should I notice a horse has not changed leads in a couple of races, I will be leery of playing the horse.

Summary
Evaluating trouble, noting horses that act up in the gate, watching how a horse wins, and watching how a horse runs, including changing leads, can be important in evaluating a horse's effort. To gain further insight, watch what actually happens in a race and don't rely on the observations of others. To quote Mark Twain: "Get your facts first; then you can distort those facts as much as you please."

Many times I have heard a person say something like "Did you see the trouble the #5 horse got into? He would have won easily." I then watch the replay with that person, who looks at the race and says, "Watch — checked, checked, steadied, now blocked. What is that rider doing? That horse will be a great bet back." In reality, the horse might have had a little trouble, maybe a half-length's worth. The person isn't interested in your opinion but just wants you to agree that the horse would have won. The person will then bet this horse blindly the next time.

Regular players aren't the only ones looking for justifications; you might read or hear similar comments in post-race interviews with owners and trainers. People see what they want to see. Also, trainers may need to make excuses for their horse's efforts in big races to satisfy their owners and future breeders. Sometimes they will resort to blaming circumstances that are impossible to prove, such as "the track was cupping out on my horse," or "the speed didn't come back to the horse." These things can't be disproved and can be used for lack of a legitimate excuse.

One last comment: Be aware that if a horse encounters significant trouble and still runs huge, the trainer may have prepped the horse to run its best that day. Consequently, the horse may not repeat that type of effort in its next start.

You will be much better off if you are able to note and evaluate trouble objectively, whether or not you played the horse. Again, many players will see what they want to see, in some cases trying to justify why their horse lost. In other cases players who do not pay attention to the entire field may not recognize the trouble a horse encountered. Significant advantages can·be obtained by noticing any trouble, especially subtle trouble, such as a horse being ridden contrary to its style. These advantageous observations can only be obtained by watching the entire field.

Track Bias

In handicapping the word "bias" implies that the track surface gives certain horses an advantage on a particular day. For example, the surface may favor horses that race along the rail because the inside is "better" than other parts of the track.

Some players refuse to recognize (or are unaware) that the track surface can be better in certain places or will favor a certain type of running style, such as horses that come from behind (closers). Other players believe not only that there is there a track bias every day, but also that the bias will change throughout the day.

Biases do exist. Most are related to the weather and track maintenance. Players familiar with biases will analyze results daily to determine if one existed. However, that determination isn't easy and, for the most part, is subjective.

Some players, especially those who are very familiar with their home track, may be able to predict when a bias will appear. For example, at the track you play regularly, you may become aware that after it rains and the surface starts to dry out, the inside of the track dries faster, thus favoring horses that race along the inside. Knowing this before others catch on can give you a huge advantage in those first few races.

Biases can make the results of any given race fairly random.

Some results are based on which horse was able to get to the best part of the surface first, and, thus, these races can be very frustrating for owners and handicappers alike. Often the bias may be obvious to an observer, but it may not be obvious to trainers and/or jockeys.

Additionally, once in-house commentators start mentioning it, and everyone knows about it, the riders may change their strategy to try to get to the best part of the track, a tactic that can skew the results even more. For example, if the rail is good, several riders will hustle their mounts early and create a brutal dogfight for the lead, leaving a closer the most likely winner despite the bias.

When I perceive a bias during a racing day, I will shut down my betting somewhat unless I am fairly certain that the horse I like will benefit. I don't want to bet on whether the trainers and jockeys are clued into the bias because the race may be reduced to the smartest or luckiest rider rather than the best horse. Don't get me wrong; I'll try to take advantage of a bias during the racing day, but I am very aware that luck is also involved when I bet horses on days when the track surface is the main factor in determining which horse wins.

Sometimes when I have perceived a strong track bias, I haven't been able, even as an owner, to get the trainer or jockey to recognize it exists and ride the horse accordingly. Several years ago while running a horse at Yakima Meadows during the winter, we drove from Seattle across the Cascades to watch him run. We were in the fourth race, and after the first three races it was obvious to me that the rail was very good. To have any chance of winning, a horse definitely had to race along the rail. The horse we owned didn't have much early speed, but I felt that if he stayed inside, he still had a pretty good chance. He had drawn a post position in the middle of the gate and was one of the favorites. There was one other horse that I felt he had to beat, a horse with good early speed that had drawn an inside post.

When I went to the paddock before the race, I mentioned to our assistant trainer that I thought the rail was the place to be and strongly recommended he instruct the rider to try to get the horse to the inside and stay there. I didn't know this assistant very well (our trainer was based at a different track and his assistant trained a string of horses at Yakima), and he didn't know me. The assistant, looking surprised, said, "We will keep that in mind."

When the rider came out in the paddock, he didn't wait around to chat with us — it was very cold. The assistant trainer said to him something like, "He likes to come from behind, so keep him wide and clear." The jockey just hopped on the horse and took off. I was so stunned by what I had heard that I didn't get a chance to say anything to him. I knew then that our horse had no chance, so I went straight upstairs and bet the other horse. Unfortunately for our horse, I was right about the bias.

Confirming Bias

If I feel that a bias is affecting the results during any racing day, I will note it. Then after calculating my variants (for both pace figures and final speed figures) and watching the replays and even reviewing the vet's list for bleeders, injuries, etc., I will try and confirm it. I have found many times that after calculating speed figures and watching the replays, the results were more a byproduct of some extreme pace situations or rough trips by the contenders in some races. Or the results were just random, not the upshot of a bias.

Also, realize that eight or nine races on any given day may not be enough of a sample to determine the existence of a bias (Chapter 9).

Using a Bias to Your Advantage

Although being able to identify a bias correctly during a racing day can give you an advantage, a bigger benefit is being better able to evaluate horses that ran on a biased track the next time out. You will be able to throw out either really good or bad past performances because you know they were mainly the result of the bias and not the abilities of the horse. You might find a horse that ran a big "hidden" performance.

For example, if you believe there is a rail bias, a horse that finished well after being three wide on the turn while forcing or chasing a fast pace will have run an effort much better than it looks on paper, especially to those unaware of the bias. Also, a horse on the same type of track that races five wide on the turn and makes a little run before tiring and ends up well beaten will also have hidden a good performance.

Don't underestimate the effect of a track bias on a horse's finish. Some horses will have no chance and never be in contention because they are running in the "quicksand" while others in the same race are running on "cement." A horse's performance can be aided greatly, sometimes absurdly, by a bias.

When the horse Edneator was entered in the Longacres Mile, the Northwest's premier race, on August 20, 2000, many regulars including me, were asking, "Why is he in here?" as he appeared badly overmatched. After the first several races that day and as the Mile approached, it became very evident that the inside was like a well-paved highway. I wasn't able to determine which horse would make the lead or which would get to the inside in the Mile because there were several horses capable of running the first quarter-mile in :22 and change, so I skipped the race.

Edneator ended up being that horse, and he rode the bias to a huge upset win at odds of 41-1. As you can see, by looking at the Beyer speed figures in the *Daily Racing Form* in Figure 2.2 (104 for August 20), his performance was several lengths faster than he had ever run, even after running the half-mile in a blistering :44$\frac{3}{5}$. After his Mile win, when he came back for the Washington Championship, he again rode a similar strong bias to an easy, big-figure win. I knew both of his efforts were hugely inflated due to the bias, so this is the type of horse I would look forward to betting against when he is racing on a fair surface.

Figure 2.2

eator

10EmDfst	1$\frac{1}{16}$	:23^3	:46^3	1:09^3	1:40^2	3↑ [S]WashChmpH60k	**106**	7	1^2	1^2	1^4	1^4	1^6	Mitchell G V	**LB**122 b	*.30e	96- 16	Edneator122^6 Kittys Link120$^{4\frac{3}{4}}$ Dash Eight117$^{1\frac{1}{4}}$	Cleared, much the best	7
-7EmDfst	1	:22^2	:44^3	1:07^4	1:33^1	3↑ LgaMileH-G3	**104**	6	1^{hd}	1^1	1^2	1$^{2\frac{1}{2}}$	1$^{1\frac{1}{2}}$	Mitchell G V	**LB**111 b	41.60	100- 11	*Edneator*111$^{1\frac{1}{2}}$ Big Ten119$^{1\frac{3}{4}}$ Crafty Boy114$^{\frac{3}{4}}$	Dueled, clear, held	11
-7EmDfst	1$\frac{1}{16}$	:23	:45^4	1:09^3	1:42^1	3↑ MtRainrBCH85k	**93**	8	1^{hd}	1$^{2\frac{1}{2}}$	1^2	2$^{\frac{1}{2}}$	5^2	Mitchell G V	**LB**113 b	13.00	85- 20	Bold Words117^{hd} Crafty Boy117$^{\frac{3}{4}}$ Zanetti119^{no}	Set pace, outfinished	11
-8EmDfst	1	:24^1	:47^3	1:11^1	1:36^1	3↑ Clm 60000(60-50)	**95**	4	1^1	1$^{1\frac{1}{2}}$	1$^{1\frac{1}{2}}$	1$^{1\frac{1}{2}}$	2$^{\frac{3}{4}}$	Loseth C	**LB**122 b	3.50	84- 15	MoonlightMeeting118$^{\frac{3}{4}}$ Ednetor122$^{1\frac{1}{4}}$ JzzyMc116^6	Cleared, game, denied	5
-8EmDfst	1	:23^2	:46^2	1:09^4	1:34^4	3↑ OClm 50000	**93**	1	1^1	1^1	1^2	1^1	2^{hd}	Cooper B B	**LB**121 b	7.30	92- 16	Archatrave118^{hd} Edneator121$^{3\frac{1}{4}}$ Weekender118$^{1\frac{1}{4}}$	Speed, game, denied	8
-8EmDsly	6$\frac{1}{2}$f	:22^1	:45	1:10^1	1:17	4↑ OClm 60000	**75**	4	2	2^1	2$^{\frac{1}{2}}$	4$^{3\frac{1}{4}}$	4$^{8\frac{3}{4}}$	Cooper B B	**LB**121 b	8.10	78- 18	Inclinator120$^{1\frac{1}{4}}$ Red River Valley120^4 Knave120$^{3\frac{1}{2}}$	Pressed, lugged out	6
-5EmDfst	6$\frac{1}{2}$f	:21^1	:42^4	1:08^1	1:14^3	3↑ FOXSprtNtH35k	**46**	2	4	4$^{3\frac{3}{4}}$	4$^{5\frac{1}{2}}$	8^{11}	7$^{19\frac{1}{2}}$	Cooper B B	**LB**120 b	6.40	79- 10	Thtruthsoutthr117^{hd} *KdKtbtc*119$^{1\frac{1}{2}}$ YovGotActon117$^{2\frac{3}{4}}$	Gave way after 1/2	8

Most "bias" plays look something like the following example. On April 20, 2001, the track strongly favored early speed and horses that raced along the inside. The running lines of three horses that raced that day — High Tailing, Midnight Cruiser, and Thunder Zoot — are shown in Figure 2.3 (the following page).

In the April 20 race Midnight Cruiser dueled with High Tailing

Figure 2.3

High Tailing

20Apr01–7EmDfst 5½f :21^{3} :44^{3} :57 1:03^{3} Clm 16000N2X 59 7 2 2½ 2^{hd} 22½ 25½ Gonsalves F A LB118 b 15.10 88– 10 MidnightCruisr1185½ HighTiling118¾ ProudNtiv1181 Pressed 3 w, held 2

Midnight Cruiser

20Apr01–7EmDfst 5½f :21^{3} :44^{3} :57 1:03^{3} Clm 16000N2X 75 3 3 1½ 1^{hd} 12½ 15½ Ventura H Jr LB118 *2.50 94– 10 Midnight Cruiser1185½ HighTailing118¾ ProudNative1181 As rider please

Thunder Zoot

20Apr01–7EmDfst 5½f :21^{3} :44^{3} :57 1:03^{3} Clm 16000N2X 53 9 9 9^{14} 9^{10} 7^{10} 57¾ Whitaker J7 B111 b 6.20 86– 10 MidnightCruiser1185½ HighTiling118¾ ProudNtiv1181 Passed tiring riva

through a rocket half-mile in :44⅗ and drew away for a five and a half-length win. High Tailing held on for second place.

Thunder Zoot, well back and wide throughout, never had a chance and placed fifth. While I haven't included the result charts for the entire day, many of the other races had similar outcomes: front runners drawing away for big wins.

These three horses faced off again on May 5, but this time, the surface was fair. Players who noted the bias on April 20 went home rich: Thunder Zoot won at 20-1 (Figure 2.4); Midnight Cruiser and High Tailing were beaten while each was well bet.

Figure 2.4

Fifth Race Emerald Downs- May 5, 2001

6½FURLONGS. (1.14⅘) CLAIMING. Purse $10,000 FOR THREE YEAR OLDS WHICH HAVE NEVER WON TWO RACES. Weight 121 lbs. Non-winners of a race in 2001 allowed 3 lbs. CLAIMING PRICE $16,000 (maiden races, claiming and starter races for $12,500 or less not considered). NWRA reserves the right to retain possession of all registration papers for any horses claimed at Emerald Downs until the conclusion of the current race meet.) (PLUS UP TO $975 TO WA-BREDS).

Value of race: $10,000. Winner $5,500; second $2,000; third $1,500; fourth $750; fifth $250. Mutuel pool $46,358.00. Exacta pool $25,294.00. Trifecta pool $25,934.00. Superfecta pool $6,529.00.

Last Raced	Horse	Med/Eqp	A	Wgt	PP	St	1/4	1/2	Str	Fin	Jockey	Cl'g Pr	Odds $1
20Apr01 ^{7}EmD^{5}	Thunder Zoot	Bb	3	118	7	8	7^{1}	6^{3}	2^{hd}	$1^{1/4}$	Matias J	16000	20.19
14Apr01 ^{8}PM^{5}	Bullero	B	3	121	4	7	8^{4}	$7^{1/2}$	5^{2}	2^{nk}	Perez M	16000	16.10
20Apr01 ^{7}EmD^{1}	Midnight Cruiser	LB	3	121	3	1	$3^{1\,1/4}$	2^{1}	1^{1}	$3^{1\,1/4}$	Ventura H	16000	0.80
27Apr01 ^{5}EmD^{1}	Alandem	Bb	3	118	5	2	$4^{1\,1/2}$	4^{hd}	$4^{1/2}$	$4^{1\,1/4}$	Russell B	16000	a-3.70
27Apr01 ^{7}PM^{1}	Fly Buddy Fly	Bb	3	118	6	9	9	9	6^{2}	$5^{1\,3/4}$	Conklin J	16000	14.20
20Apr01 ^{7}EmD^{2}	High Tailing	LBb	3	118	1	3	1^{hd}	1^{hd}	$3^{1/2}$	$6^{3/4}$	GonsalvesF	16000	a-3.70
20Apr01 ^{7}EmD^{4}	Chili Rehanno	LBb	3	113	8	5	$6^{3\,1/2}$	8^{5}	$7^{1/2}$	$7^{3/4}$	WhitakerJ	16000	16.10
20Apr01 ^{7}EmD^{3}	Proud Native	LBb	3	118	9	6	5^{hd}	$5^{1/2}$	8^{5}	$8^{12\,3/4}$	Lopez L	16000	5.30
22Apr01 ^{3}EmD^{1}	Arctic Comet	LB	3	118	2	4	2^{hd}	3^{hd}	9	9	Baze V	16000	22.30

a—Coupled: Alandem and High Tailing.

Off Time: 3:35 **Time Of Race:** :22⅗ :45⅗ 1:11⅗ 1:18
Start: Good For All But Fly Buddy Fly. **Track:** Fast. **Won driving.**

$2 Mutuel Payoffs:

6	Thunder Zoot	42.20	13.40	4.40
4	Bullero		16.00	5.60
8	Midnight Cruiser			3.00

$1 Exacta 6-4 Paid $193.10; $1 Trifecta 6-4-3 Paid $1,063.20; $1 Superfecta 6-4-3-1 Paid $2,543.00.

Summary

Sometimes a horse will be aided by a bias and run a big speed figure; then when the horse next runs, many will discount its previous performance because of the bias. But realize that winning a race sometimes does help a horse (it may gain confidence; see

Chapter 7), and the horse may jump up and run another big race on a fair surface.

Be aware of the danger in evaluating a horse that runs huge (I mean really big) against a bias. For example, on a day when the rail was dead, a horse forced a rocket pace (several lengths quicker than par) while racing along the inside throughout, battling against the bias every step of the way and still ended up earning a good final figure (above par). The horse had just run its eyeballs out. It is natural to want to bet the horse heavily if the horse comes back in a good spot in its next race. However, on occasion, the horse comes back in a good spot only to run poorly. The explanation is that the big effort against the bias took too much out of the horse (to use a sheet term, the horse "bounced"), and the horse needed more time to recover before being able to repeat that big effort.

This is one reason I don't use Ragozin or Thoro-Graph sheet speed figures. These figures are represented as including everything important in a horse's effort, and the sheet users proceed to evaluate a horse's line based on those figures. But races like the above scenario — forcing a fast pace while racing on a dead rail — and others like it happen every day. Since the sheet figures don't include these relevant factors, they wouldn't see the horse in the example above as running a huge race and also as a potential bounce candidate. But when you are aware of all the factors that are at work in a horse's final speed figure, you will be better equipped to evaluate that horse more effectively.

Watching the races for trouble or other trip information and being aware of a possible bias are just two of the things that many players do to evaluate a horse's performance better. Keep in mind that the two sometimes conflict. For example, a horse is sitting in perfect position — a couple of lengths behind a two-horse speed duel — then looms up while wide, battles through the stretch, but is outfinished late. Most trip handicappers would conclude that the horse had a perfect trip but hung.

But after calculating pace and final speed figures, you realize that the horse chased a pretty fast pace for the day; in other words, although the horse appeared to get the perfect stalking trip, it may have been too close to a fast pace. Taking it a step further, after reviewing the results for the day, you realize that the inside of the track was very good. You now know the horse was racing on the slower part of the track while chasing a fast pace, so you become impressed with the horse's effort while others may downgrade the effort because it looked like a perfect trip.

Wind

While wind will affect the moisture content of the racetrack and thus the final times on that surface, wind also has other effects on horses during a race.

On windy days, some horses may take the worst of the wind and others may be protected from it. On Breeders' Cup Day 2001 at Belmont Park, horses faced a strong headwind as they ran down the backstretch. After the day, many players felt that the surface favored horses that came from behind — there was a closing bias.

However, others had a different explanation for the advantage that closers appeared to have had. Those players made a strong argument that the surface itself was fair, but the wind and the nature of Belmont Park were the reasons closers did well that day. Most of the dirt races at Belmont Park that day were one-turn races with long runs on the backstretch. The effect of the strong wind in the faces of horses running on or near the lead, coupled with the amount of time those horses were on the backstretch, probably left those horses pretty tired when they finally reached the turn, thus aiding closers. Those closers may have been protected from the headwind somewhat early in the race and also were not asked to run as hard into that wind.

Whether you thought the surface favored closers or thought the combination of headwind and track layout aided closers, the result was the same. On Breeders' Cup Day 2001, all of the dirt races (except for the Classic) started on the backstretch. Had this been a normal day of racing at any track (one-mile tracks) around the country,[1] the wind would have affected only the front runners that were sprinting because it may have evened out in a race in which the horses traveled two turns. In this case many

[1]Belmont Park is a one and a half-mile track, but most of the dirt races on Breeders' Cup Day were either one and one-sixteenth miles or one and one-eighth miles which are one-turn races at Belmont. At most other tracks, those distances would be two-turn races.

players might not have noticed or considered the effect of a head-wind on horses in the one-turn races.

The wind has other effects. First, some horses will become riled up by the wind and noises associated with it. Others may be intimidated by the wind and noise. Second, as a side note, wind will affect raw fractions and final times on any given day. Sometimes, because of an approaching storm or quickly passing storm cell, the wind speed will vary greatly throughout the day. On-track players who are keeping track of significant wind changes will have an advantage when calculating speed figures for that day.

Summary

A variety of factors affect each horse and where that horse finishes during a race. Trouble is a big one. Related factors include how a horse runs (its action) and, in some cases, how it wins. Some trouble is obvious, but the bigger advantage is in noting subtle things such as the way a horse runs or the way the horse was ridden in its last race and then using that information to evaluate a horse's previous race better. Other players, for the most part, are just looking for the slow starts and wide trips.

Biases are another factor that can also be tricky to evaluate, but if you can correctly identify a bias and use that information to evaluate a horse's previous efforts better, you will have a significant advantage.

Race-to-Race Changes:
When Are They Important?

W hile many factors affect a horse's performance during a race, changes in medication, equipment, appearance, and workouts can also be influences.

Changes in Medication

Horses can receive various medications between races and/or on race day. The list of these medications is long and constantly changing. While medication laws vary from state to state (including what medications and in what amounts are allowed in a horse's system on race day), most players concentrate on the diuretic Salix (formerly known and still commonly referred to as Lasix).

Lasix

Lasix (generically known as furosemide) is one of the most common equine medications. Knowing why horses receive Lasix and the possible rules surrounding its use can become important when a handicapper is evaluating a horse's previous and future efforts.

Why Horses Receive Lasix

Many Thoroughbreds experience respiratory problems during a race. These problems can result in a poor performance when a horse either "bleeds," "flips its palate," or "entraps it epiglottis." Exercise-induced pulmonary hemorrhage, known as bleeding, is the most common.

During strenuous exercise, some blood vessels in the horse's lungs may burst, coating the lungs with blood and preventing the horse from processing oxygen efficiently. While most bleeding is not externally visible, on rare occasions you will see blood trickle out of a horse's nostrils after a race. Sometimes a horse will cough after a race, which can be a sign of bleeding.

The severity of bleeding can affect the horse's performance. If a horse is expected to run well and doesn't, its trainer usually will request a veterinary examination to determine whether the horse bled. Bleeding can be discovered by "scoping" — looking down a horse's throat with a small camera. If the horse is a bleeder, it is placed on Lasix for its next race.

As a diuretic, Lasix helps remove excess fluid (water) from a horse's system, but its main use in racehorses is to diminish the severity of bleeding or hopefully prevent bleeding altogether. In addition to giving a horse Lasix, a trainer has other options to help keep the horse from bleeding in future races. These include changing a horse's feeding program, not running the horse on hot/humid days when it's harder to breathe, or turning the horse out (giving the horse a rest). Additionally, the amount (dose) of Lasix can be changed. Some old-time trainers might even place copper wire around a horse's tail, a folk remedy believed to keep a horse from bleeding.

Rules Surrounding Lasix

Again, when a horse has been determined to have bled, a veterinarian will place it on Lasix for its next race and issue a certificate stating that the horse has bled. If the bleeding was severe, the horse may be placed immediately on albuterol or clenbuterol, bronchodilators that help the horse recover more quickly. Most states have a law that does not allow albuterol or clenbuterol in a horse's system on race day, as those medications are considered performance enhancing. If either of these medications has been used recently, a horse may be forced to miss a start to let the medication clear from its system.

If a horse bled in its last race, it usually will receive a small dose of Lasix before its next workout. After the workout, the horse will be scoped to make sure no bleeding has occurred. Before its next race the horse receives a dose of Lasix at a set time established by that state's racing commission, usually four hours before post.

Most horses are put on Lasix before they even run in their first race. They are scoped after a workout prior to their first start and are "determined" to have bled in that workout.[1] Normally, the horse will appear on the vet's list[2] as having bled and you can match it with a published workout.

The fact that some trainers are quick to get a horse on Lasix soon after it starts its career (assuming it isn't already on Lasix) while other trainers won't put a horse on Lasix until it actually bleeds in a race can be very frustrating. You may find yourself playing a horse that you feel should win, but the horse runs poorly and then appears on the vet's list as having "bled." As a handicapper, you wonder why the connections didn't already have the horse on Lasix. From your perspective they essentially wasted a race, one you thought they would win, by not using Lasix as a preventive measure.

Obtaining information about a horse that has bled and then receives Lasix for the first time is easy. It is usually published on the vet's list or in either the program or *Daily Racing Form* as "1st time Lasix" or "1L."

Effects of Lasix

If after some good races a horse runs poorly and is found to have bled, the horse will most likely return to its previous performance level if given Lasix. Some horses will even improve. Lasix can expand a horse's lung capacity, making it easier for that horse to process oxygen, or it can calm a nervous horse. Any of these effects can lead to an improved performance.

Sometimes, Lasix will have a negative effect on a few horses, "flattening them out" or depleting their energy. In such cases, either the dose will be reduced or the horse will be taken off Lasix completely.

On occasion, a horse given Lasix will be scratched just before a race. For example, the horse loses its rider or runs off in the post parade. The horse is unhurt, so the trainer enters the horse right

---

[1]Some states allow horses to be placed on Lasix with no proof of bleeding at the trainer's discretion. Other states want a veterinarian's certificate. In this case, the vet will say that the horse bled, even if the horse really didn't. This happens often and isn't a big deal, the connections of the horse are abiding to the exact letter of the state law and get the vet to qualify the horse for Lasix.

[2]Most tracks post a vet's list daily in the customer service center. Reasons for being on the list are bleeding, lameness, sickness, soreness, etc. In most cases after a horse appears on the vet's list, the horse must work out while being observed by the state vet in order to be taken off the vet's list and allowed to enter a race.

back in an upcoming race. Remember that the horse already was given Lasix prior to the race from which it was scratched. A few days later the horse is given Lasix again. Giving a horse Lasix twice in a short time can sap its energy and result in a dull effort.

Bleeding Through Lasix

It is not uncommon for horses to bleed while on Lasix ("bleed through Lasix"). How do trainers know their horse bled through Lasix? Anytime a horse's effort wasn't up to par (even if the horse is already on Lasix) or if it shows any signs of a breathing/bleeding problem such as coughing, most trainers have their vets scope the horse. By knowing whether the horse bled through Lasix, the trainer can make changes prior to running the horse again; additionally, the trainer will know why the horse ran poorly.

Most trainers and private vets keep this information quiet because in many states the laws restrict a horse that bled through Lasix from running for a certain time, for example, ten days. While waiting ten days to enter isn't normally a problem, if the state vet finds out that the horse bled through Lasix a second time, the restricted time is usually longer — thirty days, sometimes months. That lengthy delay from racing is why most trainers and private vets do not want it publicly known that a horse bled through Lasix during a race.

So, as a handicapper, what are you to do? In some cases you may be guessing if you think a horse bled through Lasix in its last start. Or you may never know. I keep track of days that are warmer than normal because warm or hot days increase the chances of a horse's bleeding through Lasix. If a horse I expected to run well runs poorly on a hot day, I might ignore the effort and make the assumption that the horse bled despite receiving Lasix, or I'll at least consider the possibility. As a side note, heat does affect all horses differently. This is another reason I keep track of which days were hot. I may excuse a bad race if the horse ran on a hot day.

Other Medications

While most players will concentrate on Lasix and its potential effect on a horse's performance, there are other medications horses can receive between race days and even on race day. Many of these medications are not considered performance enhancing and are not tested for; others are restricted to limited amounts on race day.

One of the medications you are probably familiar with is Butazolidin (Bute). Bute is an anti-inflammatory and can help with common aches and pains experienced by any athlete in training. Bute is allowed in a horse's system on race day, but most states strictly regulate race-day amounts. If a horse is found to have too much Bute in its system, the trainer may be fined.

Another common medication, Adequan is given to help horses that may be susceptible to joint or cartilage deterioration and/or inflammation. Many horses have joint deterioration and/or inflammation as a result of age or the rigors of training. Over time this joint deterioration can affect a horse's performance. Adequan can help stop this deterioration by improving joint lubrication, and it can relieve pain by reducing inflammation in the joint. Finally, it can promote cartilage growth.

Adequan isn't cheap, and it doesn't help every horse, although it has helped some of our horses significantly.

When I glanced at a recent vet bill, there were other substances that were being given to our horses between race days. These included anabolic steroids for muscle mass, non-steroidal anti-inflammatories, and electrolytes.

As a handicapper, you should keep in mind that when a horse changes barns (either via claim or private sale), it may be given new medications. Some of these medications, such as Adequan, could result in an improved effort. Unfortunately, you will not know what or when other medications are given to a horse because their use is not disclosed to the public, so evaluate the horse accordingly.

Changes in Equipment

Equipment changes can sometimes improve a horse's perform-ance. For example, handicappers should consider whether a horse has added blinkers, is now running in bar shoes, etc. Noting these changes may help in predicting the outcome of a race.

Blinkers

Blinkers are used to restrict a horse's range of vision and to make it focus on racing or to keep it running straight (for horses that race erratically or lug in or out during a race). Blinkers can improve a horse's effort, sometimes greatly. Also, putting blinkers on for the first time may result in the horse's showing increased early speed. The combination of first-time Lasix, blinkers, and a nice workout prior to a race can signal significant improvement and thus a nice betting angle.

The removal of blinkers ("blinkers off") can be viewed as both positive and negative. Removal of blinkers sometimes can signal an act of desperation if the horse isn't running well and the horse's connections decide to try something different. On the positive side the removal of blinkers can help a horse relax during a race (its vision isn't restricted, thus taking away its fear of not being able to see), or it can wake up a horse to the competition.

Shadow Rolls

A shadow roll is a thick band of fleece on the noseband that prevents the horse from seeing the ground. Some horses see shadows of themselves, the rail, or other horses and try to jump those shadows. A shadow roll is also used on horses that race "high-headed" in an effort to help them run a little more smoothly.

Tongue-tie

A tongue-tie is a thin piece of string/cloth that secures the tongue to keep it from interfering with breathing. Most trainers use tongue-ties whenever their horses race, though some trainers prefer instead a certain type of bit that also keeps a horse's tongue in place. For example, a spoon bit keeps the tongue pressed down, or a Sure-Win bit holder (also called a Seattle Slew bit) keeps the bit back in the mouth and makes it less likely the tongue will get over the bit

Some players try to keep track of horses that are using a tongue-tie for the first time. The addition of the tongue-tie may imply that the horse had trouble breathing in its last race. Most tongue-ties can be easily seen if you are near the paddock. You will see a thin piece of cloth tied around the bottom part of the mouth.

Leg Wraps — Front Leg Wraps

A leg wrap is a combination of cloth and elastic wrapped around a horse's lower leg and ankle. The wrap may be placed on any or all of a horse's legs. Wraps are typically used to help prevent nicks and scrapes during a race. Front wraps also can help support the legs/ankles of a horse that has some physical problems (with tendons or ligaments).

Additionally, front leg wraps can be used to deter a claim or to attempt to get a horse claimed. If a horse is being dropped suspiciously in claiming price and also comes out wearing front wraps for the first time, the addition of those wraps may discourage claims. Interested trainers may see the wraps as a sign that the horse has a physical problem, and that indeed might be the case. However, a trainer, knowing that other trainers/owners will not be as likely to claim a horse with front leg wraps, might add the wraps specifically to discourage people from claiming the horse.

One time at Emerald Downs my partners and I were interested in claiming a horse because it had been badly overmatched in its races. The horse finally was dropped to a level where it fit very well. The trainer didn't have a big barn and protected this horse for months by running the horse at high claiming levels. When the horse was walked over for the race, it had every possible piece of equipment on: extension blinkers, which implied the horse lugged out; patches on its hind ankles, which implied the horse speedy cut; copper wire wrapped around its tail, which implied he was a bleeder. The trainer didn't miss a thing. For us, this was perfect. In our minds putting all that stuff on him was just for show and to prevent a claim; it told us that the horse was fine despite the big drop in claiming price and we claimed the horse.

Another time I was interested in a horse that also was being dropped in class. This horse had worn front leg wraps in its past races, all good efforts. The race meet was coming to an end, and I assumed this horse's connections wanted another win and didn't care if they lost the horse because this trainer didn't race during the winter. She usually just turned her horses out until the next year. When the horse came over to the paddock for the race, it was not wearing the front leg wraps. I took this to be a bad sign. By taking the front wraps off, the trainer was signaling to prospective buyers that the horse's legs were fine and claims were welcome. In this case, although the horse's legs were fine, it had developed a breathing problem, thus the trainer's push to get the horse claimed.

One last comment about front leg wraps. Some players don't want to bet on a horse that has been wearing front leg wraps or is wearing them for the first time. On occasion, front wraps do signal leg troubles, but in most cases they are used just for protection. Our partnership has started several horses that raced in front wraps. In every case the wraps were worn for protection.

Rear Leg Wraps and Patches

Wraps on the rear legs or patches on the rear legs (commonly called felt patches; they look like a large white Band-Aid), in addition to being used to protect a horse that "runs down" (burns from contact with the ground), may be used to help protect a horse that "speedy cuts" or "interferes."

Speedy cuts occur when a horse overextends its stride, causing its rear legs to come in contact with its front hoofs or when its rear legs hit (interfere) with each other. Either causes the horse pain and can open some nasty gashes. Speedy cuts result from a horse being rank and can stop a horse cold in a race. The rider, while fighting the horse for control, causes the horse to run awkwardly and strike itself. Speedy cuts can also result from bad conformation and bad action but usually occur when a horse slips on the turns. Speedy cuts can be corrected by different shoeing or by the jockey's giving the horse "room" (racing wide) on the turn so as not to slip.

When a horse has injuries from speedy cuts or interfering, rear leg wraps will be used to protect the horse if the cuts are occurring right above the coronet band (where the hoof starts). Felt patches or high ankle wraps will be used if the cuts are occurring higher on the leg.

Felt patches also can protect a cut that a horse receives in the barn. As with front leg wraps, most horses run fine with rear leg wraps or felt patches; just be aware that their addition could signal some trouble, especially when they are on to protect a horse who speedy cuts or interferes.

Bar Shoe

When a horse has a foot problem, most likely a quarter crack, a bar shoe can help protect the hoof and prevent the crack from expanding. The bar shoe usually covers the entire base of the foot, and its addition usually is noted in either the program or on the overnight sheet.

If the foot problem is minor, the bar shoe is used to keep the horse in training. The trainer hopes the shoe will not affect the horse's performance but allow the foot to heal without losing valuable training time. The trainer's only other option is to rest the horse and wait for the problem to heal itself, a solution that can take a long time and cause expenses to mount.

This isn't realistic if you have a horse that, for example, is a Kentucky Derby or Breeders' Cup candidate. Those are usually once-in-a-lifetime races, so trainers will try to get away with using the bar shoe in training prior to the race and sometimes for the race.

Bar shoes on the horse's rear feet don't bother me as much as on their front feet, but the presence of any bar shoe is not a good sign. I prefer to watch the horse run with the bar shoe before considering betting on it.

I do not hesitate to take a stand against a heavily bet horse that is running in a bar shoe for the first time because very few horses will win with the bar shoe, especially when it is on one of the front feet since much of the stress during running is placed on the front legs/feet, not the rear feet/legs.

Summary

Many other pieces of equipment may be important in relation to a horse's performance. I haven't listed every possible piece of equipment, just some of the more common ones.

In most cases the equipment changes may be minor, but they could be important for any individual horse, so every player should become familiar with them.

Changes in Appearance

In the early 1980s many players found themselves calculating speed figures, but because of the increased popularity of those speed figures, the "high-figure" horse would become heavily bet. The same thing started to happen to those who used trip handicapping on horses that had obvious rough trips in their prior start. So, some players began looking for other information that could give them an advantage over the regular players who were concentrating on speed figures and trip handicapping.

I found myself in this position. During the 1983 and '84 seasons, I had my share of nice winning days, but by the time each season was over, I still showed a loss. Between the 1984 and '85 race meets I came across a book about horses' body language (*The Body Language of Horses* by Tom Ainslie and Bonnie Ledbetter, William Morrow, 1980). This, I thought, would be the information I needed to get an edge over the other handicappers (who concentrated exclusively on speed figures and never really looked at the horses) and to help me win for an entire season.

In addition to reading a couple of books on body language, conformation, and breeding, I watched videotapes on those subjects and attended a one-day class on general horsemanship at a local barn — all to learn how to evaluate a horse's appearance before the race. I felt that my strength (calculating and evaluating speed figures) was also my weakness because I knew that horses are not numbers, and I was depending too much on those numbers.

I learned quickly about sharp horses, dull horses, dappling, washing out, irritated horses, stiff horses, etc. I thought, "This is it!" One of the main reasons my choices were losing was that the horses were not physically right. The horses on the track were not necessarily the same ones, appearance- and condition-wise, that my figures were pointing to from past races. I would now be able to notice this and not play those top-figure horses that often ended up losing.

Armed with all this research, I wanted to give my new angle a try. The Longacres meet was still a couple of months away from opening, so I decided to drive to Portland Meadows for the weekend. I went to the library to get recent results charts; I did the variants to calculate speed figures and used trip/bias notes of some Longacres regulars that also went to Portland. The first day that weekend I came across a horse whose speed figures off its last two starts were substantially higher than those of the rest of the field, and he appeared to earn them without perfect trips. I sat out the first few races that night and instead watched the post parade of those early races to see if I could notice any "sharp" horses or any "dull, stiff, or lame" horses. Not seeing any and not having an opinion on the races anyway, I waited for that big-figure horse to start out my betting weekend. I was almost certain that he would look the picture of health, dappled and alert, all the things that I had learned about over the winter.

Before the post parade, I had expected the horse to be well bet, even money or so, but he was about 3-1. I didn't worry about the higher-than-normal price; a high-figure horse is usually well bet, but there are other times when it isn't as heavily bet for any number of reasons (such as low-percentage connections).

When the horse came onto the track with the rest of the horses, I couldn't believe my eyes. This horse fit, to the tee, the description of the dull, uninterested horse. His coat had no shine, he walked flat-footed, his head hung, and the rider wasn't even holding onto the reins. All the horses turned around and cantered off except this one. He continued to walk slowly toward the starting gate, and it appeared that this horse wasn't going to warm up at all.

In the very first bet I was going to make for the weekend, and for that matter the year, the horse couldn't have stood out more in terms of speed figures and at the same time fit the description of a poor body-language horse, the type I was hoping not to bet on this year in order to become a long-term winner. I really didn't know what to do.

At that time I continued to look at a horse in terms of figures, so I concluded that I would bet this horse despite his looks. My reasoning went something like this: "This horse stood way out on figures but did appear dull, so (my mathematical-oriented mind concluded) the dull looks might cost the horse two or three lengths but he would still win." Even though I had spent all winter learning about body language, I really hadn't thought out how to apply body language in combination with my speed figures and trouble/bias notes. I just assumed that it would be obvious: sharp horses would win; dull horses would lose.

To make matters worse, as the horses were loaded into the gate, this horse didn't want to go in. I had read that a reluctance to load into the gate signaled trouble — the horse "knew" something wasn't right and was signaling that by refusing to enter the gate. But the gate crew got the horse in, and when the gates opened, the horse shot out and went right to the lead with another horse. The horse I had bet on took a short lead into the turn. A different horse came up to challenge, and again he took a short lead leaving the turn. One last horse appeared to move up to him, but again he responded and ended up winning by a half-length. I didn't know whether to celebrate or to walk down the stairs to cash quietly (I almost felt as if I had done something wrong by betting such a dull-looking horse).

When I was in line to cash my ticket, I came across an acquaintance who also had bet the horse. He said he had been waiting a couple of weeks for the horse to come back and run. I said that I also thought the horse stood out in the race but that I had been worried about its "looks" in the post parade. My acquaintance said, "Oh, you're right — but that horse always looks like that."

From that experience I quickly learned that although a horse's appearance might be important, what is really important is a *change* in a horse's appearance from previous races. I then decided on my approach to using a horse's appearance. I would make a note in the program if I saw something out of the ordinary, such as a very sharp horse, one that looked a bit off to me, one that looked washed out (sweaty), or anything else. The next time the horse was going to run, I could compare its looks with the last time it raced. That way, if the horse always looked good or always looked dull, I would know and thus wouldn't have to re-evaluate the horse based on its appearance.

Many "body language" experts strongly recommend going to the paddock before a race. In addition to getting an up-close look at a horse's skin and coat, you can see which ones are hard to saddle (they are either taken to a special stall or saddled while walking around) and which ones are acting a bit nuts or too excited. This might be a horse making its first lifetime start or coming back after a layoff. Sometimes, in anticipation of the actual race, the horse is too excited and is a candidate to get hot (wash out) later. It is also easier to spot tongue-ties in the paddock. On occasion, you will see horses spook, rear up, and/or flip over, main reasons for paddock scratches. Handicappers with an eye for such things can see horses that are acting a bit stiff, are off on one leg, or have a change in a knee or ankle.

Many players like going to the paddock when there are several first-time starters, especially two-year-olds, in the hopes of being able to separate them on looks, size, muscle mass, body type, etc. You may also see horses (usually two-year-old males) that act studdish: their minds are not on racing.

I personally don't go to the paddock much because I find the post parade more useful. Many horses can look flat/dull in the paddock but then will perk up when taken out to the track. Also, if a horse is getting washy, signs (sweat marks between the legs, under the tail, on the chest or neck area, or under the saddle-cloth) are more obvious in the post parade.

While I don't mind worked-up horses that are running in sprint races, I'm cautious if the race is a route, especially a turf route. Horses that appear excited in the post parade are more likely to be unable to relax early (be rank). The rider will have the choice of either taking a hard hold on the horse (which usually results in a defeat because the horse will make a big move when finally allowed to run, then weaken in the stretch) or letting the horse go early, hoping to hang on late. Don't get me wrong, I want the horse to look good, but a horse that is too excited also is more likely to lose it mentally before or during the race.

Writing specific descriptions of a horse's body language is difficult, but just as there are good books on speed figures, there are also some on body language that might help. *Horses Talk: It Pays to Listen* (by Trillis Parker, Parker Productions, 1989) is another good book in addition to *The Body Language of Horses*. I find it easiest just to compare one horse's appearance in the post parade to another's. I think you will quickly find it easy to notice differences in the way horses look and move. Also, as they break away from the post parade, I like to see which horses break into a canter easily and eagerly when asked, which have to be pushed into a canter, and which continue to trot throughout most of the warm-up.

Watching a horse's ears also can be helpful. For example, a horse that pins its ears and swishes its tail might be irritated. A horse with ears forward and/or flicking back and forth is paying attention to its surroundings — a good sign. Again, look for a change in appearance from the horse's previous race.

One of the advantages of attending live races is keeping track of and evaluating a horse's appearance. If you are betting from a simulcast facility or watching a signal imported to your track, you may not get much of a glimpse of the horses prior to the race. For players who concentrate on a horse's appearance, being at the track is a must.

Sometimes the television shot will show you something important such as a horse that has washed out badly or one that looks like it feels good. Although you may be able to notice how some of the horses look by watching television, you will be better able to compare and analyze them if you are at the track in person.

Some players spend more time looking at horses' appearance than I do, betting them for looks rather than past performance. I view a horse's appearance mostly as a minor factor. But just like medication changes, equipment changes, and workouts (the next section), a horse's appearance can be an important factor in certain situations.

Changes in Workouts (Breezes)

Many players believe that workouts (breezes) can offer clues to a horse's current form. These players may place a lot of emphasis on workouts while other players may ignore them. On occasion a workout (or lack of a workout) can be a key to predicting a horse's performance. Other times the presence of (or lack of) a workout is a very minor factor.

Evaluating workouts can be fairly tricky. First, the workout time needs to be evaluated. Second, it needs to be evaluated in conjunction with other factors. Most players may not be aware of some of the variables that affect workout times. For example, whether the workout time was fast or slow, the same questions can be asked:

• Was the horse being asked during the workout, or did it work without prompting? If the horse was asked, how much? Note that some horses can't be restrained much; they always work fast without being asked.

• Did the horse work in company or by itself? Workouts in company tend to be faster. Some horses will not work well by themselves; they need another horse to help get their mind on running.

• Was the workout along the rail or did the horse work while wide on the turns?

• Was the workout right after a track renovation, or later, after several horses had galloped or worked over the surface? Workouts right after a track renovation tend to be faster.

• Did a 110-pound apprentice jockey or a 140-pound exercise rider work the horse? Obviously, workout times will be affected to some extent by the weight of the rider.

If I am not able to attend the workouts daily, I will make an assumption when looking at the times that the workout was under "normal" conditions — but I won't know that for sure. Those who watch and time the workouts on a daily basis can obtain significant advantages.

Those who watch and time workouts (other than official clockers) know when the conditions surrounding a workout are not "normal." For example, observers might upgrade a seemingly slow time if a horse worked well after the renovation with a 140-pound exercise rider while traveling wide on the turn. Some players will subscribe to a local workout report (if available) to get this information, but you can get conflicting information from competing reports.

A workout or a lack thereof may be important in certain situations, but the time of that workout isn't a factor. However, there are certain situations in which a workout could be a good clue to the possible performance of a horse. For example, most trainers will work a horse in a new piece of equipment (such as blinkers) before using that equipment in a race. Therefore, a horse adding blinkers, or Lasix, and showing a fast workout prior to a race may signal improvement. That good, fast workout is a sign the change may help.

A young horse starting to show faster workouts, especially after running for the first or second time in its career, might signal improvement in its next start.

The fact that a first-time starter shows several workouts from the gate could signal that the horse is a bad actor in the gate or has problems breaking sharply from the gate. Either way, this is a negative sign. However, seeing a gate workout after a horse had previously broken poorly or acted up in the gate is a good sign as the trainer is taking steps to solve the problem.

I also watch for the "for sale" workout, usually a fast work accompanied by a large drop in claiming price. A trainer trying to get a horse claimed will try to signal with a nice, fast workout that the horse is perfectly okay. It doesn't have to be a large drop in claiming price; it can be a slight drop after some excellent efforts against tougher horses. On the other hand, if I see a very slow workout before a large drop in claiming price, that may be a sign the trainer is trying to scare people away from claiming the horse.

A few years ago I knew an owner who had a pretty nice horse. The horse had shown stakes potential as a two-year-old but ran mediocre in its first couple of starts at three. It turned out that the horse had developed a "hind end problem" and wouldn't be much in the future. Knowing this, the owner had the horse treated by both a vet and a chiropractor. He did everything he could to get the horse feeling good so that the horse could run its best race. This was also accompanied by a drop into a $25,000 claiming race. While the horse ran a much improved race (placing second) in that start, the owner and trainer knew it was the absolute best effort the horse could possibly give.

In the paddock before the $25,000 claiming race, my friend's trainer noticed other trainers looking at his horse. Although no one dropped a claim that day, the trainer thought that since the horse ran better and appeared to improve in the $25,000 claiming race, a drop to a $20,000 claiming race would be enough not to arouse too much suspicion and get the horse claimed. The trainer had the horse breeze a rocket five furlongs six days before the drop to $20,000. This workout told all who were interested that the horse must be doing well because the workout was good and long (in distance). If those trainers had watched the workout, they might have seen the rider hustling the horse from the start. Anyway, enough trainers, whether they saw the workout or not, were interested in the horse and lined up at the claim box. The horse ran poorly that day, slowly descended the claiming ranks to the bottom, and never won again.

Many variations of the "for sale" workout exist, such as a well-bred first-time starter or a high-priced yearling purchase in for a claiming tag with fast workouts. The list is long. One note: Horses falling into the above categories (appearing to be "for sale") may run well on that particular day and even win — the horse's problem is still minor but may become more of an issue later. The point is to realize there may be a problem or potential problem with the horse.

Another type of workout I look for is the "too fast" blowout before a race. Some trainers will breeze their horses three, four, or five days prior to a race. Sometimes, if the horse is very sharp or gets away from the exercise rider, it can go too fast, leaving its race on the track. If I encounter a horse that I thought should have run well but did not and I see this type of workout prior to that effort, I might assume the fast workout took too much out of the horse. Horses are not like humans in their ability to recover from work; they will sometimes take several days to recover from a strenuous workout or race. What may be an innocent four-furlong blowout in :47 a few days before a race could be enough to dull the horse on race day.

For instance, Crossatyourownrisk was entered at Emerald Downs on June 23, 2001, in a one-mile stakes. She had come off a couple of sprints in which she was hurt by her inside post draws but still ran very well in those races when facing the top sprinter on the grounds, Fleet Pacific (Figure 3.1). She was now going to a route and I expected a big race from her.

Crossatyourownrisk

Figure 3.1

When she ran poorly (seventh place, beaten by ten lengths), I didn't understand why and thought she had to have some excuse (Figure 3.2). After the race and prior to her next start, the trainer said the horse had gotten away from her exercise rider and worked much faster than they wanted on June 21, two days before her race. That wasn't the case when she ran against the same horses on July 15 (Figure 3.3).

Figure 3.2

Ninth Race Emerald Downs- June 23, 2001

1 MILE. (1.33½) KING COUNTY HANDICAP. Purse $40,000. Fillies and mares, 3-year-olds and upward. By subscription of $100 each, which shall accompany the nomination, $250 to enter, $250 additional to start with $22,000 guaranteed to the winner, $8,000 to second, $6,000 to third, $3,000 to fourth and $1,000 to fifth. Weights: Wednesday, June 20, 2001. High weights preferred. Nominations closed Saturday, June 16.

Value of race: $40,000. Winner $22,000; second $8,000; third $6,000; fourth $3,000; fifth $1,000. Mutuel pool $41,472.00. Exacta pool $17,506.00. Trifecta pool $22,471.00.

Last Raced	Horse	Med/Eqp	A	Wgt	PP	St	1/4	1/2	3/4	Str	Fin	Jockey	Odds $1
2Jun01 ⁸EmD¹	Latter Day Paula	LBb	4	113	7	8	$8^{2\%}$	9^3	8^3	5_4	$1^{1\%}$	RussellB	a-3.00
3Jun01 ⁹EmD²	Taste the Passion	LBb	4	117	2	6	7^1	5^{hd}	5^1	3^1	$2^{2\%}$	GnslvesF	5.00
13May01 ⁹EmD⁷	Run a Copy	LBb	4	115	6	4	$1^\%$	1^1	$1^\%$	$2^{1\%}$	$3^{1\%}$	MatiasJ	10.10
3Jun01 ⁹EmD¹	Fleet Pacific	LB	7	123	9	1	2^3	2^4	2^2	1^{hd}	4^{hd}	MitchellG	1.50
3June01 ⁹EmD⁴	One Number Short	LBbf	5	117	4	2	4^4	3^{hd}	3^2	$4^\%$	$5^{2\%}$	CedenoA	6.30
2Jun01 ⁸EmD²	Icicle Angel	LBbf	4	113	8	3	$6^{1\%}$	$7^\%$	$6^\%$	6^1	6^2	CedenoO	29.70
3Jun01 ⁹EmD³	Crossatyourownrisk	LB	4	118	1	7	5^{hd}	6^{hd}	7^2	7^4	$7^{5\%}$	BazeG	a-3.00
3Jun01 ⁹EmD⁶	Rollette	LBf	5	118	3	9	9	8^2	9	8^{hd}	$8^{1\%}$	LopezL	14.10
3Jun01 ⁹EmD⁷	Miss Pixie	LB	4	115	5	5	$3^{2\%}$	4^5	4^1	9	9	ChavesN	14.20

a—Coupled: Latter Day Paula and Crossatyourownrisk.

Off Time: 5:22	**Time Of Race:** :22'₅	:45	1:10	1:23½	1:37
Start: Good.	**Track:** Fast.			**Won driving.**	

$2 Mutuel Payoffs:

1A	Latter Day Paula	8.00	3.60	3.00
2	Taste the Passion		4.80	4.20
6	Run a Copy			7.00

$1 Exacta 1-2 Paid $14.70; $1 Trifecta 1-2-6 Paid $145.80.

©EQUIBASE

Figure 3.3

Ninth Race Emerald Downs- July 15, 2001

1⅟₁₆ Miles. (1.39½) 6th Running of THE BOEING HANDICAP. Purse $40,000 Guaranteed. A HANDICAP FOR FILLIES AND MARES, THREE-YEARS-OLD AND UPWARD. By subscription of $100 each which shall accompany the nomination, $250 to enter, $250 additional to start, with $22,000 guaranteed to the winner, $8,000 to second, $6,000 to third, $3,000 to fourth and $1,000 to fifth. Weights: Wednesday, July 11, 2001. Starters to be named through the entry box by the closing time of entries. High weights preferred. Nominations closed at 1:00 p.m., Saturday, July 7, 2001.

Value of race: $40,000. Winner $22,000; second $8,000; third $6,000; fourth $3,000; fifth $1,000. Mutuel pool $57,447.00. Exacta pool $29,109.00. Trifecta pool $28,304.00. Superfecta pool $6,529.00.

Last Raced	Horse	Med/Eqp	A	Wgt	PP	St	1/4	1/2	3/4	Str	Fin	Jockey	Odds $1
23Jun01 ⁹EmD⁷	Crossatyourownrisk	LB	4	119	2	4	5^{hd}	$6^{1\%}$	3^{hd}	$1^{2\%}$	$1^{4\%}$	Matias J	a-1.90
23Jun01 ⁹EmD¹	Latter Day Paula	LBb	4	116	7	7	$4^\%$	4^2	4^1	$4^\%$	2^{nk}	Russell B	a-1.90
23Jun01 ⁹EmD²	Taste the Passion	LBb	4	117	4	5	$6^{1\%}$	5^1	5^3	5^{10}	$3^{2\%}$	GnsalvesF	3.40
23Jun01 ⁹EmD⁴	Fleet Pacific	LB	7	121	1	1	1^{hd}	$1^\%$	$1^\%$	3^{hd}	4^{nk}	Mitchell G	2.00
23Jun01 ⁹EmD⁹	Miss Pixie	LB	4	113	3	3	3^1	3^{hd}	$2^{1\%}$	2^{hd}	5^{12}	WhitakerJ	22.10
27Jun01 ⁵Hol⁶	Paige's Sister	LB	5	114	6	6	7	7	7	6^5	$6^{20\%}$	McFadden	15.90
16Jun01 ⁷Hst¹	Grooms Derby	LB	4	121	5	2	2^5	2^5	6^2	7	7	Loseth C	4.20

a—Coupled: Crossatyourownrisk and Latter Day Paula.

Off Time: 5:28	**Time Of Race:** :22½	:45½	1:10½	1:36½	1:42½
Start: Good For All.	**Track:** Fast.			**Won driving.**	

$2 Mutuel Payoffs:

1	Crossatyourownrisk	5.80	5.20	3.40
1A	Latter Day Paula		5.20	3.40
4	Taste the Passion			3.00

$1 Exacta 1-4 Paid $8.20; $1 Trifecta 1-4-2 Paid $22.90.

©EQUIBASE

One last type of workout pattern that I note is the "rush job." This occurs when a horse has been running well but is forced to miss some training, usually due to a minor injury or illness, and is coming off a short rest. Since the horse has been unable to train for a few days or a week, the trainer, pointing for a race that is coming up quickly, will rush the horse in its workouts. You may see this type of horse entered that shows no workouts for a certain time after the horse's last race, then three or so works within a couple of weeks right before the race. This horse is probably not ready for its best effort.

In general, when looking at any workout or series of workouts, I try to look for consistency regarding the workout pattern for that trainer. For example, if the trainer breezed the horse five days before the horse ran last time, and the horse ran well, I would look for a similarly spaced workout. In this case, the actual time doesn't mean too much to me. The same would apply to a first-time starter; I would prefer consistent, evenly spaced workouts. Gaps in the workout pattern of first-time starters could signal trouble.

One other area to be aware of when evaluating workouts is the accuracy of workout times. The trainers usually are required to notify the clockers prior to working a horse, and most will. As an owner, I know of too many occasions when the horse we owned breezed and the official time was either inaccurate, credited to the wrong horse, or the horse was missed completely. (Both the trainer and I timed the work then compared our time to the official time; other works were not published at all.)

Watching and keeping track of official workouts can be a potentially profitable activity. Since most players can't watch workouts live, you should be aware that much of the information regarding the circumstances of any particular workout isn't available. This awareness will help you decide how much emphasis to place on published workouts. Most states have a law saying a horse must show a published work if it has not run in awhile. For example, if a horse has not raced in thirty days, it must show one work of three furlongs or longer; if it has not run in sixty days, it must show two works of at least four furlongs in distance. These works do not have to be at the track; they can be at a training facility that has an official timer recording the works.

Backstretch Decisions:
Reading Between the Lines

The *Daily Racing Form* and/or a track program present racing information in a tidy package. Races are listed in order, horses are listed by post position, riders are named, and so forth so that players can easily use the information to handicap.

However, a lot has happened prior to the publication of the *Form* or program. Much of the information gathered is based on decisions trainers and owners make prior to running their horses, such as choosing a race from the condition book in which to enter the horse, picking a rider (and dealing with jockey agents), and deciding on what tactics the connections may decide upon before the race (such as sending the horse to the lead early, sitting just off the lead early, or taking the horse back to come from behind). Being aware of the restrictions that govern these decisions and the rules surrounding claiming races (which comprise the majority of races) may provide a handicapper valuable information.

Choosing a Race/Entering a Horse
The Condition Book

The racing secretary is responsible for publishing the condition book, a small pamphlet-like book that lists the races offered at a track during a specific period. The racing secretary writes races that hopefully will fit the local horse population and give most every horse on the grounds a chance to compete. Condition books, which can be obtained from a track's racing

Past Performances are © 2004 by Daily Racing Form, Inc. and Equibase Company. Reprinted with permission of the copyright owner.

office, also usually contain the track's rules on when a horse can scratch and its rules for claiming.

Trainers choose races for their horses from the condition book. The entry rules can vary greatly from one state to another and from one track to another. The horse is entered in the race by the trainer, jockey agent, or sometimes the owner. (Trainers also use the condition book to plan their daily training for each horse — knowing a race for a certain horse is coming up in two weeks, the trainer may breeze that horse five or six days prior.)

On any particular day the condition book usually will offer eight or nine scheduled races plus one or two extras. Most tracks have a minimum number of required entries (for example, six) before a race in the book can "go," or fill. If the minimum number of entries is not met, the racing secretary will use one of the "extra" races (alternate races offered in case the scheduled ones don't fill). In addition to the one or two extras printed in the condition book, the overnight sheet may list additional extras,[1] sometimes several, if the secretary thinks many of the original races aren't going to fill. Overnight sheets are also available at the racing office.

While the races in the condition book are numbered one through eight, they will not necessarily go in that order. Field size (number of horses entered) and purse size (for the feature race) may determine the order. Larger fields are usually scheduled later in the day to make certain exotics, such as the pick fours or superfectas, more attractive to players who otherwise might leave early or look to other tracks. The last race is usually a bottom-level claimer or maiden race; you may hear a comment such as "Gary Stevens is staying around to ride this horse, he must like it" — when, in fact, the race could have originally been listed as the second of the day but was moved because of the field size. Stevens and his agent don't know in advance where on the card the race will be scheduled.

Choosing a Jockey

Some players draw conclusions based on which horse a jockey

---

[1]An overnight sheet is a one-page sheet that lists the races that have just been drawn and also the new extras for the next day.

chose to ride, especially if that jockey had previously ridden two horses that are running against each other. These players assume the jockey chose one horse over the other because he thinks he has a better chance of winning with that horse.

The reality is he, or usually his agent, may not choose the better horse, but not from lack of trying. The challenge is the jockey or agent obviously won't know what post positions will be drawn or what other horses will comprise the field. For example, the agent and rider may have a choice between a front runner and a closer. They go with the front runner, but that horse draws a poor post in a race that drew several other front runners. At that point they probably wished they had chosen the closer.

There are other reasons a rider may end up on one horse over another that may have nothing to do with which horse is better. For instance, the rider may have "first call" for a certain barn and must ride that stable's horses before any others, regardless of other horses' chances of winning.

Also, trainers commonly wait and enter a horse right before entries close. Sometimes a horse's regular rider might have already committed to riding another horse, and the trainer must find a new rider. It may appear that the rider chose one horse over the other when, in fact, he didn't.

Most agents have more than one rider. If one rider has to choose between two good mounts in the same race, an agent will try to get the other rider to pick up the call on the leftover horse. By doing this, the agent probably ensures the mount of the first jockey for future races.

Another possibility is that the trainer decides to make a rider change. Maybe a horse is running well for a certain rider but is not winning, so the trainer decides to use another rider, hoping to get a win.

So, overall, don't give too much significance to a rider's leaving one contender for another.

Shipping a Horse to a Race

While most horses are stabled at the track where they run, some have to be shipped in from a training facility off track or another racetrack. Most of these horses arrive by van, and some may not handle the ride well, especially a long trip. These horses can become very nervous and stressed during shipping, which can affect how they run. Additionally, new surroundings can stress a horse, upsetting its ability to rest or eat.

For example, many horses are shipped between northern and southern California. If a horse stabled in southern California is entered to run at Bay Meadows on a Sunday, that horse will usually be shipped either Friday, after entries are drawn, or Saturday. The trip takes eight hours or more, and I might be leery of playing a horse that has just shipped in after a long van ride. At the same time I might excuse a poor race in which I know a horse had to run after a long ship. Some horses handle shipping fine, but I would look for evidence that the horse shipped and ran well in its previous races.

Most trainers will not ship a horse until they know the horse actually has a spot in a race. Certain races such as stakes races will fill with no problem, so a trainer usually will ship the horse early, a couple of weeks or so in advance. This gives the horse time to recover from traveling and also to acclimate to the new surroundings. Published workouts at the track will indicate whether a horse has been on the grounds for a couple of weeks. Other times you may have no way of telling when a horse might have shipped.

Filling a Race

Races are usually "drawn" (entries taken) two days in advance, but some are drawn as far ahead as four days.

The number of horses entered is updated throughout the morning entries are accepted. Some trainers will enter a horse early in the morning; others may wait until the final minutes before entries close. If a race doesn't fill, it could be carded back the next day or in the next few days as an extra. For example, if four or five horses are entered in the original race, the racing secretary may know he can move the race back a day or two and get some more entries to fill it. Also, that race could be carded at a different (usually shorter) distance to draw more horses. If that fails, the race is dropped.

Most trainers would like to race their horses every two to four weeks, but if the race for a certain horse is not filling, the horse will have to stay in the barn longer or the trainer will have to find a less-than-ideal race in which to run. Time between races also can increase in the event of bad weather, and sometimes months can elapse before a trainer finds the ideal race for a horse. As a handicapper, you might excuse a short layoff between starts as you know the horse hasn't run because races were not filling, not because of injury or sickness. Or you might see a horse entered in a race where it looks overmatched or misplaced and figure out that the trainer can't get the right race to fill, so he is running the horse where it does not belong to keep the horse fit. You then would want to ignore the performance of that horse (from the race where it appeared misplaced) when evaluating that horse in the future.

Let's look at an example from Emerald Downs of races that

Figure 4.1 — Condition book (races 6-9 and substitute races not shown)

THIRTY SEVENTH DAY – FRIDAY, JUNE 20, 2003
Entries Close on Wednesday, June 18, 2003

1 FIRST RACE   **MAIDEN/CLAIMING**
PURSE $5,500. (PLUS UP TO $536 TO WA-BREDS) FOR MAIDENS, TWO YEAR OLDS.
Weight .... 118 lbs.
CLAIMING PRICE $8,000

FIVE FURLONGS
NWRA reserves the right to retain possession of all registration papers for any horses claimed at Emerald Downs until the conclusion of the current race meet.

2 SECOND RACE   **WASHINGTON MAIDEN/CLAIMING**
PURSE $5,500. (PLUS UP TO $536 TO WA-BREDS) FOR MAIDENS, FILLIES THREE YEARS OLD (BRED IN WASHINGTON).
Weight .... 120 lbs.
CLAIMING PRICE $8,000

SIX FURLONGS
NWRA reserves the right to retain possession of all registration papers for any horses claimed at Emerald Downs until the conclusion of the current race meet.

3 THIRD RACE   **MAIDEN/CLAIMING**
PURSE $8,400. (PLUS UP TO $819 TO WA-BREDS) FOR MAIDENS, THREE YEAR OLDS AND UPWARD.
Three Year Olds .... 117 lbs.   Older .... 123 lbs.
CLAIMING PRICE $16,000, if for $14,000, allowed .... 2 lbs.

ONE MILE
NWRA reserves the right to retain possession of all registration papers for any horses claimed at Emerald Downs until the conclusion of the current race meet.

4 FOURTH RACE   **CLAIMING**
PURSE $6,500. (PLUS UP TO $634 TO WA-BREDS) FOR THREE YEAR OLDS AND UPWARD.
Three Year Olds .... 117 lbs.   Older .... 123 lbs.
Non-winners of a race since April 19 allowed .... 2 lbs.
A race in 2003 .... 4 lbs.
CLAIMING PRICE $6,250, if for $5,000, allowed .... 2 lbs.
(Maiden races, claiming and starter races for $5,000 or less not considered).

ONE MILE AND ONE-SIXTEENTH
NWRA reserves the right to retain possession of all registration papers for any horses claimed at Emerald Downs until the conclusion of the current race meet.

5 FIFTH RACE   **CLAIMING**
PURSE $6,300. (PLUS UP TO $614 TO WA-BREDS) FOR FILLIES THREE YEARS OLD WHICH HAVE NEVER WON TWO RACES.
Weight .... 120 lbs.
Non-winners of a race in 2003 allowed .... 3 lbs.
CLAIMING PRICE $8,000
(Maiden races, claiming and starter races for $6,250 or less not considered).

ONE MILE
Alternate Distance SIX AND ONE-HALF FURLONGS
NWRA reserves the right to retain possession of all registration papers for any horses claimed at Emerald Downs until the conclusion of the current race meet.

were first offered (Figure 4.1) and the races that actually ended up filling for Friday, June 20, 2003.

When the overnights came out on June 19, the racing secretary listed seven "extra" races for the June 20 card (Figure 4.2), so there were a total of *eighteen* races of which the track would use nine.

Figure 4.2 — Overnight extras

EXTRAS FOR FRIDAY, JUNE 20, 2003

X3 EXTRA RACE NO 3 — MAIDEN SPECIAL WEIGHT
PURSE $13,750. (PLUS UP TO $1,341 TO WA-BREDS) FOR MAIDENS, THREE YEAR OLDS AND UPWARD.
Three Year Olds .... 117 lbs.   Older .... 123 lbs.
SIX AND ONE-HALF FURLONGS

X4 EXTRA RACE NO 4 — MAIDEN/CLAIMING
PURSE $8,400. (PLUS UP TO $819 TO WA-BREDS) FOR MAIDENS, FILLIES AND MARES THREE YEARS OLD AND UPWARD.
Three Year Olds .... 116 lbs.   Older .... 122 lbs.
CLAIMING PRICE $16,000, if for $14,000, allowed .... 2 lbs.
SIX FURLONGS
NWRA reserves the right to retain possession of all registration papers for any horses claimed at Emerald Downs until the conclusion of the current race meet.

X5 EXTRA RACE NO 5 — CLAIMING
PURSE $7,400. (PLUS UP TO $722 TO WA-BREDS) FOR FILLIES AND MARES THREE YEARS OLD AND UPWARD.
Three Year Olds .... 116 lbs.   Older .... 122 lbs.
Non-winners of a race since April 19 allowed .... 2 lbs.
A race in 2003 .... 4 lbs.
CLAIMING PRICE $8,000, if for $7,000, allowed .... 2 lbs.
(Maiden races, claiming and starter races for $7,000 or less not considered).
SIX AND ONE-HALF FURLONGS
NWRA reserves the right to retain possession of all registration papers for any horses claimed at Emerald Downs until the conclusion of the current race meet.

X6 EXTRA RACE NO 6 — CLAIMING
PURSE $8,400. (PLUS UP TO $819 TO WA-BREDS) FOR THREE YEAR OLDS AND UPWARD.
Three Year Olds .... 117 lbs.   Older .... 123 lbs.
Non-winners of a race since April 19 allowed .... 2 lbs.
A race in 2003 .... 4 lbs.
CLAIMING PRICE $10,000
(Maiden races, claiming and starter races for $8,000 or less not considered).
SIX FURLONGS
NWRA reserves the right to retain possession of all registration papers for any horses claimed at Emerald Downs until the conclusion of the current race meet.

X7 EXTRA RACE NO 7 — CLAIMING
PURSE $5,400. (PLUS UP TO $527 TO WA-BREDS) FOR FILLIES THREE YEARS OLD WHICH HAVE NEVER WON TWO RACES.
Weight .... 120 lbs.
Non-winners of a race in 2003 allowed .... 3 lbs.
CLAIMING PRICE $6,250 / *1 ft for $ 5,000 Allowed*   ONE MILE
NWRA reserves the right to retain possession of all registration papers for any horses claimed at Emerald Downs until the conclusion of the current race meet.

X8 EXTRA RACE NO 8 — MAIDEN/CLAIMING
PURSE $6,400. (PLUS UP TO $624 TO WA-BREDS) FOR MAIDENS, FILLIES AND MARES THREE YEARS OLD AND UPWARD.
Three Year Olds .... 116 lbs.   Older .... 122 lbs.
CLAIMING PRICE $10,000, if for $8,000, allowed .... 2 lbs.
FIVE AND ONE-HALF FURLONGS
NWRA reserves the right to retain possession of all registration papers for any horses claimed at Emerald Downs until the conclusion of the current race meet.

X9 EXTRA RACE NO 9 — CLAIMING
PURSE $4,800. (PLUS UP TO $468 TO WA-BREDS) FOR FILLIES AND MARES THREE YEARS OLD AND UPWARD WHICH HAVE NEVER WON TWO RACES.
Three Year Olds .... 116 lbs.   Older .... 122 lbs.
Non-winners of a race in 2003 allowed .... 3 lbs.
CLAIMING PRICE $5,000
FIVE AND ONE-HALF FURLONGS
NWRA reserves the right to retain possession of all registration papers for any horses claimed at Emerald Downs until the conclusion of the current race meet.

Five of the original nine races filled as did the second substitute race and three of the "extras." These were the races that were used (Figure 4.3). Two of the original nine races were carded back for Sunday at different distances and surfaces.

If you note the circles on the actual card — in this case "1st Race (X9)" and "9th Race (4)" are circled — "1st Race (X9)" means this will be the first race of the day, but it originally was carded as extra #9. "9th Race (4)" means this is the ninth race of the day, but originally it was carded as race four (4).

The above is typical at most racetracks throughout the country. Again, many times a race that is in the condition book doesn't fill or is carded back later in the week, etc. This can explain why a horse hasn't run in a while or why a horse appears misplaced in a race.

Figure 4.3 — Overnight sheet

THIRTY SEVENTH DAY		**EMERALD DOWNS**			**FRIDAY, JUNE 20, 2003**	
POST TIME: 6:00 PM					**NO SCRATCH TIME**	

1st RACE (X9)
F&M 3 & UP CLAIMING $5,000
PURSE $4,800 (PLUS UP TO $468 WA-BRED) — 5 1/2 FUR

#								
1	TAKE ISSUE	ML	B.F.4	119	G Mitchell	R-05/29/03	Vann Belvoir	V Belvoir
2	WHISTLE TESTER	ML	Ch.F.4	122	D Velazquez	E-05/18/03	H. E. Maggard	M Jones
3	REASON TO BUCK	ML	Gr/Rn.F.3	116	A Cedeno	R-05/01/03	Bob Thomas	R Terry
4	GREEK BALLET	ML	Ch.F.4	122	K Radke	R-05/08/03	Remmah Racing, Inc	M Molina
5	BORGIA BASKET	ML	Dk.B./Br.M.5	122	H Ventura Jr	E-05/01/03	Mr & Mrs Elwin Gibson	B Gibson
6	SWEETIE BELLE	ML	Dk.B./Br.F.4	119	J Gutierrez	R-06/08/03	Karl Toye &/or Duane Hamamura	J Toye

6

2nd RACE (2)
F 3 YO MAIDEN/CLAIMING $8,000
PURSE $5,500 (PLUS UP TO $536 WA-BRED) — 6 FUR

#								
1	SNOHOMISH GEMINI	ML	B.F.3	120	K Murray	R-06/05/03	Martin or Sylvia Kenney & J. L. Ingalls	M Kenney
2	CLASSIE GREEN	ML	B.F.3	120	G Mitchell	R-06/06/03	James McClellan	J Navarro
3	ES MUY STORMY	ML	Dk.B./Br.F.3	120	S Saito	R-06/06/03	Chris Stanelle	C Stanelle
4	SHORE WEAVE	ML	Gr/Rn.F.3	120	J Gutierrez	R-06/06/03	Jack Porter	F Lucarelli
5	BET A HEATHER	ML	Gr/Rn.F.3	120	G Baze	R-05/31/03	Monogram Stable	M Lloyd
6	CLASSIC HIT	ML	Ch.F.3	120	K Radke	N-	Allen & Tim Floyd	T McCanna
7	ALL FOR THE GAME	ML	Ch.F.3	120	B Russell	R-05/04/03	Betty Wolf	L Wolf

7

3rd RACE (S2)
F&M 3 & UP CLAIMING $3,200
PURSE $4,300 (PLUS UP TO $419 WA-BRED) — 6 FUR

#									
1	JANA O' GAILL	ML	Dk.B./Br.M.6	122	B Russell	R-06/05/03	Leon D. Winrich	G Colello	
2	ROLLS JOYCE	ML	Dk.B./Br.M.5	122	K Murray	R-05/22/03	Martin or Sylvia Kenney	M Kenney	
3	ANNA'S BIRTHDAY	ML	Dk.B./Br.M.6	122	H Ventura Jr	R-05/22/03	Philip Rile II & Karen Tilden	M Jones	
4	BREEZY BULLETTE	ML	Ch.F.4	122	J Gutierrez	E-06/12/03	Patty or Dave Runyon	R Fergason	
5	CARRIE'S WILD GIRL	ML	Ch.F.4	122	Y Lasso	R-05/28/03	Moreno Farm, LLC	C Moreno	
6	BOONE'S GATE	ML	Ch.M.5	122	K Radke	S-06/05/03	Quadrun Farms, LLC	T McCanna	
7	JAZZY HOSTESS	ML	Dk.B./Br.M.5	122	G Mitchell	R-06/05/03	Kevin Mertens	S Koler	Blk On
8	ZANY BABY	ML	B.M.6	122	D Velazquez	R-05/30/03	Jim Nunnally	J Nunnally	

8

4th RACE (X8)
F&M 3 & UP MAIDEN/CLAIMING $10,000-$8,000
PURSE $6,400 (PLUS UP TO $624 WA-BRED) — 5 1/2 FUR

#									
1	JORJA'S SUITE	ML	B.F.3	116	D Doll-Carriere	E-04/19/03	William Craig	A Bozell	$10,000
2	GLORY TRAIN	ML	Dk.B./Br.F.3	116	J Gutierrez	R-06/05/03	Patrick DeFeo & Richard Dondero	J Navarro	$10,000
3	JAZZIN JULIE	ML	Dk.B./Br.F.4	122	A Cedeno	R-05/08/03	Joe & Judi Kitchen	J Fergason	$10,000
4	QUICK CHARGE	ML	Dk.B./Br.F.3	116	K Radke	E-04/29/03	Guy Roberts	T McCanna	$10,000
5	STORM TEMPEST	ML	Ch.F.4	122	H Ventura Jr	R-06/01/03	Rico Troiani	R Troiani	$10,000
6	SELINA'S STARLET	ML1	Gr/Rn.F.3	122	K Murray	E-04/19/03	M/M Calvin E. Bagby	C Bagby	$10,000
7	SILVER SWING	ML	Gr/Rn.F.3	116	G Mitchell	R-06/05/03	Seawind Stable	D Kenney	$10,000

7

5th RACE (5)
F 3 YO CLAIMING $8,000
PURSE $6,300 (PLUS UP TO $614 WA-BRED) — 6 1/2 FUR

#								
1	PETE'S LADY	ML	Dk.B./Br.F.3	117	S Barber	R-06/08/03	Teresa Nelson	D Lavenway
2	SAHARA KNIGHT	ML	B.F.3	117	A Cedeno	R-06/06/03	Standish Stables	J Fergason
3	ZOEZEEBEAR	ML	Ch.F.3	120	K Murray	R-05/31/03	Jim L. Ingalls	M Kenney
4	HI DIXIE	ML	Dk.B./Br.F.3	117	Y Lasso	R-06/06/03	Dave & Pam Wood	E Bischoff
5	ITS A LADYS GAME	ML	B.F.3	117	S Saito	R-05/31/03	Sam Lanlow	T Gillihan
6	MISTY LEADER	ML	Ch.F.3	117	J Gutierrez	R-06/06/03	Yo Racing	J Nance
7	CHITTER BOX	ML	B.F.3	117	G Baze	R-06/06/03	Blue Diamond Stable, Cliff O'Brien, Iron Horse Ent	R Lumm
8	TEASE N' DELETE	ML	Dk.B./Br.F.3	117	K Radke	R-06/07/03	Eric & Robin Schwelger	B Kolstad

8

6th RACE (X4)
F&M 3 & UP MAIDEN/CLAIMING $16,000-$14,000
PURSE $8,400 (PLUS UP TO $819 WA-BRED) — 6 FUR

#									
1	LIFE ESTATE	ML	Dk.B./Br.F.4	122	K Murray	R-06/08/03	Martin or Sylvia Kenney & J. L. Ingalls	M Kenney	$16,000
2	CROWNING ADVENTURE	ML	B.F.4	122	S Saito	R-06/05/03	Louis H. Wickham	D Harwood	$16,000
3	STRUDEL LOU	ML	B.F.3	116	A Cedeno	R-05/29/03	K & W X.L.C. & J & L Kirschman	S Ross	$16,000
4	DAZZLE CAT	ML	Dk.B./Br.F.3	116	N Chaves	E-05/11/03	Janel Griffin or Jim Gilmour	N Knapp	$16,000
5	LG'S GOLD	ML	Ch.F.3	116	J Gutierrez	R-06/05/03	L G Farms	L Wolf	$16,000
6	HELLO LILLY	ML	Dk.B./Br.F.3	116	K Knapp	E-04/29/03	Charles J Barth	C Barth	$16,000
7	GRAMMA JO'S PRIDE	ML	Dk.B./Br.F.3	116	K Radke	R-05/22/03	T & J Twiggs, K McMillian & C Twiggs	O VanHorne	$16,000
8	MAYNE ATTIRE	ML	B.F.4	122	G Baze	R-06/05/03	Chilako Stable	C Phillips	$16,000

8

7th RACE (7)
F&M 3 & UP CLAIMING $10,000
PURSE $8,400 (PLUS UP TO $819 WA-BRED) — 6 FUR

#								
1	ALFIE	ML	B.M.5	118	J Gutierrez	E-06/20/03	Mauro Comenscoli	R Terry
2	KALOWANA SUNRISE	ML	B.M.6	118	K Murray	R-05/25/03	Seawind Stable	D Kenney
3	EMOSWA GOLD	ML	Ch.M.5	118	A Cedeno	E-05/16/03	Michael & Sharon Malarkey	J Penney
4	VAMPIRA	ML	B.F.4	118	G Mitchell	R-06/08/03	Ron Maug & Bob Wagner	F Lucarelli
5	CONQUER THE DAY	ML	Dk.B./Br.F.4	122	S Saito	R-05/29/03	Hoot N' Holler Subway Stable	B Beamer
6	BLESS MY SOLES	ML	B.F.3	118	G Baze	R-05/23/03	Riverbend Stable	S Ross
7	VENTURE FOREVER	ML	B.M.5	118	D Velazquez	R-05/15/03	Arturo Arboleda	A Arboleda
8	LITTLE NAT	ML	B.M.5	*113	J Olvera	R-05/23/03	Jerry Weaver	D Mungar
9	FRESH BROCCOLI	ML	Ch.F.4	122	K Radke	R-06/07/03	Herry LePley	T McCanna

9

8th RACE (9)
3 & UP CLAIMING $16,000-$14,000
PURSE $10,400 (PLUS UP TO $1,014 WA-BRED) — 1M & 1/16

#									
1	MELCAPWALKER	ML	B.G.4	123	S Saito	R-06/05/03	Art McFadden	B Klokstad	$16,000
2	NOMISSTAKEN KRIS	ML	B.G.4	*114	N Wright	-	R & V Gilker	R Gilker	$18,000
3	S. S. HAWKEYE	ML	Ch.G.7	117	G Mitchell	R-06/05/03	Ron & Marion Vatne	D Markle	$14,000
4	THUNZARR	ML	Dk.B./Br.G.6	119	K Radke	R-05/25/03	Maggie Dunton	D Doutrich	$16,000
5	POINT BLANK	ML	Dk.B./Br.G.5	121	B Russell	R-06/05/03	Remmah Racing, Inc	M Molina	$16,000
6	STAR OF REHAAN	ML	Dk.B./Br.G.6	119	J Gutierrez	R-06/06/03	Mr. Ed Stable & Steve Bullock	S Bullock	$16,000
7	FIT TO BE ROYAL	ML	Ch.G.6	119	G Baze	R-05/24/03	Rick Beal	S Ross	$16,000
8	SCORING SLEW	ML	Dk.B./Br.G.6	119	K Murray	S-05/24/03	Jim L. Ingalls	M Kenney	$16,000

9th RACE (4)
3 & UP CLAIMING $6,250-$5,000
PURSE $6,500 (PLUS UP TO $634 WA-BRED) — 1M & 1/16

#									
1	THE RIGHT PRIZE	ML	Dk.B./Br.G.4	117	G Mitchell	R-05/29/03	Martin Pimental	C Roberts	$5,000
2	SNACKBASKET	ML	B.G.7	119	B Russell	R-05/24/03	Sharon Ross & Dave Cooke	S Ross	$6,250
3	THUNDER ZOOT	ML	Gr/Rn.G.5	121	K Radke	R-05/29/03	Abella Racing	N Norton	$6,250
4	MOLOCH	ML	B.G.6	119	J Gutierrez	R-06/06/03	Oak Crest Farm	S Bullock	$6,250
5	IDEL ZACK	ML	Ch.G.4	123	G Baze	R-06/06/03	William & Bret Stiles	R Baze	$6,250
6	FIRST KNIGHTER	ML	B.G.7	117	J Whitaker	R-05/06/03	Rising Star Stable	H Belvoir	$5,000
7	HERBE VERT (BRZ)	ML	B.G.7	119	A Cedeno	E-05/25/03	Rick Beal	S Ross	$6,250
8	DAILY SPORT	ML	B.G.4	117	K Murray	R-06/06/03	Churchyard Farms	S Maloney	$6,250
9	MISCONCEPTION	ML	Dk.B./Br.G.6	119	S Saito	R-05/25/03	Frank & Phyllis Gaunt	A Villyard	$6,250

Late Extras

Trainers might not know about the possibility of running their horse until they see the extras (assuming that the extras are not recently carded races that almost filled in the previous days) and thus might not have time to prepare the horse properly. Consequently, those late extras tend to be cheaper claiming or maiden claiming races for horses that run often.

Finally, sometimes a trainer will request that the racing secretary offer a late extra. The trainer might have a horse that is ready to run, but the current condition book doesn't have a race that fits that horse.

Getting a Race to Fill

As just shown, a trainer may want to run a horse, but many times the race may not fill. However, trainers have some options, such as entering a second horse in the race. As a handicapper, you will encounter this situation, particularly with a small field. If the trainer has two horses entered and one of those horses appears misplaced, you can probably conclude the trainer believes his other horse has a good shot at winning and has made sure the race filled.

Finally, there are many days where, because of a horse shortage, the track is in danger of not carding its usual number of races. On occasion, a trainer may enter a horse to help the track/racing secretary fill a race. The trainer may get the favor returned when he needs a certain race to be written for a horse. These misplaced horses can be spotted fairly easily, a horse coming back to race very quickly or a router in a sprint, etc. You may want to ignore a bad effort when evaluating these horses in the future.

Scratching

The rules about scratching after horses are entered vary from state to state and track to track. Some tracks have an "enter to run" policy, which prohibits a trainer from scratching without the stewards' permission after he enters his horse, regardless of the field size. Other tracks allow scratches down to a certain minimum number of horses (for instance, if ten enter, the track may allow scratches down to eight without any questions, but if more than two horses want to scratch, they will have to draw). Once a field is down to eight, a trainer can scratch only with permission of the stewards (for sickness, soundness, track condition, etc.). The rules for stakes races may differ slightly.

Trainers also can scratch horses in fields smaller than eight by having a vet declare their entry ineligible. Let's say a horse enters an eight-horse field but is overmatched and has a poor post. Officially the trainer is stuck, but suddenly the horse develops a cold and is excused as a vet scratch. There is probably nothing wrong with the horse, and a handicapper can sometimes view this type of scratch as being positive: the trainer/owner wants to win but didn't like the way this spot came up, so the trainer/owner will look for a better race in a week or two. Trainers usually are not allowed to enter horses in a new race for a certain time after a vet scratch, usually five days.

Also, the rules on weather-related scratches vary from track to track, but the most commonly applied is this: If the track is "fast" when a horse is entered and then it rains, resulting in a wet surface, the trainer can scratch regardless of field size. If the track is wet when a trainer enters his horse, the horse probably will have to run if the track is wet on race day unless the horse was entered "conditional" of a fast track. A trainer can only scratch with the stewards' permission in this case (for instance, a vet scratch). For some East Coast turf races, horses can be entered for a particular race for "main track only," which means it will run only if the race is moved to the dirt. This is common during the winter when weather can wreak havoc with turf racing.

Summary

Knowledge of racing rules pertaining to entering, scratching, and running can be important in evaluating a particular horse. A trainer may have had to give his horse a short layoff because he could not find the right race in which to run him, or maybe the horse was listed as "sick" on the vet's list five day ago and you conclude the trainer was really looking for a better spot. In either case, as a handicapper you may be able to make better decisions when evaluating these types of scenarios if you are aware of what goes on before the *Daily Racing Form* and program are printed.

Race Strategy

Throughout any given meet, the same horses will race each other many times with different results due to a variety of factors. One of those factors is the strategy used by the jockeys. Part of handicapping the races (and finding potential wagers) is to predict rider strategies successfully.

If you are able to predict what race strategies are going to be used, you will have an advantage over other bettors. Knowing the effect of post position and how trainers and jockeys may approach any given race will give you an edge in determining race strategy and an advantage at the betting window.

In determining these possible strategies, you have to be aware that most, if not all, of the horses' owners/trainers/jockeys will study the past performances published in either the program or the *Daily Racing Form*, and those same owners/trainers/jockeys are basing their strategy on *their* expectations of what will happen. Also realize that the owners/trainers/jockeys read the comments by handicappers for the local newspapers, *Daily Racing Form*, or the program, and sometimes the comments influence their strategy.

You may be able to find races in which you have a good idea of what will happen early on and thus be better able to decide which horses may win. But to do so, you have to be aware of what factors affect strategic decisions.

Post Position

One of the main factors that will help you to determine possible race strategy (tactics) that the connections of a specific horse may decide on in a race is the post position drawn. For the most part, trainers/jockeys hope to draw an inside post for routes and an outside post for sprints. Most sprints have a long run to the turn and drawing outside gives more options to the rider of a horse with tactical speed — if the horse breaks well, the rider can send the horse to the lead. If other riders that drew inside also send, then the rider that is outside can sit just off the lead.

The worst post for a horse that has some early or tactical speed is the #1 hole. Assuming a good break, this horse has to be sent to keep its position. If the rider doesn't send, horse and rider risk being crowded into the rail, bumped, shuffled back, or blocked.

The other choice is to take back and try to circle the field. The horse might run well, even with the extra effort to get outside but would probably run better with an outside post.

For example, Holy Heart had been unlucky in her post position draws in her first four races at Emerald Downs in 2001 (Figure 4.4). She either was forced to try for the lead early or she was forced to drop back and move outside. Also, in each of those four races, she broke a length or two slowly, likely intimidated by the inside post.

Figure 4.4

ly Heart

1-4EmDfst	6f	:22	$:45^2$	:58	$1:11^1$	ⒻClm 10000N2X	**59**	1	6	5 2½	4^2	3 2½	3 2¼	Russell B R	**LB**117	3.20	81- 19	VentureAfleet118 1¾ Puckerupnkissme119½ *HolyHert*117 1¼	Steady advance	7
1-1EmDfst	6½f	$:22^3$	:46	$1:11^4$	$1:18^4$	3↑ⒻClm 12500(12.5-10)N2L	**59**	2	5	4 1¼	4 2½	4¾	3 1½	Cedeno O	**LB**114	6.30	76- 19	Spice Twice119 1½ Twit Wilson119hd HolyHeart114 1½	5w rally, gradual gain	6
1-5EmDsly	6f	$:22^2$	$:45^2$	$:57^4$	1:11	ⒻClm 10000N2X	**57**	2	6	2½	4 2½	3 3½	3 5½	Cedeno A	**LB**118	4.20	78- 14	Triton Cove117hd *Rolls Joyce*120 5½ Holy Heart118nk	Pressed, weakened	9
1-7EmDfst	5½f	:22	$:45^3$	$:57^3$	1:04	ⒻClm 16000N2X	**48**	3	5	4 3½	4 1½	5 2¼	5 4¼	Cedeno A	**B**118	13.50	88- 10	MichllsCp117¾ AnniNWill118nk Rsonforrjction117 2	Middle move, faltered	6

Here are my notes on her trips:

May 10, she broke from #3 post: broke 2 lengths slow, 3 wide turn.

May 28, she broke from #2 post: broke 2 lengths slow, rushed up to leaders, okay while ran evenly late.

June 23, she broke from #2 post: broke 1 length slow, 5 wide turn.

July 20, she broke from #1 post: broke 1 length slow, rail early, moved to 4 wide mid-turn, 5 wide entering.

On August 4, she finally drew outside (#6 post in a seven-horse field). She broke better from the gate, had a nice trip, and was able to win while running an improved Beyer speed figure (Figure 4.5).

Figure 4.5

ly Heart

01-7EmDfst	6f	$:22^1$	$:45^3$	:58	$1:11^1$	Ⓕ[S]Clm 10000N2X	**68**	6	4	3½	4^1	2hd	1nk	Radke K	**LB**117	5.30	83- 16	Holy Heart117nk Easy Lisa118 1¾ *Easy Liv'n*118 3	Split foes, prevailed	7
01-4EmDfst	6f	:22	$:45^2$	:58	$1:11^1$	ⒻClm 10000N2X	**59**	1	6	5 2½	4^2	3 2½	3 2¼	Russell B R	**LB**117	3.20	81- 19	VentureAfleet118 1¾ Puckerupnkissme119½ *HolyHert*117 1¼	Steady advance	7
01-1EmDfst	6½f	$:22^3$	:46	$1:11^4$	$1:18^4$	3↑ⒻClm 12500(12.5-10)N2L	**59**	2	5	4 1¼	4 2½	4¾	3 1½	Cedeno O	**LB**114	6.30	76- 19	Spice Twice119 1½ Twit Wilson119hd HolyHeart114 1½	5w rally, gradual gain	6
01-5EmDsly	6f	$:22^2$	$:45^2$	$:57^4$	1:11	ⒻClm 10000N2X	**57**	2	6	2½	4 2½	3 3½	3 5½	Cedeno A	**LB**118	4.20	78- 14	Triton Cove117hd *Rolls Joyce*120 5½ Holy Heart118nk	Pressed, weakened	9
01-7EmDfst	5½f	:22	$:45^3$	$:57^3$	1:04	ⒻClm 16000N2X	**48**	3	5	4 3½	4 1½	5 2¼	5 4¼	Cedeno A	**B**118	13.50	88- 10	MichllsCp117¾ AnniNWill118nk Rsonforrjction117 2	Middle move, faltered	6

In routes or two-turn races, especially at a mile or a mile and one-sixteenth on a one-mile track, most trainers/jockeys prefer an inside post. With a short run to the first turn, drawing inside gives a horse a better chance to get to the lead, get position within the field, or save ground on that turn. The short run to the turn does force the hand of many jockeys, and the final results of many routes can be determined after the first quarter-mile. A quick first quarter fraction with two or more horses dueling may doom the front runners. A slow first quarter gives the horses racing near that pace a big advantage; they are on or near the front without having to expend any energy, forcing those behind either to move early or just hope the front-runners stop.

What Happened Last Race

Another factor that may help you in determining the possible race strategy is what happened in the previous race, especially when two or more horses just raced against each other and are meeting again.

For example, on April 22, 2001, Best Judgement, Shandra Smiles, and Sophisticated Slew all met. In that race, Sophisticated Slew drew post #1 and Shandra Smiles drew post #6. They both broke well and flew through the first quarter-mile in :21⅘ and the half-mile in :43⅘ while Best Judgement sat third. Shandra Smiles put Sophisticated Slew away but was unable to hold off Best Judgement late. These horses met again two weeks later. Below are their past performances going into their race on May 6, 2001 (Figure 4.6).

Figure 4.6

Shandra Smiles

22Apr01-8EmDwf	6f	:212	:434	:562	1:094	ⒻUSBank35k	**83**	6	3	1hd	2½	2hd	2¾	Mitchell G V	**LB**119 b	5.00	89- 10	BestJudgement119¾ *ShandraSmiles*1193½ AnitMri1173	Dueled, held g
18Aug00-6EmDsly	5½f	:221	:453	:583	1:053	ⒻMd 40000	**44**	6	2	21	31	32½	23½	Mitchell G V	**LB**117 b	4.10	80- 18	ShestheKind1173½ ShndrSmiles1173½ KnightWv1173¾	Prompted, 2n
30Jly00-5EmDfst	5½f	:223	:454	:582	1:051	ⒻMd 40000	**32**	5	4	2hd	32	45	410½	Mitchell G V	**B**117 b	2.30	75- 18	PersonlDecison1178 *Whtdidshesy*1171 *MttisStr*1171½	Vied 3 wide, flat

Best Judgement

22Apr01-8EmDwf	6f	:212	:434	:562	1:094	ⒻUSBank35k	**85**	4	4	33	32	1hd	1¾	Baze G	**LB**119 f	*.80	90- 10	BestJudgement119¾ *ShandraSmiles*1193½ AnitaMri1173	3-wide, hard
10Sep00-4EmDsly	1 1/16	:223	:461	1:112	1:44	GottstnFut100k	**72**	1	42	43	21½	33½	59½	Baze V	**LB**117 f	6.00	68- 20	Jumron Won1203¼ Dr. Slew1202¼ *Legendary Weave*1202	Bid, wea
19Aug00-9EmDfst	6½f	:22	:441	1:091	1:16	ⒻWTBALassie54k	**80**	6	6	41½	31½	21	1½	Baze V	**LB**119 f	7.60	92- 08	Best Judgement119½ Amocat1192½ Collect Call1193½	4-wide, up fin

Sophisticated Slew

22Apr01-8EmDwf	6f	:212	:434	:562	1:094	ⒻUSBank35k	**66**	1	1	2hd	1½	31	47¼	Perez M A	**LB**116 b	5.70	83- 10	BestJudgement119¾ *ShandraSmiles*1193½ AnitaMri1173	Dueled, wea
1Apr01-9TuP fst	6f	:213	:443	:57	1:101	ⒻKthrynDoll23k	**46**	4	3	1½	1½	22	412¼	Mawing L A	**L**121	15.90	77- 19	*Channing Way*1217¾ The Queen and I1173 Lucy T1191½	Set pace, wea
24Mar01-7TuP fst	6f	:22	:451	:574	1:12	ⒻMd Sp Wt 9k	**55**	4	2	11	13	12½	1¾	Mawing L A	**L**121	*1.60	80- 17	SophistictedSlw121¾ ShuttlTickt1216 BrokinBlirsdn121no	Tiring, h

In the May 6 race, their respective post positions were different. Shandra Smiles drew inside of Sophisticated Slew with Best Judgement between them. I had to decide if Shandra Smiles and Sophisticated Slew were going to hook up early again, setting up the race for someone else, as had happened with Best Judgement in the previous race. Since Shandra Smiles drew inside of Sophisticated Slew, I thought that Shandra Smiles had to go early. Also realize that Sophisticated Slew did draw post #1 last time, which essentially committed her to the lead in that race, and she had been buried by dueling with Shandra Smiles. Now that she was moved a bit to the outside, you could make a strong case that the connections of Sophisticated Slew would probably not send her as hard early.

Deciding what strategy the connections would use was the key to this race. While Sophisticated Slew's connections didn't decide to "lay off" completely that day, neither rider "sent" his horse as hard early as he did last time; this time the first quarter was run in a significantly slower :22⅗. Figure 4.7 shows the result chart: Shandra Smiles won handily with Best Judgement third at 4-5, and Sophisticated Slew in sixth.

Figure 4.7

venth Race Emerald Downs- May 6, 2001

URLONGS. (1:14⅘) FEDERAL WAY HANDICAP. Purse $45,000. Fillies, 3-year-olds. By subscription of $50 each, which shall accompany the nomination, $200 to enter, $200 itional to start. Weights: Wednesday, May 2. Starters to be named through the entry box by the closing time of entries. High weights preferred. Nominations close Saturday, il 28.

ue of race: $33,378. Winner $16,500; second $6,000; third $6,525; fourth $3,265; fifth $1,088. Mutuel pool $65,943.00. Exacta pool $37,919.00. Trifecta pool $47,526.00. erfecta pool $18,681.00.

st Raced	Horse	Med/Eqp	A	Wgt	PP	St	1/4	1/2	Str	Fin	Jockey	Odds $1
Apr01 ^{8}EmD^{2}	Shandra Smiles	LBb	3	117	2	1	1^{hd}	1^{hd}	$1^{2½}$	$1^{3¾}$	Mitchell G	4.10
Apr01 ^{5}EmD^{1}	Aunt Sophie	LBb	3	115	6	5	7^{8}	$6^{1½}$	5^{5}	$2^{1¼}$	Cedeno O	4.40
Apr01 ^{8}EmD^{1}	Best Judgement	LBf	3	120	3	3	$4^{½}$	$3^{½}$	2^{hd}	$3^{¾}$	Baze G	0.80
Apr01 ^{8}EmD^{3}	Anita Maria	LB	3	117	4	4	$6^{1½}$	4^{2}	$4^{½}$	$4^{2½}$	Gonsalves	7.40
Aug00 ^{9}EmD^{9}	Silver Echo	LB	3	117	1	8	8	8	8	$5^{¾}$	Matias J	11.80
Apr01 ^{8}EmD^{4}	Sophisticated Slew	LBbf	3	115	5	2	2^{1}	$2^{1½}$	3^{hd}	$6^{2½}$	Perez M	25.50
Aug00 ^{9}EmD^{10}	Pharosos	LB	3	114	7	6	5^{hd}	5^{hd}	6^{3}	$7^{5½}$	Russell B	42.90
Apr01 ^{4}EmD^{1}	Jeni's Tough Night	B	3	115	8	7	$3^{½}$	7^{8}	7^{hd}	8	Chaves N	36.20

Time: 4:23 **Time Of Race:** :22⅗ :45⅕ 1:09⅗ 1:16⅕

rt: Good For All. **Track:** Fast. **Won driving.**

Mutuel Payoffs:

Shandra Smiles	10.20	5.00	2.80
Aunt Sophie		4.80	2.40
Best Judgement			2.20

Exacta 2-6 Paid $21.50; $1 Trifecta 2-6-3 Paid $53.10; $1 Superfecta 2-6-3-4 Paid $199.30.

QUIBASE

Another strategic situation is one in which a horse running on the outside forces the early pace. For example, let's use a seven-horse field. Horse #1 is pretty quick and goes to the lead. Horse #5 also is quick early and has run well from on or off the lead, but horse #7 has a similar style. Very early in the race, horse #1 has opened a one-length lead with horse #5 a length back and horse #7 another length back.

The rider on horse #7, seeing a situation in which he will be wide and chasing a lone speed horse, asks his horse a bit early, so horse #7 moves closer to horse #5. At this point the rider of horse #5 has a choice: take his horse back a bit and let #7 by or hustle his horse to keep in front of #7. Many times when a horse in #5's position sees another horse come up to challenge on the outside, the horse will naturally speed up. Meanwhile, horse #5 puts pressure on horse #1, leaving horse #7 sitting third off a two-horse speed duel.

Smart riders who are on horses with tactical (early) speed who also draw outside posts may take advantage of that outside post and force the horses inside to press each other early in a race. Obviously, if these three meet again with different post positions, the riders may have different options.

Knowing how trainers/owners/jockeys strategize is also important. Some jockeys are known for a certain style. For example, some have a tendency to send a horse to the lead while others prefer to rate (take back) horses.

You will be better able to evaluate probable race strategy if you pay attention to media interviews in which trainers at your local track say how they like to run their horses. For example, some trainers will reveal they want their horses on or near the lead early when possible. Those trainers are aware that horses on or near the lead early will have a better chance of winning any given race. You may learn that other trainers prefer their horses to race from behind. Those trainers may think that teaching a horse to rate will lead to success at longer distances. Additionally, those trainers may think that if a horse is not a front runner, it has less chance for injury.

As a side note, another advantage of reading and listening to those interviews is that you will find out which jockeys/trainers are "clued-in" to track biases and those who are not. All this information can be important in evaluating probable race strategy, and thus your betting strategy.

Considering Jockey Instructions

Many players assume each rider is given instructions by the trainer. But while some trainers and/or owners want to offer specific instructions, most think it is better to let the rider make decisions based on what happens after the gates open. Obviously, the trainers (and the owners) will talk to their rider, mentioning things about the horse and expected race shape. In most cases a trainer will tell a jockey riding the horse for the first time of the horse's preferred style of running. The trainer may say, "Look, this horse runs its best race on the lead," or "This horse needs to be taken hold of and then don't ask it until the quarter-pole."

Depending on the circumstances, the trainer may also tell the jockey not to be too aggressive with the horse. For example, if a horse is returning after a layoff or making its first start, the trainer may say, "Try to get the horse in good position, sit on the horse early, ask the horse at the three-eighths pole, and then if it gets tired, ease it home." Other times, if a horse is expected to run well, the trainer may say nothing other than, "This horse is doing well; I will let you decide on where the horse needs to be placed early, depending on what the other horses are doing." The most common instructions go something like, "Get away cleanly from the gate, try to get some position, and then do what you think is best."

Obviously when significant trouble arises early, a jockey can't do what the trainer/owner wants. But other times the jockey may ignore the instructions, thinking he has a better view of what will happen (in terms of strategy).

When playing a race based on the probable strategy you foresee, be aware of the different scenarios that may occur. Say you are betting horse C because you think it will benefit from an expected speed duel between horses A and B. Knowing that your bet depends on horses A and B hooking up early, you may want to seek protection in case they don't (either horse may break slowly or one of the riders could choose to take back early). For example, if you are playing pick threes keying horse C, you may want to use some backup tickets with A and B. Or you may want to box horse C with horses A and B in the exacta, in addition to betting C to win. Either way, the final result of the race depends on one turn of events predicating another, so hedge your bets.

Summary
Players trying to figure tactics sometimes have obvious clues, such as a quick horse that draws the rail and has to be sent to the lead or a new rider who is known as being a sender or sitter. Other

times you can't really determine what will happen early in a race. What actually happens is more a matter of how the key horses break and what split-second decisions their riders make. Also, be aware that it is pretty tough for a rider to change his mind after committing for the lead or laying off.

The Claiming Game

The majority of races nationwide are for claiming horses and create a separate poker game between many owners and trainers who are trying to win the race and keep the horse, win the race and lose the horse, or just lose the horse. Most players are aware of this poker game and recognize that it needs to be factored into their handicapping because the owners'/trainers' intent should be considered when evaluating any horse in any claiming race.

Players must also evaluate a claiming horse that is making its first start for a new barn. Will the horse improve off its previous race, run a similar race, or regress? Players also should look at horses dropping in class after a layoff or horses dropping in claiming price after a good effort against better. Players who are involved in claiming horses must decide when a horse may be a good bet but may not be a good claim — the horse may win but have a limited future.

Rules of Claiming

Claiming races come with their own set of rules, separate from the regular maiden, allowance, and stakes races, and these rules differ depending on the racing jurisdiction. Most state racing commissions prohibit a trainer from shipping out a horse that was recently claimed and running it at another track (usually out of state) until the current meeting ends, unless the racing secretary of the track where the horse was claimed grants permission. This protects the track from losing horses to out-of-state trainers/owners for that meet. However, the track may let a horse ship out for a stakes race.

After a horse is claimed, state rules often restrict the level at which a horse can be raced for a certain period, most commonly thirty days; however, the rules surrounding "jail time" can vary from state to state. At some tracks, there is no jail time; a trainer can run the horse at any level he wants at any time after claiming it. At other tracks, if the horse lost the race from which it was claimed, the trainer can run it again anywhere, any time. If it won that race, the trainer has to move it up at least one claiming level to run it in the next thirty days. Other tracks have a similar rule that covers all claimed horses regardless of where they finish. After the thirty days are up, a horse can race at any level.

After a horse is claimed, the new owners are usually not permitted to transfer ownership of the horse (via private sale) for thirty days.

Having an understanding of the claiming rules at the track you are playing can help you make more informed handicapping decisions.

Say you follow a track that allows the new connections of a claimed horse to run it anywhere after the claim. Although those connections are allowed to run right back for the same price of the claim, they decide to move the horse up in claiming price. You might conclude that the new connections expect a better effort from that horse.

Let's use The Novelist (see Chapter 2) again as an example. After my partnership claimed him at Emerald Downs for $5,000, we could have run him right back for the same price or lower anywhere (since he didn't win) because Washington state doesn't restrict a horse if it does not win the race. But we were confident that the horse would run well, and we also didn't want to lose the horse, so we put him in a $10,000 claiming race because we felt he could win at that level (Figure 4.8). A handicapper might see this as a positive move and expect improvement.

Novelist

Figure 4.8

Claiming Trainers

Placement of a recently claimed horse can give you a good idea of how the new connections perceive that horse. However, most players instead concentrate on looking at the history of the horse's trainer to predict improvement in the horse's effort. Has that trainer had previous success with claims? Many players keep records of those trainers who claim and their results. This leads to the question: What makes a good claiming trainer?

Good claiming trainers know all the other horses on the track and try to watch them in the morning and during a race. They know and compare a horse's coat condition to that of the last time they saw it. They know how it pulled up after its last race. They can get information about a horse and its problems from that horse's previous trainers/grooms.

One morning I went to the backstretch and watched Ron Glatt (who was training my first claim at the time) training some horses. One of Longacres' top stakes horses was breezing, and as the filly, who was not trained by Ron, went by, he said she wasn't moving very well. Of course, I couldn't tell that she was moving poorly because to me she looked like all the other horses breezing. I didn't think much about his comment until she was favored in a stakes race later than week and ran last.

Claiming horses can be very similar to buying a used car. You can get a look at the car's exterior, sometimes a good look at the outside of the engine, but you really don't know what you are getting until you have owned the car for a while. Good claiming trainers will figure out how to run that car (horse) efficiently.

Good claiming trainers go over a horse completely when they claim it. They probably scope the horse after the race, worm it, float its teeth, put it on their feeding program, or use different medications. Claiming trainers may train the horse differently, make equipment/shoeing changes, put the horse in a quiet part of the barn, or provide it with a companion animal such as a goat. They may also school the horse in the paddock or starting gate if it has shown some problems with washing out (becoming very sweaty, usually from nerves) or acting up in the gate. The list is endless. Many times even the best claiming trainers need to start a horse once in a race before they can figure it out. Sometimes they may never figure it out. Mostly the key is to get a horse happy and fit. Once a horse is fit and feeling good, a trainer doesn't need to do much in regard to training.

Near the end of one of Emerald Downs' racing seasons, I claimed a horse I liked for my partnership. She had been in the barn of another top trainer, and I really didn't think she would improve when changing barns, but she was a quick filly that we thought would do well in California. Repeating her Emerald Downs efforts in California would be good enough for us. She did run very well after shipping to California and was claimed away. I asked Ron about how he had trained her and he said she was a horse that didn't need or, in fact, was much better without a lot of training between races. He joked that "the way to train this horse is, once she is fit, take her from her stall to the walker and then back to her stall each day; don't gallop her, don't breeze her. Then enter her and run."

After she was claimed from us, her new connections appeared to train her often (galloping and breezing her more often than Ron had), and she didn't do as well. Later in the year, after she ran poorly in several races and was dropped below the claiming price at which we lost her, Ron claimed her back. She then improved significantly with him because he had learned the best way to train her.

There are some situations where one trainer will not claim from another trainer and vice versa. You may become aware of some of these relationships at your home track and that knowledge will help you better evaluate claims. For instance, it is not considered "good sportsmanship" to claim a horse from a neighboring barn (if you want to know where trainers are stabled, get a barn list from the racing office). While working in their barns, trainers daily see the horses of the barns either across from or next to them. Thus they have intimate knowledge of those horses and won't take advantage of this information by claiming those horses.

Some trainers agree not to claim off each other (this can involve two or more trainers). These trainers usually are at the smaller tracks and are the top or better claiming trainers, or just are friends. As a result of this tacit agreement, sometimes top claiming trainers will try to "get away" with jamming a horse in a race (placing a horse right back at the same level after a win or dropping the horse down in price after a win) in which the horse is probably worth more than the claiming price, knowing that the other top claiming trainers won't drop a claim tag. While this doesn't guarantee that a horse won't get claimed, it does lessen the chances.

On occasion one of these claiming trainers may drop a "protection" claim for another trainer. Let's say you and I are friends and we don't claim off each other, but I train a horse and want to place it in a race in which the horse looks pretty good to win. I don't want to lose the horse so I ask you to drop a claim tag, thinking that if someone else drops, you could win the shake. After the race, if you get the horse, we won't start it until thirty days are up, and then we will transfer it back into my name. A handicapper may see that a horse was claimed but didn't race for thirty days and now appears with the previous connections listed as owner/trainer (not the connections who claimed the horse). The handicapper may view this protection claim as a positive because it means the connections didn't want to lose the horse.

Effect of the Claiming Game

Being familiar with the claiming game helps handicappers evaluate horses that are running for any claiming price (whether or not the horses were claimed in their previous race). Remember that some trainers/owners are looking to claim horses; other trainers/owners are looking to lose a horse via a claim — in this case, winning the race isn't the primary goal. Players also must evaluate first-time starters that debut in a maiden claiming race and horses that are suspiciously dropped in class.

First-Time Starters in Maiden Claiming Races

When you are looking at first-time starters, you can tell a lot about a horse's potential by where it is placed. Is the horse placed in a cheap maiden claiming race or a maiden special weight? Be aware that no matter how poorly a horse works out, until it actually runs, most owners will think their horse has ability. An old saying at the track is "Nobody who owned an unraced two-year-old ever committed suicide."

Also, realize that the cost of bringing a horse to a race, either a homebred or an auction purchase, is very expensive. No one wants to lose the horse (via a claim) in its first race and also lose money on the horse (purchase price, which is usually listed in the *Daily Racing Form*, plus expenses, less claiming price and any purse earned). If the horse's connections enter it below the cost of getting it to that first race, it usually indicates a physical problem or a potential physical problem or that it can't run much and the owner/trainer doesn't mind losing the horse. This is important because, again, any horse can get claimed in a claiming race and no one normally gives away anything of value, especially a young, potentially good horse. So always be leery about betting this type of horse.

Remember C.J.'s Dancer? (See Chapter 2.) When he was entered in his first start for $10,000 claiming, I was suspicious, even though he'd had nice, fast workouts. After he won easily by four and a quarter lengths in 1:09⅗ (which earned a good speed figure), I didn't understand why he had been entered so cheaply until I watched the head-on replay. His right front leg "paddled" so badly that it was clear this horse wouldn't stand up to much racing before becoming injured.

He was claimed out of his first race, but the new connections didn't jump him up much (he probably came back out of his maiden win a bit "off"). If they thought they had made a nice claim, they probably would have entered him in a much higher claiming race (Figure 4.9). He was 3-2 in that second start, but I knew what his problem was and I stayed away from betting (or claiming) him. The horse ran okay (fifth) but did lose when well bet and ran only one more time in his career.

Figure 4.9

s Dancer
ıth Jetty Stables

Dk. b or b. g. 6 (May)
Sire: Petersburg (Danzig) $1,500
Dam: Satin Morn (Prince O'Morn)
Br: Lila M Furukawa (Wash)
Tr: Kenney Daniel(0 0 0 0 .00) :(86 9 .10)

Life	**3**	**1**	**0**	**0**	**$4,045**	**71**	**D.Fst**	**3**	**1**	**0**	**0**	**$4,045**	**71**
2000	**3**	**1**	**0**	**0**	**$4,045**	**71**	**Wet(362)**	**0**	**0**	**0**	**0**	**$0**	**-**
1999	**0**	**M**	**0**	**0**	**$0**	**-**	**Turf(274)**	**0**	**0**	**0**	**0**	**$0**	**-**
Bel	**0**	**0**	**0**	**0**	**$0**	**-**	**Dst(313)**	**0**	**0**	**0**	**0**	**$0**	**-**

5EmDfst	6f	:22^{1}	:45^{3}	:58^{2}	1:11^{1}	Clm 6250N2L	–	8	6	1^{hd}	-	-	-	Landeros J^{10}	**LB**111	*1.10	-	10	BnnrofLght121½ FortunsSoldr121^{1} *AlsknGmblr*118^{1½}	Pulled up, vanned off	8
3EmDfst	6f	:22	:45^{1}	:57^{3}	1:10^{4}	Clm 14000(16-14)N2X	**56**	5	2	3½	2^{1½}	4^{5}	5^{10}	Perez M A	**LB**116	*1.50	76-	18	PlayWellTC118^{1¼} CherokeeStr118^{6½} Muscovy117^{nk}	Came in, no response	7
1EmDfst	6f	:22	:44^{4}	:56^{4}	1:09^{2}	[S]Md c-10000	**71**	3	2	1½	1^{hd}	1^{1½}	1^{4¼}	Perez M A	**LB**121	6.20	93-	11	C. J.'s Dancer121^{4¼} Dr. Evil121^{3¼} Sly Schemes121¾	Dueled, kicked away	9

ed from Bridges, Bill D. and O'Connor, Bill for $10,000, Harris Ben Trainer 2000(as of 5/19): (-)

The time to be suspicious that a horse has potential problems is when the horse appears to have been placed well below its worth based on that horse's performance in its first start. When a horse starts in a cheap race and wins by a wide margin or a comparatively fast time, I would be suspicious of that horse for the rest of its career.

As in many areas of handicapping, there are always exceptions. Sometimes a horse may make its first start in a lower-level maiden claiming race, run well, and not have any serious or potentially serious problems. Here are some examples:

1. If the purchase price (auction price) is fairly cheap, let's say $1,500, the owner/trainer can pretty much run that horse anywhere for two reasons: Other trainers/owners who see such a low purchase price may shy away, assuming the horse went cheap because of some obvious problem (such as a conformation defect). Or, the current owners wouldn't care if they lost the horse via a claim because it didn't cost them much anyway.

2. If a horse is by a little-known sire and/or an unraced or unproven mare, most trainers/owners won't claim it the first time out.

3. If a horse's owner is also the breeder (a homebred) and the horse is claimed away and continues to earn money, the previous owner gets breeding awards. In addition, the mare (owned by the breeder) and the value of the mare's future foals will increase.

Also, the rare owner/trainer sometimes realizes that the purchase price of the horse is sunk, and he places the horse at its proper ability level regardless of the price paid. That type of horse can do well, and I would not be too suspicious of it in the future. Keep track of these trainers to differentiate them from a trainer who drops his horses in the hope of their being claimed because of a potential problem.

Regular Claiming Races

As you know, suspicious drops in claiming races occur every racing day. For example, you may encounter a horse that just ran second in a $20,000 claiming race and is dropped to $10,000 claiming. This horse probably looks like an easy winner in today's race if it is able to repeat its previous effort. However, most players are leery of these big drops for one big reason: if the horse looks too good to be true, it probably is — there is an old saying at the track that directly relates to these suspicious droppers: "Christmas only comes once a year." The claiming game forces you as a handicapper to evaluate any big drop in claiming price and decide whether the horse will be a good bet. In most cases you should be wary of playing a horse that is dropping way down in claiming price after some good efforts. Other times these horses may be played with confidence. The different scenarios are discussed in the next few paragraphs.

Munjiz illustrates why you should be suspicious of a horse that is dropping in claiming price after some good efforts. Figure 4.10 shows his past performances. Munjiz was claimed on May 18, 2002, for $32,000; he won his next start for his new connections on June 8 for a claiming price of $50,000. After this he ran twice more for $50,000 claiming and lost both times; in his last race at that level, on July 21, he ran a dull ninth. At this point Munjiz was a turf horse with no real success on the dirt.

Figure 4.10

Here is where things get suspicious. After his dull turf race on July 21, the connections probably knew that a problem was developing so they dropped the horse in for a claiming price of $25,000 and also moved him to the dirt. Hollywood Park and Del Mar do not normally card claiming turf races for less than $40,000 so Munjiz's connections had to run him on the dirt. He actually didn't run that badly, finishing fifth despite drawing the #1 hole.

His connections then decided to ship him to Bay Meadows, where the horse could run on the turf for a much lower claiming price than in southern California. In this case the connections were probably trying to win the race and also probably didn't mind if the horse was claimed away. The drop to a claiming price of $12,500 did the job; he was claimed away. His new connections, instead of running him right back for $12,500 claiming, placed him in a $32,000 claiming race where he ran a dull seventh at odds of 7-2. Then he was dropped back in for $12,500 claiming and failed in three straight races, two of which he was well bet. On January 12 he appeared for $4,000 claiming, was 2-1, and ran second. In his next two starts after this race, he failed to win again as the favorite (Figure 4.11).

Munjiz (Ire)

Figure 4.11

When Munjiz was offered for a claiming price of $25,000 and placed on the dirt, I became suspicious. At that point I would have been very hesitant to play the horse in any more races. While he ran well in six of his next eight starts, he lost in all eight, four times when favored and three times when the second choice.

Each situation in which a horse is suspiciously entered must be looked at separately, taking into account the history of the owner/trainer, the purse, etc. If you are uncertain and the odds of the horse in question are low, as with Munjiz, skip the race.

On occasion a large drop in price may be for a reason that makes perfect sense, and the horse can be played confidently. One sign that a horse is just fine is when the horse is claimed back by its previous connections. If the owner wanted to lose the horse, he obviously wouldn't claim it back. So if you see a horse that is claimed back by its previous owners, in most cases you can assume the horse is physically fine. Similarly, if a horse is claimed several times by different trainers, that horse is probably pretty sound.

Here are some other examples:

1. Some owners are not interested in running claimers; they will drop a horse that has no real physical problems but has no stakes potential. They think that if they lose the horse, fine. Most of these owners will concentrate on young horses and don't have too many older horses unless they are competitive in stakes.

2. A few owners/trainers at every track who actively play the claiming game are not afraid to take chances and drastically drop

a horse off a good effort or drop horses off wins. They aren't as interested in keeping any particular horse; their interest is to make a quick dollar.

At most tracks you can claim a horse and still make money if the horse wins its next race and is claimed away because the purse size is enough to justify such moves. For example, at Bay Meadows, the purse for an open, older $8,000 claiming race is $11,000. If you claimed a horse for $10,000 and dropped it into a $8,000 claiming race and the horse won the race you would receive (after paying the trainer and jockey 10 percent each) about $4,800, which would cover the $2,000 loss if the horse was claimed from you.

In addition, large drops in which the horse wins and doesn't get claimed set up future drops (for different horses). If the connections were able to get away with a big drop last week (they won the race but the horse wasn't claimed), they may drop another horse way down in claiming price, only this time wanting to lose the horse. Another trainer/owner, remembering what happened last week, thinks, "They got away with it last week, but this time I will claim the horse."

3. Certain owners just like to win races and are not opposed to cashing a bet, so losing the horse via a claim isn't their main concern. In other words, they may be able to bet enough to cover any loss (cost of the horse versus today's claiming price) should the horse win. These owners want to win races and cash tickets.

4. Owners who have had success with a horse after a claim may be "out" on that horse (already have earned back its purchase price plus expenses) and are free to place the horse where they want.

While the above scenarios occur often, it is a pretty good assumption that, in general, horses that have good current form but are taking big drops in claiming price probably have something wrong that may not show up that day but will probably show up in the near future. The horse may have an obvious leg problem or something that is not visible. The horse may be a "problem child" in the barn. Maybe the horse is a bit nuts or is a weaver or cribber. Maybe the horse has trouble maintaining weight, needs a rest, bleeds, or has a breathing problem, or any other number of things that make the horse tough to train and race. Realize that many trainers (and players) can see problems in ankles and knees just by looking at a horse, but other problems or potential problems (such as a breathing problem) cannot be seen.

Once a horse has been claimed, a new "cost" (the price of the claim) is in effect when you are evaluating suspicious class drops. When owners make a good claim, they want to keep the horse because good horses are hard to find. If an owner made a bad claim, he will want to turn that horse over to someone else quickly to cut his losses. I am always suspicious of any horse that is dropped below its recent claimed price, especially if the horse shows good current form because it is possible that the horse has developed or will develop some problems. If the horse is heavily bet, why get involved in playing the horse?

Finally, if you are involved in claiming horses in addition to handicapping, you know that the peaks and valleys of betting are magnified when you are claiming and racing horses. You have to hope you are "right" about the horse you claimed being worth at least what you paid and hopefully more. When you are right, you can have a ton of fun and even make significant money. But just as with betting on the horses, making money claiming horses is tough, plus you can't just walk away from a horse you own. Don't get me wrong; having an ownership interest in any type of racehorse can be very enjoyable even if you don't make money. Some people love it; others don't want to deal with the stress associated with owning horses.

Summary

As handicappers you must be aware of the strategies and maneuvering used by owners and trainers in the claiming game to evaluate better why a horse is in a certain race and/or to predict improvement or regression by a recently claimed horse. Also, you should learn more about the trainers who claim regularly at your home track. Knowing how they operate their stable will help you in evaluating any suspiciously placed horse.

Beaten Favorites

I am sure you have come across the phrase "beaten favorite." These are horses that were favored or well bet in their previous start and ran poorly for no apparent reason. Many players will play a horse just because the horse was well bet or the favorite in its previous race. Their thinking is that the horse was bet in the prior race for a reason and may have had an excuse for running poorly that is unknown to the general public. On occasion this thinking has validity, and playing a horse back that ran poorly with no apparent excuse or giving it another chance is the thing to do.

For example, several years ago when Longacres was still open, I knew the owners of a horse that was deservedly a strong favorite in a race but ran very poorly for no apparent reason. I did not talk to the owners that day, but I knew the horse pretty well and he looked fine to me in the post parade and after the race. The next time the horse entered, I talked to the owners prior to the race and asked them what had happened the last time.

They told me that a few weeks earlier a circus had come to town, and the circus had been allowed by Longacres to house the animals near the horse barns. It turns out that this particular horse was closest to the circus animals and could hear and see two or three lions. Most horses that encounter unfamiliar animals react with fear or nervousness.

This horse was terrified at the sight of the lions (predators) and their noise. Apparently the horse didn't sleep or eat normally and was a nervous wreck the week or so the circus was in town. The circus left about two days before the race in which the horse ran poorly as a heavy favorite. Even though the horse did have two days without the circus next door, the damage had been done, and he needed more time to recover both physically and mentally. Is there a note in the *Daily Racing Form* "bothered by lions?" Anyway, players who threw out the dull race and played the horse back were rewarded because the horse did return to his previous form after that one bad effort.

Another example: A couple of years ago, our partnership raced a horse that had won three straight races. He did have a minor breathing problem and raced with a tongue-tie. When he went to the gate for his next start, the assistant starter reached up to grab his bridle and instead mistakenly grabbed the tongue tie, loosening it, and, of course, it fell off soon after the start of the race. The result was a very poor effort by the horse. The next time the horse ran, players who were looking at him as a beaten favorite may have just assumed that something unknowable to the public had gone wrong and evaluated him off his previous efforts.

While the above two examples are about horses with which I was very familiar, one you may be familiar with was the favorite for the 2001 Kentucky Derby, Point Given. Point Given was deservedly a strong favorite to win the Derby. While he did run poorly and also ran the worst race of his career that day without any apparent visible excuses (there are several views on why Point Given ran poorly), some just assumed he wasn't himself and gave him another chance to prove himself in the Preakness. Sure enough, Point Given redeemed himself not only in the Preakness but also the Belmont (Figure 4.12).

Point Given

Figure 4.12

9Jun01-10Bel	fst	1½	:48 1:11^3 2:00^3 2:26^2	Belmont-G1	**114**	9	3^1	1^{hd}	1^2	1^7	1$^{12\frac{1}{4}}$	Stevens G L	L126 b	*1.35	107- 02	*Point Given*126$^{12\frac{1}{4}}$ A PValentine126$^{\frac{3}{4}}$ Monarchos126^1	5 wide, strong u
19May01-11Pim	fst	$1\frac{3}{16}$	:47^1 1:11^4 1:36^2 1:55^2	Preaknes-G1	**111**	11	9^{10}	6$^{7\frac{1}{2}}$	3^{nk}	1$^{\frac{1}{2}}$	1$^{2\frac{1}{4}}$	Stevens G L	L126 b	*2.30	94- 11	*Point Given*126$^{2\frac{1}{4}}$ A P Valentine126^{nk} *Congaree*126$^{1\frac{1}{4}}$	Brk slw,5wd,lug i
5May01-8CD	fst	1¼	:44^4 1:09^1 1:35 1:59^4	KyDerby-G1	**99**	17	7$^{6\frac{1}{4}}$	7$^{3\frac{3}{4}}$	2$^{1\frac{1}{2}}$	4$^{4\frac{1}{2}}$	5$^{11\frac{1}{2}}$	Stevens G L	L126 b	*1.80	92 -	Monarchos126$^{4\frac{3}{4}}$ Invisible Ink126^{no} Congaree126^4	Broke in bmp,flatt
7Apr01-5SA	wf	1⅛	:46^2 1:10^4 1:35^2 1:47^3	SADerby-G1	**110**	1	2^1	2^1	1^1	1$^{2\frac{1}{2}}$	1$^{5\frac{1}{2}}$	Stevens G L	LB122 b	*.70	97- 08	Point Given122$^{5\frac{1}{2}}$ CraftyC.T.122^3 ILoveSilver122$^{2\frac{1}{2}}$	Led in hand,ridder
17Mar01-7SA	fst	$1\frac{1}{16}$	:22^3 :46^1 1:10^2 1:41^4	SnFelipe-G2	**105**	8	5^5	5^4	1^{hd}	1^2	1$^{2\frac{1}{4}}$	Stevens G L	LB122 b	*.40	95- 13	*PointGiven*122$^{2\frac{1}{4}}$ ILoveSilver116$^{1\frac{1}{2}}$ JamicnRum119^7	5wd move, led, cle
16Dec00-4Hol	fst	$1\frac{1}{16}$	:23 :46^4 1:10^4 1:42^1	HolFut-G1	**101**	4	4^5	3$^{\frac{1}{2}}$	3$^{\frac{1}{2}}$	2^{hd}	1^1	Stevens G L	LB121 b	*.30	89- 15	*PointGiven*121^1 *MillnniumWind*121^7 GoldnTickt121^5	3wd,lugged in bit
4Nov00-8CD	fst	$1\frac{1}{16}$	:23^2 :46^4 1:11^1 1:42	BCJuven-G1	**99**	1	10$^{6\frac{1}{2}}$	12^7	14^{10}	6^7	2no	Stevens G L	L122 b	8.10	100 -	Macho Uno122^{no} *Point Given*122$^{1\frac{1}{2}}$ *Street Cry*122$^{\frac{1}{2}}$	10w strtch,closed
14Oct00-9Bel	fst	$1\frac{1}{16}$	:22^3 :45 1:09^2 1:41^2	Champagn-G1	**95**	2	4^1	1^{hd}	3^{nk}	2^{hd}	2$^{1\frac{3}{4}}$	Desormeaux K J	L122 b	4.60	88- 09	A P Valentine122$^{1\frac{3}{4}}$ Point Given122$^{\frac{3}{4}}$ Yonaguska122^1	Vied inside, ga
16Sep00-12TP	fst	$1\frac{1}{16}$	:22^1 :45^3 1:12 1:47	KyCupJuv-G3	**81**	7	8$^{9\frac{1}{2}}$	6$^{7\frac{1}{2}}$	5^3	1^3	1$^{3\frac{1}{2}}$	Sellers S J	L114 b	3.30	68- 23	Point Given114$^{3\frac{1}{2}}$ Holiday Thunder114^4 *The Goo*116$^{\frac{1}{2}}$	Broke a bit i
26Aug00-7Dmr	fst	7f	:22^3 :45^2 1:10^2 1:23^2	Md Sp Wt 47k	**93**	1	6	4$^{\frac{3}{4}}$	1$^{\frac{1}{2}}$	1^1	1^2	Espinoza V	LB118 b	*1.20	88- 10	*PointGiven*118^2 HighandLowVixen118^4 Qwqeb118^8	Inside duel,clear,
12Aug00-6Dmr	fst	5½f	:22^1 :45^1 :57^2 1:04	Md Sp Wt 47k	**74**	9	6	10$^{9\frac{3}{4}}$	9$^{9\frac{1}{2}}$	7$^{9\frac{3}{4}}$	2$^{5\frac{1}{2}}$	Take Y	LB118 b	19.00	86- 17	HighCascade118$^{5\frac{1}{2}}$ *PointGiven*118$^{2\frac{1}{2}}$ WestwrdAngel118^{no}	4wd turn,late

If you are an owner, you know many things can happen to any horse between races, things that will affect its performance, sometimes greatly. Because this information is generally not available to the public, players are usually left in a position of having to forgive a horse for a dull race and assume it had a legitimate excuse.

PART II

Value and Wagering

Aweek or so before the 1998 Super Bowl matching Denver and Green Bay, I read an interview with an oddsmaker who discussed the making of the game's point spread. Green Bay was a favorite by approximately twelve and half points. The oddsmaker said that if this were a regular-season game on a neutral field, he would make Green Bay, the National Football Conference representative, a seven-point favorite. However, since this was the Super Bowl and the NFC had won thirteen Super Bowls in a row, he made the spread twelve and a half points because he knew the public would need at least that many points before any money would be placed on Denver, the American Football Conference representative.

After reading the article, I didn't have to know anything about football to understand that at twelve and a half points, Denver was a strong play as an "overlay." Anyone who played Denver was getting a five-and-half point bonus only because of the hype surrounding the Super Bowl. It didn't matter to me if Denver actually covered the point spread or not, just as the results of one race, or in this case one game, are not the issue.

A successful handicapper wins over time by making good plays at fair prices. The main thing you should do is find an approach to establishing value coupled with an approach to wagering that incorporates your goals, personal strengths, handicapping style, etc. Establishing value and having an approach to wagering are critical to any individual player's success or potential success.

Value: The Key to Winning?

When it comes to determining value, players use all kinds of methods. Some use a very strict approach; others acknowledge the importance of value but don't address it in their wagering.

Some players go to the extreme of confining their betting to horses that are overlays (underbet) — horses whose odds are significantly higher than what those players determine to be their true chances of winning. Their view is they may not win that individual bet, but by repeatedly betting such overlays they will come out ahead over time. This is correct if the handicapper is right about a horse's "true chances."

The converse view is that a winner always pays, however small the amount, while the loser pays nothing. There is no real "minimum price" for this type of player. If he is confident the horse can win, he will bet it regardless of the odds.

I imagine most players' view of value falls between these two extremes. This section gives a few general ways to establish value, as well as my approach.

An Extreme Value Player
(Betting Any Horse That Is an Overlay)

Some players look at a race with the goal of establishing accurate probabilities; they are not attempting to select an individual horse to bet.

For example, they may conclude horse #1 has a 20 percent

chance of winning; the #2, an 8 percent chance; the #3, a 12 percent chance; and so on. After establishing those probabilities, they compare the actual odds against those probabilities and bet any horse whose actual odds are significantly different from its assigned probabilities. This approach reduces betting to playing *any* horse only because it is an overlay.

They might play a horse in a race because it is going off at 2-1 and think it should be 6-5, or they might play a horse because it is 60-1 and think its actual chances equate to 20-1. Of course, this pretty much limits those players to considering only the win pool because trying to come up with probabilities for most exotic wagers (such as the trifecta or pick three) can be very complicated and difficult to implement.

A More Effective Value Player
(Handicap First, Then Bet the Overlays)

A similar but more common type of value player will, instead of looking at every horse in the field, narrow the field to a few main contenders (two, three, or maybe four horses), assign win probabilities to those horses, and then compare those probabilities against the actual odds. If this type of player can accurately determine main contenders and probabilities, his chance of success is excellent.

The only drawback with this approach is it still limits those players to the win pool and maybe the exacta pools. Since a majority of wagering is done in exotics such as the trifecta, pick threes, etc., a narrow view of establishing value like this won't work for most players.

A Player Who Bets the Morning Line

Another method is to look at value in relation to the morning line printed in the program. This approach would be great if the morning line was accurate. While many morning line makers are very good, just because a horse is listed at 6-1 in the program and actually goes off at 12-1 doesn't mean it is an overlay.

Remember, the morning line is a person's opinion of what the public will do (similar to the way the spread is set by oddsmakers in sports betting) and not that person's opinion of what the odds should be. The best morning line makers are very good at judging the public and don't impose their view of what the odds should be.

Also, as you probably already know, those morning lines are usually done a day in advance without the knowledge of late changes, changing weather, track conditions, etc.

Finally, those morning lines printed in the program tend to make potentially strong favorites "high." No track wants a morning-line maker who will list horses accurately when they will probably be 3-5 or 4-5 because bettors might skip the race or turn to other tracks. Instead, the favorite is usually listed at a higher price than its final odds.

How I Determine Value

When first looking at a race to try and establish fair value, I will do the following:

1) try to determine which horses are likely to be overbet/underbet (underlaid/overlaid) in the win pools;

2) look at the exotic possibilities so I can still play a horse that I like but that may be overbet in the win pool or to enhance my total return by playing exactas, trifectas, etc.;

3) combine steps one and two with my view of the race to form my betting strategy.

Determining Which Horses Are Likely To Be Overbet/Underbet

As I handicap any given race, I try and determine whether a particular horse will be overbet/underbet, and I estimate the likelihood of obtaining fair value.

If I select a horse whose strengths are obvious, I know I won't be alone in noticing the horse, and I'll conclude it will probably be overbet. On the other hand, if I like a horse for reasons not obvious to most others, I will be fairly confident of getting at least a fair price.

For example, if a horse has the highest speed figures and is starting for the leading trainer with the leading rider aboard, that horse is probably going to be overbet. Underbet horses may be horses that, while not encountering obvious trouble, have not had things go their way in their past few starts and/or have low-profile connections. As mentioned in Chapter 1, if you are aware of how your competition is thinking, you will be better able to determine which horses are likely to draw money and, thus, which horses might be overbet or underbet.

Before considering exotic wagers, I suggest you establish a minimum win price you would accept on a horse you think can't lose. However, no matter what you end up deciding that minimum price is, in terms of odds, you must be aware of the assumed risk of any wager and include that in your evaluation of any horse's chances. Regardless of how much of an advantage a particular horse appears to have over the field, the risk of the unforeseen — a bad stumble out of the gate, a significantly troubled trip, an obvious or not-so-obvious condition such as bleeding, entrapped epiglottis, flipped palate, or any of the other common to bizarre things that can happen during a race or before a race must be considered in that minimum price.

On occasion I will accept 4-5 as my minimum price. For instance, late scratches one day reduced a race at Emerald Downs to four horses. The field consisted of three plodders and one front runner; in addition, the front runner also had better final speed figures than the other three horses in the race. In this case I thought 4-5 was a pretty good price on the front runner. Translated into probability, I expected it to have a high chance or better of winning. To overcome the assumed risk of racing, a price of 4-5 is enough for me.

I don't play 4-5 shots often. In fact, unless the right circumstances exist (such as in the example above), I rarely play horses to win at those reduced prices. The point is this: 4-5 is my minimum, and I won't play any horse below 4-5; it just isn't worth it to me with the assumed risk on any horse. Your minimum becomes your base. You would work up from that base when determining the lowest price you would accept on any particular horse.

Looking at the Exotics Possibilities

Before I even go to the track, I look at the exotic options while I estimate overlays and underlays in the win pool. If a horse actually is overbet in the win pool, I look to the exotics for value so I can still wager on that horse. Also, if I feel a horse will, at the least, be a fair value in the win pool, I also will consider exotics to improve my return.

Combining My View of the Race

The final part of my initial analysis of a race is to assess the likelihood of the success of my selection(s). For me, races fall into a limited number of categories. The first category is races I can't figure out and won't play regardless of the odds of any particular horse. I can't find a horse or horses that I think have an advantage, or the field contains too many unknowns (shippers, horses off layoffs, first-time starters, etc.). Part of successful handicapping/betting is to skip races in which you don't have an advantage or an opinion.

The second category is races in which I have no strong opinion about any individual horse but can narrow the contenders down. Though I don't estimate probabilities for each horse, I do have an expectation of what the odds will be. If the actual odds on a horse I view as a contender are significantly different from what I anticipated, I play that horse only because it is a *significant* overlay.

Similarly, if I think a heavy favorite is vulnerable, I may play the race if I have some opinion of which horse could beat that favorite.

I am sure you have looked at a race and had the thought "that horse (the favorite) is way overbet." I thought Fusaichi Pegasus was way overbet in the 2000 Preakness Stakes. It is not unusual for such a horse to have a lot of hype because of the press he received before and after the Kentucky Derby. In fact, the national/local press often touts a particular horse as unbeatable or dominating in these top races. In some of these cases, the horse's previous efforts did justify the hype. One of the results of this hype is that on occasion, the connections of the horse (trainer/jockey) decide to give the horse a conservative, confident ride believing the horse is so superior that it can overcome any sort of bad (or wide) trip.

When Fusaichi Pegasus went into the 2000 Kentucky Derby with excellent connections and good speed figures, he looked like a definite and deserving favorite. He won only after receiving an absolutely perfect trip. He had a perfect pace setup, he saved ground throughout much of the race, and despite a large field, he was never forced to check. Figure 5.1 shows the chart for the 2000 Kentucky Derby.

Prior to the Preakness, people were saying the Triple Crown was a foregone conclusion and had already anointed Fusaichi Pegasus as the "super horse" racing fans so desperately wanted to see. When Fusaichi Pegasus drew an outside post, I was a little

Figure 5.1

EIGHTH RACE
Churchill
MAY 6, 2000

1¼ MILES. (1.59^{2}) 126th Running of THE KENTUCKY DERBY. Grade I. Purse $1,000,000 guaranteed. 3-year-olds. With an entry fee of $15,000 each and a starting fee of $15,000 each. Supplemental nominations may be made upon payment of $150,000 and in accordance with the rules set forth. All fees, including supplemental nominations, in excess of $500,000 in the aggregate shall be paid to the winner. Churchill Downs Incorporated shall guarantee a minimum gross purse of $1,000,000. The winner shall receive $700,000, second place, $170,000, third place, $85,000 and fourth place, $45,000 from the guaranteed purse. Colts and Geldings shall each carry a weight of one hundred twenty-six pounds (126); Fillies shall each carry one hundred twenty-one pounds (121).

Value of Race: $1,338,400 Winner 1,038,400; second $170,000; third $85,000; fourth $45,000. Mutuel Pool $29,288,707. Exacta Pool $13,352,999. Trifecta Pool $13,466,683. Superfecta Pool $2,642,948.0

Last Raced	Horse	M/Eqt.	A.Wt	PP	¼	½	¾	1	Str	Fin	Jockey	Odds $1
15Apr00 ^{9}Aqu^{1}	Fusaichi Pegasus	Lf	3 126	15	$15^{3\frac{1}{2}}$	$13^{\frac{1}{2}}$	$11^{\frac{1}{2}}$	6^{1}	1^{hd}	$1^{1\frac{1}{2}}$	Desormeaux K J	2.30
15Apr00 ^{9}Aqu^{3}	Aptitude	L	3 126	2	$13^{\frac{1}{2}}$	$14^{1\frac{1}{2}}$	10^{hd}	8^{1}	$4^{3\frac{1}{2}}$	2^{4}	Solis A	11.80
15Apr00 ^{9}OP^{3}	Impeachment	L	3 126	14	19	19	17^{hd}	$13^{1\frac{1}{2}}$	7^{hd}	$3^{\frac{1}{2}}$	Perret C	a-6.20
15Apr00 ^{9}Kee^{2}	More Than Ready	L	3 126	9	3^{hd}	3^{hd}	$3^{\frac{1}{2}}$	4^{hd}	2^{hd}	4^{nk}	Velazquez J R	11.30
15Apr00 ^{9}Kee^{3}	Wheelaway	Lb	3 126	3	6^{hd}	$8^{\frac{1}{2}}$	7^{hd}	5^{1}	$3^{\frac{1}{2}}$	5^{3}	Migliore R	f-20.80
25Mar00 NAS^{1}	China Visit	L	3 126	11	12^{5}	11^{hd}	$9^{1\frac{1}{2}}$	7^{hd}	6^{hd}	6^{hd}	Dettori Lanfranco	b-23.70
25Mar00 NAS^{3}	Curule	L	3 126	18	14^{1}	15^{1}	16^{4}	$9^{\frac{1}{2}}$	$8^{\frac{1}{2}}$	$7^{4\frac{1}{2}}$	St Julien M	b-23.70
8Apr00 ^{5}SA^{3}	Captain Steve	L	3 126	7	7^{hd}	$6^{\frac{1}{2}}$	$6^{1\frac{1}{2}}$	1^{hd}	5^{1}	$8^{\frac{3}{4}}$	Albarado R J	8.10
8Apr00 ^{5}SA^{2}	War Chant	Lb	3 126	8	11^{1}	10^{1}	$12^{\frac{1}{2}}$	14^{hd}	10^{2}	$9^{3\frac{3}{4}}$	Bailey J D	9.90
15Apr00 ^{9}Kee^{4}	Deputy Warlock	Lf	3 126	6	$17^{1\frac{1}{2}}$	17^{3}	$18^{2\frac{1}{2}}$	$18^{1\frac{1}{2}}$	17^{3}	$10^{\frac{1}{2}}$	Guidry M	f-20.80
8Apr00 ^{11}GP^{1}	Trippi	L	3 126	5	$2^{2\frac{1}{2}}$	2^{1}	$2^{1\frac{1}{2}}$	2^{hd}	9^{1}	11^{1}	Chavez J F	a-6.20
15Apr00 ^{9}Aqu^{9}	Exchange Rate	Lb	3 126	16	5^{hd}	7^{hd}	8^{hd}	$12^{\frac{1}{2}}$	12^{hd}	$12^{\frac{3}{4}}$	Borel C H	59.20
8Apr00 ^{5}SA^{4}	Anees	Lb	3 126	1	16^{1}	16^{6}	$15^{\frac{1}{2}}$	11^{hd}	$11^{1\frac{1}{2}}$	$13^{2\frac{3}{4}}$	Nakatani C S	17.10
8Apr00 ^{5}SA^{1}	The Deputy-IR	L	3 126	10	$9^{\frac{1}{2}}$	$12^{2\frac{1}{2}}$	$14^{\frac{1}{2}}$	17^{hd}	16^{hd}	$14^{\frac{3}{4}}$	McCarron C J	4.60
15Apr00 ^{9}Kee^{1}	High Yield	Lb	3 126	17	$8^{\frac{1}{2}}$	$5^{\frac{1}{2}}$	$5^{\frac{1}{2}}$	$10^{\frac{1}{2}}$	15^{hd}	15^{nk}	Day P	a-6.20
15Apr00 ^{9}Kee^{8}	Hal's Hope	L	3 126	4	1^{hd}	1^{1}	$1^{\frac{1}{2}}$	3^{1}	13^{1}	$16^{1\frac{3}{4}}$	Velez R I	22.70
22Apr00 ^{9}Kee^{4}	Commendable	Lb	3 126	12	10^{hd}	$9^{\frac{1}{2}}$	13^{hd}	$16^{1\frac{1}{2}}$	18^{1}	$17^{3\frac{1}{2}}$	Prado E S	a-6.20
15Apr00 ^{9}OP^{7}	Ronton	L	3 126	19	$18^{1\frac{1}{2}}$	$18^{1\frac{1}{2}}$	19	19	19	18	Blanc B	f-20.80
15Apr00 ^{9}OP^{1}	Graeme Hall	Lb	3 126	13	4^{1}	4^{1}	4^{hd}	$15^{\frac{1}{2}}$	$14^{1\frac{1}{2}}$	—	Sellers S J	46.30

Graeme Hall:Eased;

a-Coupled: Impeachment and Trippi and High Yield and Commendable.
b-Coupled: China Visit and Curule.
f-Mutuel Field: Wheelaway and Deputy Warlock and Ronton.

OFF AT 5:29 Start Good. Won driving. Track fast.
TIME :22^{2}, :45^{4}, 1:09^{4}, 1:35^{3}, 2:01 (:22.47, :45.99, 1:09.99, 1:35.74, 2:01.12)

$2 Mutuel Prices:				
	12–FUSAICHI PEGASUS	**6.60**	**5.60**	**4.00**
	5–APTITUDE		**9.80**	**5.80**
	1C–IMPEACHMENT (a-entry)			**4.00**

$2 EXACTA 12–5 PAID $66.00 $2 TRIFECTA 12–5–1 PAID $435.00 $1 SUPERFECTA 12–5–1–9 PAID $1,635.40

B. c, (Apr), by Mr. Prospector–Angel Fever, by Danzig. Trainer Drysdale Neil. Bred by Arthur B Hancock III & Stonerside Ltd (Ky).

FUSAICHI PEGASUS broke to the inside, was unhurried while working his way to the rail by the first turn, continued tosave ground in hand while advancing on the backstretch and around the second turn, swung out with a deft move approaching the final quarter to be seven wide when straightened for the drive, was roused three times with the whip on the right side and edged clear under vigorous hand urging. APTITUDE, with the winner entering the backstretch while four or five wide between concerned (Pimlico has a reputation of favoring inside post positions and early speed).

However, my real concern was that the connections of Fusaichi Pegasus thought (or at least read the news articles and believed what they read about him) their horse was so superior he could handle a wide trip and they wouldn't be too worried about getting position and/or saving ground on the turns.

Although I picked him to win the Preakness, I also felt the favorite was a little vulnerable and there wasn't much room for error. In my opinion, he needed to improve off his Derby race or get a perfect trip.

Like many other players, I thought Red Bullet was the main threat as he had run second to Fusaichi Pegasus in the Wood Memorial and then skipped the Derby to run fresh in the Preakness. I had not really planned to play the Preakness because I assumed that Fusaichi Pegasus would be a deserved 4-5 and Red Bullet the second choice at about 5-2. But a few minutes before the post, Fusaichi Pegasus went to as low as 2-5 while Red Bullet was about 6-1. I concluded that Fusaichi Pegasus was being extremely overbet and that the race warranted a play. While the outcome wasn't the issue, finding and playing the value in this situation turned out to be profitable. Figure 5.2 on the following page shows the chart for the 2000 Preakness.

The last category of races is one in which I do have a strong opinion, usually involving one horse. Well before the actual odds appear on the tote board, because of the first two steps in my approach, I should have a general idea of the odds. Based on my estimate of closing odds and view of the race, I will have to decide on win betting versus exotic betting. If I am confident that I will get a decent win price, I will make sure to invest part or most of my bet on a win ticket before considering the exotics.

On the flip side, if I am pretty sure the horse will be overbet in the win pool, I will concentrate on the exotic possibilities offered within and around the race. These options become most useful if I can narrow the number of horses I will use with the key horse. With so many options such as pick threes, daily doubles, exactas, trifectas, etc., I probably will be able to find other horses to use with that key horse to try to overcome an underlaid win price.

Figure 5.2

TENTH RACE

Pimlico

MAY 20, 2000

$1\frac{3}{16}$ MILES. (1.52^2) 125th Running of THE PREAKNESS. Grade I. Purse $1,000,000. 3–year–olds. $10,000 to pass the entry box, starters to pay $10,000 additional. Supplemental nominations may be made in accordance with the rules, upon payment of $100,000, 65% of all monies to the winner, 20% to second 10% to third, and 5% to fourth. Weight, colts and geldings, 126 lbs. Fillies, 121 lbs. Starters to be named through the entry box on Wednesday, May 17, 2000, three days before the race by the usual time of closing.

Value of Race: $1,000,000 Winner $650,000; second $200,000; third $100,000; fourth $50,000. Mutuel Pool $9,564,378.0 Exacta Pool $6,719,358.0 Trifecta Pool $7,157,760.0 Superfecta Pool $1,714,467.0

Last Raced	Horse	M/Eqt. A.Wt	PP	St	¼	½	¾	Str	Fin	Jockey	Odds $1
15Apr00 9Aqu2	Red Bullet	L 3 126	4	6	7⁷	7¹⁰	6¹¹⁄₂	1¹	1³¾	Bailey J D	6.20
6May00 8CD1	Fusaichi Pegasus	Lf 3 126	7	7	6¹¹⁄₂	5¹	5hd	3hd	2hd	Desormeaux K J	0.30
6May00 8CD3	Impeachment	L 3 126	3	8	8	8	8	6¹¹⁄₂	3nk	Perret C	19.10
6May00 8CD8	Captain Steve	L 3 126	6	5	5hd	6¹	7⁴	7¹²	43¼	Albarado R J	11.50
15Apr00 9OP2	Snuck In	L 3 126	2	4	42¹⁄₂	4³	4¹⁄₂	5¹	5¹	Asmussen C B	19.60
30Apr00 9Hol2	Hugh Hefner	Lb 3 126	1	3	1¹⁄₂	2¹¹⁄₂	1hd	4¹⁄₂	6¹⁄₂	Espinoza V	49.70
6May00 8CD15	High Yield	Lb 3 126	5	2	2¹⁄₂	1¹⁄₂	2¹⁄₂	2¹⁄₂	7³⁰	Day P	7.30
6May00 8CD16	Hal's Hope	L 3 126	8	1	3¹¹⁄₂	3hd	3¹	8	8	Velez R I	35.10

OFF AT 5:28 Start Good. Won driving. Track good.

TIME :23¹, :46³, 1:11¹, 1:37, 1:56 (:23.30, :46.62, 1:11.21, 1:37.06, 1:56.04)

$2 Mutuel Prices:

4–RED BULLET	14.40	3.20	2.80
7–FUSAICHI PEGASUS		2.60	2.20
3–IMPEACHMENT			3.60

$2 EXACTA 4–7 PAID $24.00 $2 TRIFECTA 4–7–3 PAID $115.80 $1
SUPERFECTA 4–7–3–6 PAID $235.50

Ch. c, (Apr), by Unbridled–Cargo, by Caro*Ire. Trainer Orseno Joseph. Bred by Stronach Frank H (Ky).

RED BULLET, unhurried early, was in hand while taking an awkward step approaching the first turn, settled well off the pace for a half, gradually worked his way forward between horses leaving the backstretch, waited patiently for room midway on the turn, split horses while making his move inside FUSAICHI PEGASUS nearing the quarter pole, charged to the front in upper stretch, opened a clear advantage in midstretch then drew away under steady left handed encouragement. FUSAICHI PEGASUS, pinched back a bit at the start, was kept to the outside while going five wide into the first turn, raced in the middle of the pack while well off the rail along the backstretch, continued five wide while making a mild move when asked for run midway on the turn, drifted in a bit nearing the three-sixteenths pole then weakened a bit while holding for the place.

©EQUIBASE

There are many times when you will be able to get a good exotic price on an underlay in the win pool. But be aware that if a horse is underlaid in the win pool, it also might be underlaid in the exotics pools. Many players, knowing a horse is underlaid in the win pool, will then look to exotics in which to key the horse but *ignore* the possibility that the horse may be overbet in the exotics pools, too.

Race Day

I now should have a pretty good idea of which races I plan to play. I also should have a good idea of those races in which I expect to play a fair-valued horse and the races in which I will be looking to the exotics. But before actually placing a bet, I have to compare the current odds of the horse with the odds I expect the horse to be at post time.

Because odds can change significantly in the minutes before

betting closes, making comparisons can become difficult. A large problem in determining value is trying to deal with the late merging of simulcast money in the pools of the track you're playing and the sometimes significant changing of odds that can occur. The problem can be compounded if you are playing a track that has relatively small pools.

Many times, for example, a horse that is 7-5 when it goes into the gate may be 4-5 by the time the race is over as the simulcast money and late on-track money are merged during the running of the race. You may think you are making a good wager (in terms of value) and then discover you didn't because the odds have changed dramatically. Merging of simulcast money requires that you estimate closing odds rather than rely on what the tote board tells you. This ability comes from experience. You can use the actual odds a few minutes before the running of the race as a guide, but don't be fooled; other players also are looking at those odds. If you see a horse, for example, that is 8-5 a minute or two before the start that you thought should and would be 4-5, it probably will end up at 4-5 after all the simulcast pools are merged.

I don't mean to use favorites for every example because you will face the same problems with longshots. You could be playing a horse that is 15-1 entering the gate and drops to 10-1 (a 33 percent decline in potential payoffs) while the field is on the backstretch.

Another problem, especially at small to mid-sized tracks, arises when a player manipulates the win pools with some "bogus" wagers. In this case someone is trying to throw off players who look at the tote board for clues. It's not hard to cause the odds on a horse to plummet by betting a few hundred dollars early. Those bets are usually cancelled within a few minutes prior to the start of the race. The point is that using the actual win odds posted on the tote board to decide whether the horse you like is going off at acceptable odds can become problematic.

One thing that can help you estimate the closing price is to look at the probable daily-double and pick-three payoffs. These potential payoffs will give a fairly good clue about a horse's closing win odds.

For example, consider if the following probable pick-three pay-offs, after the first two legs have been run, in a six-horse field are:

#1 — $120
#2 — $90
#3 — $194
#4 — $50
#5 — $400
#6 — $290

The #4 horse that is paying $50 in the pick three will probably be a heavy favorite (around 6-5) based on those probable pick-three payoffs. I recommend you use those probable payoffs rather than the actual odds on the tote board to overcome the problem of the late commingling of the pools.

If a few minutes before the start of a race the actual odds in the win pool are different from those expected based on the pick-three and/or daily-double payoffs, you can assume that by the time all the money is commingled, those odds will reflect the betting in the pick-three and/or daily-double pools. Of course, there are exceptions such as a late scratch or other late changes. Except for the first race of the day, most tracks will have some sort of probable payoffs (either pick-three pools or daily-double pools) that will be a big help in determining final closing odds for the race being handicapped.

Also, while determining the actual price at which a horse will close isn't necessarily easy, it is even tougher to establish value in any particular exotic. You will be able to see probable payoffs for bets such as the daily double, exactas, and quinellas, but you will probably not be able to determine probable payoffs for trifectas, superfectas, and pick threes because there would be too many combinations to list and too many combinations to take into consideration.

In addition, when looking at the probable payoffs for daily doubles, exactas, and quinellas to determine value, you will find the same problem as with win pools. Late simulcast/on-track money may change the payoffs significantly. With trifectas and superfectas, you may not have any idea of the actual payoffs so you bet in hopes of getting a "good" payoff if you cash.

Another problem regarding value in pick threes, pick fours,

and sometimes pick sixes occurs when one of the legs of the multi-race bet has a strong favorite (such as a 4-5 shot). What happens is that nearly every player singles the 4-5 shot, figuring he has a good chance to be alive in the pick threes, fours, or sixes. Even though the horse may be 4-5 in the win pool, in the multi-race bet pools it may act like a 1-9 shot for a couple of reasons.

First, no one wants to waste money by doubling his ticket, adding another horse in the race with the 4-5 shot. Second, since everyone appears to have a freebie in one of the legs (the 4-5 shot), more money may be spent covering even more horses in the other legs. The result of this becomes a lopsided (low) potential payoff if the 4-5 shot wins regardless of which horses win (longshots or favorites) the other legs. For an example of the above scenario, review the result charts (Figure 5.3, following page) for a pick four that started in race six at Emerald Downs on August 30, 2002.

When Bulls and Bears won the first leg of the pick four at 4-5, the resulting payoff for that pick four was $156.10. But the payoff for the pick three starting in race seven was $205.70 ($49.60 higher than the pick-four payoff).

This type of payoff or similar underlaid payoffs happens all the time in multi-race bets that include a very strong favorite or favorites. Some pick threes involving heavy favorites will pay less than a win parlay of those horses. Of course, the benefit of these horses being heavily keyed in pick threes occurs when you are able to beat one or more of those favorites; the resulting payoff will be significantly higher. When you encounter such a scenario, be aware that the heavily favored horse will probably become even more strongly bet in the pick-three, -four, and -six pools over the win pool and adjust your decision about whether to place those bets on the likely payoff.

Pick threes are touted as excellent bets because in most cases, they pay more than a win parlay of the same horses. But one reason you need a payoff that is higher than a win parlay of those three races is the significant effect of late scratches on the pick-three payoffs. I am sure you have been alive after the first or second leg of a pick three only to have your key horse run off in the post parade or flip in the gate and be scratched, leaving you with

Figure 5.3 — Example of a Pick Four

Race 6 EmD- 30Aug02 1 Mile (1:33⅕), 3 and up Clm 4000

Value of race: $5,700. 1st $3,135; 2nd $1,140; 3rd $855; 4th $428; 5th $142. Mutuel pools: $37,770. Ex $24,723. Tri $22,483. Super $9,170. Pick-3 $4,570.

Last Raced	Horse	Med/Eqp	A	Wgt	PP	St	1/4	1/2	3/4	Str	Fin	Odds $1
27Jly02 ^{3}EmD^{2}	Bulls And Bears	LBb	6	123	7	6	$5^{1/2}$	5^{4}	3^{hd}	$1^{1/2}$	1^{6}	0.80
16Aug02 ^{6}EmD^{11}	D D Stormy	LB	4	119	1	1	2^{3}	2^{3}	1^{hd}	$2^{1 1/2}$	2^{3}	11.80
13Jly02 ^{5}EmD^{7}	Bright Stout	LBbf	4	121	5	5	4^{2}	$4^{1 1/2}$	$4^{1 1/2}$	3^{3}	3^{1}	4.10
20Jly02 ^{4}EmD^{2}	Talking About	LBb	6	117	3	3	3^{3}	3^{hd}	5^{2}	$4^{1/2}$	$4^{1 1/2}$	7.50
11Aug02 ^{6}EmD^{2}	Pesky Pete	LB	4	120	6	4	6^{4}	6^{hd}	7	5^{1}	$5^{1 1/2}$	34.90
11Aug02 ^{6}EmD^{8}	Corn Mash	LBbf	6	121	4	7	7	7	6^{hd}	6^{hd}	$6^{1 1/2}$	20.10
18Aug02 ^{8}Kam^{4}	Ringside Rhythm	LBb	4	118	2	2	1^{hd}	1^{hd}	2^{1}	7	7	4.30

Off Time: 8:25 **Time Of Race:** :22⅘ :46 1:11⅗ 1:24⅖ 1:36⅘
Start: Good For All But Corn Mash. **Track:** Fast. **Won ridden out.**

$2 Mutuel Payoffs:

8	Bulls And Bears	3.60	2.60	2.20
2	D D Stormy		6.00	3.20
4	Bright Stout			2.60

$1 Exacta 8-2 Paid $16.20; $1 Trifecta 8-2-6 Paid $42.10; $1 Superfecta 8-2-6-4 Paid $87.60; $1 Pick-3 (4-5-1/8) Paid $53.10

Race 7 EmD- 30Aug02 6 Furlongs (1:07⅗), 3 and up fillies and mares Clm 12500

Value of race: $10,500. 1st $5,775; 2nd $2,100; 3rd $1,575; 4th $788; 5th $262. Mutuel pools: $55,750. Ex $40,577. Tri $38,484. Pick-3 $5,579.

Last Raced	Horse	Med/Eqp	A	Wgt	PP	St	1/4	1/2	Str	Fin	Odds $1
17Aug02 ^{6}EmD^{2}	Hot and Spicy	LBb	4	122	3	3	$4^{1 1/2}$	3^{1}	$2^{1/2}$	1^{nk}	2.20
15Aug02 ^{6}EmD^{2}	Check These Legs	LBb	4	118	2	5	$1^{1/2}$	1^{4}	1^{2}	$2^{1 1/2}$	2.60
15Aug02 ^{6}EmD^{4}	Lefa Theda	LBbf	5	122	5	1	$2^{1/2}$	2^{1}	3^{3}	$3^{4 1/2}$	3.50
15Aug02 ^{6}EmD^{1}	Sizzlin' Knight	LBf	7	122	1	6	$5^{1/2}$	6	4^{1}	$4^{3/4}$	4.00
12Jul02 ^{6}EmD^{5}	Gaiter Girl	LBf	5	122	6	4	6	4^{hd}	5^{2}	$5^{9 1/4}$	13.40
15Aug02 ^{6}EmD^{3}	Writehof	LB	5	120	4	2	3^{2}	5^{1}	6	6	7.30

Off Time: 8:58 **Time Of Race:** :21⅘ :44⅕ :56⅖ 1:09⅖
Start: Good For All. **Track:** Fast. **Won driving.**

$2 Mutuel Payoffs:

3	Hot and Spicy	6.40	3.20	2.40
2	Check These Legs		3.20	2.20
6	Lefa Theda			2.40

$1 Exacta 3-2 Paid $9.90; $1 Trifecta 3-2-6 Paid $33.20; $1 Pick-3 (5-1/8-3/4) Paid $33.40.

Race 8 EmD- 30Aug02 1 Mile (1:33⅕), 3yo fillies Clm 20000 n2x

Value of race: $11,500. 1st $6,325; 2nd $2,300; 3rd $1,725; 4th $863; 5th $287. Mutuel pools: $42,977. Ex $30,009. Tri $33,550. Super $10,441. Pick-3 $4,342.

Last Raced	Horse	Med/Eqp	A	Wgt	PP	St	1/4	1/2	3/4	Str	Fin	Odds $1
16Aug02 ^{8}EmD^{2}	Ruby Montani	LBb	3	117	2	7	8	8	6^{3}	$3^{1 1/2}$	$1^{3/4}$	3.50
9Aug02 ^{8}EmD^{05}	Perfect Plan	LBb	3	118	3	4	$2^{1 1/2}$	2^{3}	2^{hd}	2^{hd}	2^{nk}	3.60
16Aug02 ^{8}EmD^{1}	Lady Buccaneer	LBb	3	120	6	1	1^{hd}	1^{hd}	1^{1}	1^{1}	$3^{1 3/4}$	2.30
8Aug02 ^{5}EmD^{1}	Callie Mae	LBb	3	113	7	5	$3^{1/2}$	$3^{1 1/2}$	$5^{1 1/2}$	5^{hd}	4^{1}	15.00
9Aug02 ^{6}EmD^{4}	Amazing Sue	LBb	3	118	4	8	7^{4}	$6^{1 1/2}$	$4^{1/2}$	6^{4}	$5^{3/4}$	4.70
3Aug02 ^{6}EmD^{1}	Classic Jourdan	LBbf	3	120	5	2	5^{hd}	$5^{1/2}$	3^{1}	$4^{1/2}$	$6^{4 1/2}$	10.70
16Aug02 ^{8}EmD^{3}	Aquaduck	LBb	3	110	1	3	$6^{1 1/2}$	7^{hd}	$7^{1 1/2}$	7^{2}	$7^{5 1/2}$	8.50
1Aug02 ^{8}EmD^{3}	Bries N By M	LB	3	110	8	6	4^{2}	4^{1}	8	8	8	29.00

Off Time: 9:24 **Time Of Race:** :23⅕ :45⅘ 1:10⅘ 1:24 1:37⅕
Start: Good For All. **Track:** Fast. **Won driving.**

$2 Mutuel Payoffs:

2	Ruby Montani	9.00	4.00	2.40
3	Perfect Plan		4.60	2.80
6	Lady Buccaneer			2.40

$1 Exacta 2-3 Paid $19.10; $1 Trifecta 2-3-6 Paid $48.60; $1 Superfecta 2-3-6-7 Paid $387.30; $1 Pick-3 (1/8-3/4-2) Paid $23.90

Race 9 EmD- 30Aug02 1 1/16 Miles (1:39 3/5), 3 and up Clm 8000

Value of race: $8,300. 1st $4,565; 2nd $1,660; 3rd $1,245; 4th $623; 5th $207. Mutuel pools: $41,424. Ex $30,181. Tri $33,550. Super $16,401. Pick-3 $7,395. Pick-4 $7,216.

Last Raced	Horse	Med/Eqp	A	Wgt	PP	St	1/4	1/2	3/4	Str	Fin	Odds $1
22Aug02 ^{5}EmD^{1}	Barfly Begone	LB	4	123	3	5	4^{2}	4^{2}	4^{1}	$3^{1/2}$	$1^{3/4}$	10.10
22Jun02 ^{4}EmD^{1}	Themanwithebigcigr	LBbf	6	112	8	2	$2^{2 1/2}$	2^{3}	$2^{2 1/2}$	1^{hd}	2^{hd}	5.50
4Aug02 ^{7}EmD^{5}	Eye Spy	LBb	5	119	7	7	$6^{1/2}$	6^{2}	6^{5}	$4^{1/2}$	$3^{1 1/2}$	4.70
26Jly02 ^{7}Hst^{2}	Silver Sky	LBb	4	114	1	1	$1^{1/2}$	$1^{1/2}$	1^{hd}	2^{hd}	$4^{1 1/4}$	4.10
17Aug02 ^{9}EmD^{2}	Winterstarr	LBbf	4	119	2	4	3^{2}	$3^{2 1/2}$	3^{3}	$5^{1 1/2}$	$5^{2 1/4}$	1.60
3Aug02 ^{1}EmD^{1}	Harbro	LBbf	4	119	6	3	5^{3}	5^{3}	$5^{1/2}$	6^{4}	$6^{1 1/2}$	8.10
27Jly02 ^{6}EmD^{7}	Cowboy Jazz	LBb	4	119	4	6	7^{6}	7^{8}	7^{4}	$7^{1/2}$	$7^{3/4}$	12.50
17Aug02 ^{9}EmD^{7}	Trackman	LB	5	120	5	8	8	8	8	8	8	35.60

Off Time: 9:53 **Time Of Race:** :22⅗ :45⅗ 1:09⅗ 1:36⅕ 1:42⅗
Start: Good For All. **Track:** Fast. **Won driving.**

$2 Mutuel Payoffs:

3	Barfly Begone	22.20	10.60	5.60
9	Themanwithebigcigr		8.20	3.60
8	Eye Spy			3.60

$1 Exacta 3-9 Paid $58.40; $1 Trifecta 3-9-8 Paid $360.60; $1 Superfecta 3-9-8-1 Paid $6,387.00; $1 Pick-3 (3/4-2-3) Paid $205.70; $2 Daily Double 2-3 Paid $93.80; $1 Pic-4 (1/8-3/4-2-3) Paid $156.10.

the favorite, which you may or may not want at a reduced price.[1]

There are several other situations in which late scratches significantly impact your pick threes (or pick fours or pick sixes), such as when a late scratch affects the race shape, leaving your horse at a significant disadvantage.

Or, let's say you play a pick three, keying a horse in the final leg in hopes of beating a heavy favorite in that final race and that favorite is scratched and all the money on that horse is transferred to your horse. Your potential payoff is depressed, and to add insult to injury, if your horse wins, others betting the favorite also get paid.

Or, suppose you are alive to an entry and the stronger half of a two-horse entry (the one you counted on running) is scratched, leaving you with the weaker half. In playing any multi-race bets (pick threes, fours, and sixes), you leave yourself open to these possibilities, so make sure you are playing combinations that will pay enough to include those risks.

Whether you are trying to determine the final payoffs for a lone winner or as a key in the exotics, you rely on experience before making your wager. All choices come down to risk versus return. If you feel the payoffs for any wager will be low, why take the risk? If I can't find any good-paying exotics or don't have any good options in the exotics and the win price is insignificant, I skip the race.

[1]In most cases if a horse is scratched in a pick three, the wager reverts to the post-time favorite.

A pure value player looks for overlays by comparing current odds versus the player's own odds line and may end up playing one, two, or more horses in any particular race. But since I primarily try to come up with one key horse, I have to use a betting strategy that incorporates playing that key horse while avoiding underlays. My style of handicapping does limit me somewhat because I am, for the most part, looking to key one horse. But I never look at a race and say, "I love this horse at 3-1 and hate him at 2-1."

You may have read or heard that favorites are overbet early in the card and then tend to be underbet later. I have found this to be true at pretty much any track any day. No one wants to go home losing. As the last race approaches, players who are "stuck" and trying to get out for the day tend to key on exotics and ignore the win pools — especially if the horse they like is the favorite and a win bet probably won't get them even. Those who like the favorite don't play the horse to win but key that horse in exotics, which is why favorites tend to be underbet in the win pool toward the last race. Early in the card, players want to cash and will bet the favorite down — no one is chasing their losses yet.

As you are aware, the number of exotics offered, from the trifecta, superfecta, pick threes, pick fours, twin trifectas, etc., seems endless, and for many players their goal is to win a lot of money off one race. Betting a horse to win isn't enough, regardless of odds, because they want to go home rich. If you say after a race, "I loved the winner," the first question asked will be, "Did you have the tri?" While there obviously is opportunity in exotics wagering, there is nothing wrong with playing a horse to win and walking away from the exotics. Making an exotics wager by keying a horse you like and guessing on other horses to come in with your horse or hoping for a longshot after you wheel your key horse will, over time, lower your overall return. If you don't have an opinion about other horses to use with your key horse (either within the race or across several races), take the win money.

Wagering/Betting Strategy: Can You Pick Winners but Still Lose?

With most forms of gambling (many casino games, state lotteries), there is no way to win over time. However, with horse racing it *is* possible. If you don't exactly understand why you can win despite the relatively steep takeout on horse racing compared to other forms of gambling, the next few paragraphs should help.

When you walk into a casino and play $10 on "the bank" at a baccarat table (probably the best bet or lowest takeout in a casino for the fixed-odds games), you essentially donate a dime to the casino with every $10 wager. It doesn't matter if you win the particular bet; the casino edge is fixed at about 1.17 percent for that bet and does not change. Absolutely nothing (that isn't illegal) can be done to give you an edge. This is true for all forms of fixed-odds gambling, including bets made when playing craps, baccarat, roulette, and keno.

Blackjack and video poker are the only forms of casino gambling in which you might be able to overcome the casino edge. Blackjack is beatable because the edge changes, sometimes in favor of the player depending on the value of the cards (face cards versus non-face cards) removed from the deck during play. Video poker is beatable because of progressive payoffs that may go above a certain amount or because a certain payoff scale could return more than 100 percent with proper play. In either case, the player can have a slight edge.

Sports betting — with a standard bet of $11 to win $10, usually with a point spread — has a takeout (commonly called "juice" or "vig" by sports bettors) of about 4.5 percent.[1] Unlike casino gam-

[1] Many people assume that straight sports betting has a 10 percent takeout, as if you are betting $11 to win $10, you are paying 10 percent juice. In reality, the takeout is 4.5 percent — using the 1998 Super Bowl as an example, if you bet both teams, let's say $11 on Green

bling in which the odds are fixed in favor of the casino, in sports betting the odds are "made" in order for the sports book to try to attract equal amounts of money on each side. The sports books look to make a minimum of 4.5 percent.[2] Similar to the Super Bowl example at the beginning of Part II, of Denver versus Green Bay, the spread in many football games each week isn't really a "good" number because of each team's relative chances, but the number is established to get the public to bet evenly on each side. The result of the spread being "made" to get equal money is the reason sports betting can be profitable.

Horse racing falls in line with sports betting, although the takeout is fairly high. The takeout for straight betting (win, place, show) is usually between 14 percent and 20 percent, and the takeout for exotics betting is even higher.[3] Each track is different, but if you average the win/place/show takeouts with the exotic takeouts, you are looking at about a 20 percent takeout overall. Most players do not normally notice the effect of this large takeout. But realize that with an average of 20 percent takeout, you are chasing 80 cents in payoffs for every dollar you bet . Think about it for a second. This is for every race. If a track has a total handle of $1 million, the patrons together have lost about $200,000 that day.

Unlike sports betting in which the sports book sets the odds and point spreads or money lines are slightly adjusted depending on the flow of money, the bettors determine the odds in horse racing. In general, the public is pretty good, and the final closing odds are a decent representation of a horse's chances. Of course, the public isn't perfect, and many times this results in horses being overbet or underbet in relation to their actual chances.

There are several reasons horses become overbet or underbet.

Bay −12.5 points and $11 on Denver +12.5 points, you would be betting $22, and no matter which team wins, cashing for $21; the $1 you lost divided by the amount wagered ($22) is 4.5 percent.

[2] While legal sports books and illegal bookies do try to have equal money on each side of any given event, they probably make more than 4.5 percent. First, many players play teasers and parlays, which have a higher takeout. Second, many players make the same mistakes as bettors in horse racing (overbetting popular teams) and the bookies/sports books aren't afraid to take a stand on one side against the bettors.

[3] All racetracks have significantly different takeouts. If you are a once-in-a while, casual racegoer, the specific takeout probably won't affect your final results too much. If you attend

A common one is that the public has a tendency to emphasize a horse's most recent race. In popular races such as the Kentucky Derby or the Breeders' Cup, this emphasis can be magnified. The press coverage usually concentrates on a few horses, usually the ones coming off wins.

Beginning with the first Breeders' Cup (1984), there have been many short-priced horses that, because of the press they received prior to the Breeders' Cup races, were touted as being "pretty much unbeatable," yet many lost. In many cases, *just as in any race on any day,* those heavily bet horses in the Breeders' Cup were not really that much better than the other horses in those races, but the press they received resulted in the public's believing those horses would not lose. In addition, the press may have ignored a significant disadvantage that the horse could encounter. For example, if the horse encountered any trouble at all, or a pace scenario that did not favor the horse, or some other obstacle, the horse was beaten. The point is, the big races can offer regular players increased opportunity to find value as the public will concentrate on the horses receiving the most media hype.

You can win at horse racing, as playing horses that are underbet in relation to their actual chances allows the player to overcome the takeout.

Do You Need a Betting Strategy?

Most players don't spend too much time thinking about a betting strategy. They have no plan; they just bet each race as they feel best. The amount they bet on each race is usually determined by whether they are winning or losing on that given day.

In addition, while the amount varies based on how that particular player is doing that day, the type of wagers (exotics versus straight betting) also tends to vary. These players might just bet

and wager on a regular basis, the difference in takeout at one track versus another could be the difference between having a winning or losing season. For example, the win pool takeout in California is currently 15.43 percent; the win takeout at Turf Paradise in Arizona is 20 percent. If throughout the season, you bet and cashed for $50,000 in the win pool at Santa Anita and also $50,000 in the win pool at Turf Paradise, assuming similar results, you would get an extra $2,485 back in payoffs at Santa Anita because of the lower takeout there. Smart players are aware of the effect of takeout and try to avoid playing the tracks with the higher takeouts.

whatever options are offered on a particular race. If there is tri-fecta wagering, the player will bet the trifecta. If there is super-fecta wagering, the player will bet the superfecta.

A wagering strategy can vastly help you decide among all the possibilities offered in a race and also help you deal with the unavoidable streaks involved with gambling.

There are several keys to becoming a successful bettor. First, you should have a strategy that goes hand in hand with your style of handicapping. For example, if you are skilled at identifying longer-priced horses that might run well without winning, you probably want to concentrate your betting on the exacta and tri-fecta pools rather than the pick-three pools. If you are a strict "value" player, you also may find pick threes tough to bet because you may not be able to determine value since those probable pay-offs are not available.

Second, your betting strategy should mirror your ability to deal with losing streaks and reflect your realistic goal in playing horses.

Finally, your betting strategy should reflect confidence in your handicapping. For example, after a horse wins a race I might hear someone say, "I thought that horse couldn't lose," and I will ask what he or she bet on it; often the response is: "Twenty dollars across the board." That type of bet doesn't show a lot of confidence.

Since we all have different backgrounds, different strengths and weaknesses, and different goals, a betting strategy that is suc-cessful for me might not be successful for you. What follows is a brief description of my betting strategy, which incorporates my handicapping style. It could help you determine your own.

Goals

Having realistic goals when playing the races, whether it is once in a while or every day, is the first step toward a successful betting strategy. Trying to make a living as a professional player is very dif-ficult, time consuming, and probably unrealistic for most people. That doesn't mean you can't win or have fun. Many people have decided that playing the races is their recreation. They accept some losses over time, realizing that they enjoy the races and that those losses are just the cost of entertainment, no different from buying tickets to a football game. By knowing your goals, you can form a betting strategy that includes what type of player you are (professional to casual) and where you will be placing most of your wagers (attending a live track versus betting simulcasts).

Betting

The easiest and most recommended betting strategies say something like "bet more when you are winning and less when you are losing" or "scale your wagers; when you feel strongly about a horse, bet your largest amount (prime bet); conversely, bet less if you have less confidence in the horse." Wagering strategies that incorporate some of these recommendations include betting a fixed percentage of bankroll on each race. As you win, your bet goes up; as you lose, your bet decreases.

I disagree with these recommendations, and I prefer to have my bets remain fairly consistent and unaffected by whether I won my last bet, my last five bets, or my last ten bets. I try to bet similar amounts on each race that I decide to play — either I like the race and the horse or I don't. I find it hard to make dollar-amount distinctions; for example, there isn't a certain race on which I'll bet $100, a different type of race on which I'll bet $50, and a third type of race on which I would bet only $20. Of course, I leave myself some room. I don't bet an exact amount on each race but try to stay within a close range for each race I play. I try to be aggressive when I feel the time is right, but I also want to remain fairly consistent.

In addition, my approach to betting is conservative. I want to win, but I also want to come back to the track tomorrow. I prefer to concentrate on win bets and exactas, and occasionally play trifectas, pick threes, pick fours, and pick sixes. I don't think this minimizes or limits my profits, but my goal is to keep the money flowing rather than to experience the large swings associated with extreme exotics betting. It is my personal choice. I may give up some of the potential gains of a big individual score via the pick four or superfecta for the psychological advantage of cashing tickets. In my opinion too many players are trying to make the big score rather than trying to win overall.

I also distinguish between wagers I place when attending the races live at my home track and wagers I make at a track with which I'm not familiar or by simulcast. When playing my home track, I tend to be more aggressive, and I give myself less room for error. Because of the advantages associated with playing the races live at my home track, I am pretty confident in my handicapping. I will concentrate my betting around one key horse and not spread too much covering. I take the view that if I am right, I want to maximize my winnings, and if I am wrong, so be it.

I approach playing an unfamiliar track differently. If I'm playing a track that Emerald Downs imports as part of its simulcast offerings, if I am in Las Vegas skimming several tracks, or if I am visiting a track on vacation or on a Breeders' Cup weekend, I tend to bet a little more conservatively and also spread my money around a little more. My goal in playing those tracks is to cash tickets if I am partially right. I'm aware that I probably don't know the horses that well and have to rely on a little more luck. This approach could also work for a player who comes to the track just once a month or so.

Planning Your Bets

Well before the race day comes up, I should have a pretty good idea of what races I like and how I plan to bet them. Part of my handicapping of each race includes estimating odds of the horse(s) I look at for value.

After probable daily-double and/or pick-three payoff information becomes available, I combine those figures with my estimated odds; thus, I should have a good idea of whether a particular horse will be overbet (assuming I didn't already expect it).

As stated previously, part of my handicapping process includes deciding whether to look at the win pool and/or exotic pools. If I have decided to play exotics (or a combination of a win bet with exotics), I already have thought out potential exotic combinations and their costs.

Also, I need to be aware that if many of my planned bets that day involve pick threes, pick fours, pick sixes, bets in which I may have winning choices but won't cash a lot on an individual race, then I need to have enough money to place those bets and other bets later in the card. While I expect every bet I make to be a winner, I know that some will lose and I need to plan for those losses. I don't want my bets later in the card to depend on my early bets.

I won't have my exact bets planned because the actual odds, a horse's appearance, or track condition might not be what I expected, or I might have to make changes because of a late scratch. But I do have a plan to work from. There is too much going on during the races for me to be able to make good decisions if I was not already prepared. Deciding how to bet a race as you stand in line at the mutuel windows or self-betting terminal can only lead to mistakes, being shut out, and/or missed opportunities.

Deciding Among Betting Options
Straight Bets — Win

Betting a horse to win is the easiest decision. Many players like to bet to win and place, sort of a protection bet if their horse runs well but doesn't win. Additionally, if the horse they are betting is a longshot, they don't want to miss out on what they feel is a good-paying place price if the horse finishes second. I think those players would find they are better off playing a horse to win only. If they tracked their total return, they may find that betting the entire amount exclusively to win would result in a higher total return rather than splitting the bet between win and place.

If you want to protect for the horse running second, I suggest using exactas rather than a place bet. As you may know, place payoffs are determined by the amount of money in the place pool divided by the number of place tickets sold, not only to those who bet the place horse, but also to those who bet the winning horse to place. Essentially, if you are betting to place (or to show for that matter), you are hoping for a longshot to run first or second with your horse to get a higher place price because the money will be divided among fewer ticket holders. If a favorite (or heavy favorite) runs first or second, your place price may be significantly reduced. Boxing your horse in the exacta with others that you think are contenders and varying the amount of your bets based on the chances of those horses will give you a much better return over time than place betting.[4]

---

[4]One note about place and show betting. Even though I don't look at those pools too often, be aware that the public tends to overbet longshots in the place and show pools and the public tends to underbet favorites in the place and show pool.

Exotics

The most important key to exotics is to vary the amount of your bets so you get a similar return (on your main combinations) no matter what combination actually comes in. Also, adding horses to any exacta/trifecta/superfecta box increases the cost of the wager substantially, thereby significantly reducing the return. The same is true for adding horses to pick threes, pick fours, and pick sixes. Taking two horses in a race doubles the cost of the ticket. Be aware of the cost of adding horses (especially if they are marginal) and be sure they are worth the extra money. Exotics offer all sorts of possibilities. Below are some thoughts about wagering on the more common exotics.

Exactas

Many of the more successful players concentrate on exactas. There are a couple of reasons for this. The first is the ability to win more with small wagers. There is nothing wrong, for example, with having $50 to win on a 3-1 shot. But successful players, when the opportunity presents itself, will look to key that horse in the exacta. Obviously, you can obtain significantly higher payoffs than 3-1 with exactas and not add too much more risk. This probably gives most players the best chance to beat the races.

Many successful players also bet exactas when they think two or three horses have a chance to win. Boxing those horses (or varying the amounts on each combination to obtain similar payoffs) still gives many bettors the chance to play the race and obtain large returns. However, once you begin to box four or five horses, you start wasting money and lowering your potential return. These four- or five-horse boxes, in general, are a bad bet.

Trifectas

Compared to other types of wagering, the trifecta is one of the most popular bets and can draw the most money (in percentage of handle) on any given day. Similar to exactas, trifectas can offer potentially large payoffs with small costs. The best approach to successful trifecta wagering is to separate main (key) horses from marginal horses. However, most players would rather box all the horses they like in their trifecta rather than distinguish between key and marginal horses.

Boxing each additional horse greatly increases the cost of the ticket. A four-horse trifecta box ($1) costs $24, a five-horse trifecta box costs $60, a six-horse trifecta box costs $120, and so on. Rather than spend large sums boxing horses, most successful players key one or two horses and use others in second and third positions (part-wheeling). This gives the player a good chance of hitting the bet without having to spend a large amount of money boxing several horses. For example, below are some random part-wheels showing how you can approach a race, depending on your view of the contenders (these are all different races with eight-horse fields).

A: $1 trifecta: 3-5/1-3-5/1-3-4-5-8, cost $12.
B: $1 trifecta: 7/1-3-4/1-3-4-6-8, cost $12.
C: $1 trifecta: 2-4-6/2-4-6/1-2-4-5-6, cost $18.
D: $1 trifecta: 3-5/3-5/all, cost $12 (essentially an exacta bet, with the player hoping for a longshot third).
E: $1 trifecta: 8/1-2/all, cost $14 (also essentially an exacta bet).

In each case the player has keyed some horses in the first position, may have added some in the second, then added marginal horses in the third position. The effect of this type of wagering is to give yourself a good chance of cashing the bet while minimizing costs. Unlike exacta wagering, it becomes a little trickier to "tier" your wagering to overcome different payoffs and cash for similar amounts no matter what combination comes in.

Take the trifecta part-wheel shown earlier as A (3-5/1-3-5/1-3-4-5-8). If the #3 was an 8-5 shot and the #5 a 4-1 shot, you may want to play a $2 trifecta: 3/1-5/1-4-5-8 (a $12 bet) and a $1 trifecta: 5/1-3/1-3-4-8, (a $6 bet) to even out your potential payoffs. However, looking at the trifecta part-wheel example of C: 2-4-6/2-4-6/1-2-4-5-6, it becomes a little more difficult to break that bet up to account for potential different payoffs.

The point is that while the trifecta bet is very popular and will offer opportunity, potential payoffs can be a little tougher to predict. You play in "hopes" of getting a good payoff. There is nothing wrong with playing trifectas, but more successful players are probably looking at exactas because it is easier to determine value (potential payoffs available) and to tier their bets to compensate for different payoffs.

Superfectas

The same issues regarding trifectas apply to superfectas. Many players box their horses in the superfecta. They don't want to distinguish between key and marginal horses (or they may be lazy and not want to play part-wheels because more work is required). The result is the same: each additional horse in a box increases the wager's cost substantially.

I don't do a lot of superfecta wagering. I will if the right race presents itself — I might play a superfecta in a race in which I think very few horses have a chance at running first, second, and third — but I prefer exactas for the reasons mentioned above. If you enjoy playing superfectas, I suggest a strategy similar to what I use for trifectas. Playing part-wheels, keying one or two horses on top, and using marginal horses in the third and fourth positions probably give you the best chance at winning with realistic wagering amounts.

Daily Doubles/Pick Threes/Pick Fours/Pick Sixes

While betting exactas, trifectas, and superfectas involves wagering options within a race, daily doubles, pick threes, pick fours, and pick sixes offer options across multiple races. These bets share a similar characteristic with exactas, trifectas, and superfectas in that adding horses in any individual race may substantially increase the cost of the ticket. As you are aware, the main difference is that these exotics deal with the winners of races (not which horse runs second, third, or fourth). Pick threes and pick fours have become very popular because, similar to exactas and trifectas, they offer potentially large payoffs with small investments. Earlier in this chapter, I mentioned some of the drawbacks of pick threes, pick fours, and pick sixes, but the main consideration is how to play these wagers properly.

I suggest playing these similarly to playing part-wheels in trifectas and superfectas. You separate your key horses and then use marginal horses on back-up tickets. You can also vary your bet amounts on your key horses versus marginal horses.

Below is an example of playing a pick three with key and marginal horses:

	1st Leg	2nd Leg	3rd Leg
Key horse(s)	2,4	6	1,3,5
Marginal (backup) horses	5,6	1,3,5	7

I recommend the following wagers for the above scenario:

$1 pick three: 2-4/6/1-3-5-7, cost $8.
$1 pick three: 2-4/1-3-5-6/1-3-5, cost $24.
$1 pick three: 2-4-5-6/6/1-3-5, cost $12.

The total cost of these wagers would be $44. If your key horses won each race, you would have won the pick three three times (each of the above tickets would be a winner). If you were right about two of your three key horses and a backup horse won the other leg, you would have won the pick three once. Of course, you could vary the amounts of the wagers. For example, if in the first leg the #2 was even money and the #4 was 3-1, you could play $3 pick threes that key the #2 and $1 pick threes that key the #4 so as to even out your potential payoffs.

This is pretty standard wagering by most players in pick threes. The above recommendation of breaking up the bet using key and marginal horses is probably much smarter than playing a ticket with all the horses you like: $1 pick three: 2-4-5-6/1-3-5-6/1-3-5-7, cost $64. By breaking up the bet, you save some money and are playing according to your opinion. You also will cash more tickets if your key horses win all three races.

But you should select your marginal horses carefully. It becomes easy to add any number of marginal horses just to be sure you cash. The extra money, while not exactly doubling the cost of your tickets, tends to add up quickly and thus reduce your total return. This can be problematic in playing pick sixes in which using marginal horses greatly increases the total costs of the ticket.

That doesn't mean you have to part-wheel every time you play. There are times you might be better off not playing the wager because you want to use too many horses. Or there are times when, depending on your view of the race, it makes sense to play all of your choices on one ticket rather than breaking the bet into several tickets.

Creative Bets

There is another way to use all the exotics to your advantage when trying to cover marginal horses and also cover bets you already made such as a pick four. Be creative. There are times when I will use a pick three to protect a pick four or pick six.

For example, assume that I have played a pick six, singling a horse in the final leg. I have another horse I would like to use in the final leg but I can't justify adding it to the pick six because the cost of my ticket would double. If I am alive after the first three legs of the pick six, I will play a pick three with the horses I used in the next two legs of the pick six and use the horse I originally didn't play in the pick six's final leg to cover. If I am not alive, I saved doubling the cost of my pick six ticket. Of course, I risk that I may not have a winning pick-six ticket if my second choice does win the last race and I had the first five. However, in that case I will get a pick-three payoff (from my cover bet) and a pick-five consolation payoff, so all isn't lost.

One thing I have learned about playing pick sixes is that, despite how much I may like the races on that particular day, the pick six is a tough bet to win. In addition to having strong opinions and also being right about those opinions six straight times, which is hard to do, you also have to avoid bad racing luck in six straight races. Knowing pick sixes are hard to win, I will not include a marginal horse. Those savings over years of playing the pick six will be more than enough to offset the chance of winning any pick six with the questionable or marginal horse.

I considered playing this pick six ticket: 1-2-3/4-6/2-5-8/7-8/1-8-10/4-6, cost $432. The #4 in the last leg is the "marginal horse."

Instead, I played this pick six ticket: 1-2-3/4-6/2-5-8/7-8/1-8-10/6, cost $216. I have "saved" $216.

If I am three for three after the first three races, I play a pick three: 7-8/1-8-10/4, which costs $6 to cover. Of course, I can play that pick three multiple times.

If you find yourself alive in the last leg of a pick three or pick four, and you know you're going to cash your ticket because you've selected "all" in that last leg, you might want to consider looking at the payoffs to determine whether you want to make an additional "free" bet. Take this scenario for example:

Pick-Three Payoff	Odds
#1—$1,500	8-1
#2—$1,200	7-1
#3—$4,000	29-1
#4—$981	5-2
#5—$2,200	17-1
#6—$495	6-5
#7—$1,700	12-1

You can bet the #6 horse to win with some amount, let's say $100, knowing that if it loses the next best payoff is $981. If it wins, you would increase your winnings over the payoff. A lot of players don't consider this type of bet; they instead stick with the original wager and hope for the best. But you can use the additional information (now available in the form of the actual payoffs) to maximize your overall return.

This same type of betting can be used to protect trifectas and superfectas. You can use exactas to protect marginal horses or horses you are not using at all from beating you without having to spend the sometimes significant money to add them to all positions in your trifecta or superfecta. There are all sorts of creative bets you can come up with to cover marginal horses while minimizing costs. For example, consider a race in which I have one key horse, two other horses that I think are contenders, and three horses I think have a shot at hitting the board:

Key Horse: #5
Main Contenders: #7, #9
Marginal Horses: #1, #3, #4

Here is how I might approach a trifecta for such a race:

$3 trifecta: 5/7-9/1-3-4-7-9, cost $24.

$2 trifecta: 7-9/5/1-3-4-7-9, cost $16.
$1 trifecta: 5/1-3-4-7-9/7-9, cost $8.

So, what don't I have covered? Obviously, if the #5 wins, I can miss second or third. I then might look to the exactas to be sure to cash if I am mostly right but miss the third-place horse:

$9 exacta: 5/7-9, cost $18.
$3 exacta: 7-9/5, cost $6.
$2 exacta: 5/1-3-4, cost $6.

Finally, I will probably bet something to win on the #5 in case I also miss second. After making all these wagers, I have given myself a good chance of winning at least one trifecta if I am right (and having that trifecta as many as four times, if my perfect combination comes in — 5/7-9/7-9). If I am close but miss the trifecta, I should cash the exacta.

If I were looking at the superfecta for the same race, here is how I might approach it:

$1 superfecta: 5/7-9/7-9/all (ten-horse field), cost $14.
$1 superfecta: 5/7-9/1-3-4-7-9/1-3-4-7-9, cost $24.
$1 superfecta: 5/7-9/all/7-9, cost $14.
$1 superfecta: 5/1-3-4/7-9/7-9, cost $6.
$1 superfecta: 7-9/5/1-3-4-7-9/1-3-4-7-9, cost $24.

At this point, I have spent a large amount of money keying #5 in the superfecta. I still don't have many potential results if #5 wins "covered." First, I may not play the last ticket (7-9/5/1-3-4-7-9/1-3-4-7-9); instead, I may play a trifecta (7-9/5/1-3-4-7-9, cost $8) rather than spending $24 to cover #5 running second. Knowing that superfectas are hard, I may use exactas to make sure I cash something if #5 wins and I don't have the superfecta. I also will vary the amounts of those exactas to cover the cost of the superfecta tickets:

$10 exacta: 5/7-9, cost $20.
$5 exacta: 7-9/5, cost $10.

$2 exacta: 5/1-3-4, cost $6.

Again, I will probably bet something on the five to win. Also, I could use trifectas to cover the superfecta bets. The difference here compared to the trifecta recommendations is that I have to spend a fair amount of money to give myself a good chance at winning because superfectas are expensive. There is nothing wrong with this, but make sure that the total bet isn't out of line with your normal wagers in other races in which you may be playing only win/exactas.

The Most Common Mistake

The most common mistake you can make is trying to spread your money around to assure cashing something and/or at the same time betting similar amounts on different-paying combinations in hope of cashing the better-paying combination. Also, the number of horses you end up using with your key horse may depend on the key horse's expected odds.

When keying favorites, you don't have as much room to use several horses as you have when playing longer-priced horses. For example, if you start playing an 8-5 shot with more than three other horses in the exacta, you risk having a winning exacta wager pay less (total won versus total bet) than 8-5. This is assuming that the horses you use with the 8-5 shot are somewhat decently bet. Contrast this when keying a 15-1 shot. Because of the longer odds, you will be able to use more horses in the exotics without too much danger of receiving less than 15-1 should your horse come in with any of those others.

Here's an example of an interesting but ultimately wasteful approach to betting. I got to know a fellow handicapper after he cashed a $5,000 trifecta. He was sitting near me, and I asked how he hit that tri (if you had looked at the *Daily Racing Form*, there was no way you could have played the first two finishers). He said that he had wheeled the #5 horse in the third position in the tri-fecta (all/all/5). I have wheeled horses on top, and many others will wheel horses on top and sometimes also in second (top and bottom), but I had never heard of someone wheeling a horse in the third position only. I asked him whether he also would have won the trifecta if the horse had won? He said no, he had only played the horse to run third in the trifecta.

He further stated that he liked betting longshots across the board, but in many cases, even if his longshot did run well, the show price was low because of the nature of show betting. So he would now take the horse he liked and bet $10 to win, $20 to place, and, in his thinking, since show betting was a waste of time, he would wheel the horse in third only ($42 bet in an eight-horse field); this was like betting $42 to show on the horse — an interesting view. He spreads his money around in hopes of catching some longshot, and he does cash with some nicely priced horses, on occasion.

I once heard him say he liked a 20-1 shot in a particular race. I had no opinion about the race and no plan to bet it. He took the 20-1 and wheeled it in the pick three with eight-horse fields in the next two legs ($64), then wheeled the horse in second and third positions in the trifecta (the total of those bets was $84). The horse won easily but my friend didn't cash the trifecta because he had used the horse only for second and third in the trifecta. But he was looking at a big pick three because he felt the next two races were wide open.

However, for maybe the same reasons he was able to come up with a 20-1 shot, he also thought the next two races had upset written all over them. I disagreed. In each case, I thought the favorite looked pretty tough, and one of those favorites would probably be 3-5. I asked him if he had any extra tickets with the favorites, and he said no (his mentality of searching for longshots also may have hurt him because sometimes in other races where the 3-5 shot looks legit, he still tries to beat it). The favorites did win the next two races and the pick three paid $127, so he ended up losing money while keying a winning 20-1 shot.

This is not the first person to key a horse in the exotics, have that horse win, then cash little if anything. However, that isn't his main handicapping flaw. Even though his betting is bizarre, by wheeling horses either in first, second, or, in his case, third, he wastes a ton of money. It is no different when players box four or five horses in an exacta or trifecta. In each case they are playing equal amounts on horses that have different chances and different payoffs. They don't want to waste the time to break up things to account for different payoffs or chances.

As I have mentioned, while you should expect to win any wager you make, don't be afraid to lose, even if you are close. If you key horses in the exotics, you know there will be times when your key horse wins but you miss the exotics. Of course, these losses can be made up on other races in which your key horse wins and you also cash those exotics. But many players have to cash something in every race they play because they are afraid of losing. The result of this fear is that they spread their money around so much that, even when they win, they don't make much. It is strange to say, but have the confidence to be wrong.

Reviewing Your Decisions

After a day's races I will review my handicapping and betting for each race to see what I did right and where I might have gone wrong. If I lost, was it my handicapping? Did the race (pace) set up as I had anticipated, or should I have had a different view of the probable race shape or strategies used by the jockeys? Did I overlook a horse or did I get sucked into betting a horse I knew was suspiciously entered? Did some late information make me change my horse(s) or wager significantly (i.e., from a winning wager to a losing wager), and was that information (for example, a horse that appeared washed out on the track) really deserving of the emphasis I placed on it?

If my choices ran well but I didn't cash any bets, I review those bets and ask similar questions. By doing this daily, I can quickly correct any mistakes either in betting or handicapping that if I continued to repeat could lead to a losing streak.

Keeping Records

Most players who bet regularly don't keep track of their betting. Big winning days are easily remembered and losing days quickly forgotten. To improve, you must track your overall results and review those results periodically to determine if you need to make changes. These changes could increase your winnings and enjoyment of the races.

Evaluating Your Results

The easiest way to determine if you are successful is by showing a profit over a long period. But in addition to keeping track of your actual profit/loss totals, I suggest keeping more detailed information that will help you better evaluate those results.

One word of warning: many players who keep detailed track of their betting sometimes go too far in analyzing their results. For example, I have a friend (an excellent handicapper) who lives in another state and came to Emerald Downs one weekend. We both liked a horse that was going to be about 8-5. While I didn't hesitate to play the horse, my friend sat the race out. When I asked him why, he said that in the past, 35 percent of his actual plays won. He essentially was a win bettor only, so to make sure he was going to win for the year, he wouldn't accept anything less than 3-1.

At first glance this seems right, but what I believe he failed to take into account is that after keeping track of his win percentage, he didn't break it down regarding odds. His selections may have won 50 percent of the time when going off at a price around 8-5, while winning 10 percent of the time when going at a price around 8-1. If his actual results were along those lines, he would be much better off playing his selections when they were strong favorites.

Return on Investment

If you approach most of your betting like I do (mainly looking for one horse to key either in the exotics and/or playing the horse to win), I suggest that you start your record keeping by tracking the win return on investment (ROI).[5] I keep a record of all those key horses, noting when they win and what their win pay-off was. After many races (at least 200), I will total those payoffs and calculate the ROI. By knowing what the ROI is on my key horses, I will be able to draw conclusions about my handicapping and betting. For example, if you play a track where the win take-out is 17 percent, here are my thoughts on the ROI:

---

[5]ROI is short for return on investment. Most will calculate this based on a $2 win wager. For example, if you bet 10 races ($20 total) and you win a total of $18, your ROI would be $1.80 ($18 divided by 10). A ROI of $2 would be the break-even point.

ROI below $1.66: Since a random method of selection (randomly selecting any horse) would produce an ROI of $1.66 (17 percent of $2), obviously a person with this type of ROI would need significant improvement. His chances of overcoming some mediocre handicapping by smart betting would be very poor.

ROI between $1.67 and $1.80: At most tracks, if you were to make a wager on the favorite, regardless of the race, you would lose about 10 percent (betting the favorite at your track may vary for any given year, but betting the favorite, in general, will return more than playing randomly). By wagering on the favorite in every race and losing 10 percent, you would have an ROI of $1.80 at the end of the season. A person with an ROI between $1.67 and $1.80 is doing okay in comparison to others but still has a way to go before he would probably be able to show a profit betting.

ROI between $1.80 and $1.90: A player with this ROI is probably a decent handicapper. This type of person may have some winning seasons but more likely he will lose over a longer period. Don't be discouraged if you fit this category; you are doing comparatively well. This is not bad for a casual racegoer. This player would have enough handicapping skills to hit big occasionally (with pick fours, superfectas, and pick sixes) while not losing too much over time.

ROI between $1.91 and $2: This type of player is doing very well. While I don't know what the exact statistics may be, I would guess he is obtaining a return that beats about 93 percent of other bettors. This person may be able to win consistently with smart betting (by using exotics to increase value) but, of course, will have some losing seasons/years.

ROI of above $2: Again, while I don't know the exact statistics, I imagine this type of person will comprise 1 percent to 2 percent of the betting public. He should win a majority of the time.

After knowing your ROI, you can then determine if you are making smart betting decisions. For example, if you fit in the ROI category of above $2 but are showing a net loss, your handicapping is excellent, but your betting can improve. On the flip side, if you fit in the ROI category of about $1.80 but manage to show a net profit, your handicapping is okay, yet you have been able to make smart betting decisions. If you need to improve in handicapping or betting, figuring out your ROI is a good place to start.

Win Versus Exotics

In addition to keeping records on the ROI of my key horses, I keep separate totals on win versus exotic wagering and also break my exotic wagering down a bit. As with any other type of statistic, having a decent sample size is important. When playing pick fours, pick sixes, and superfectas, because you might go a long time before cashing one of those types of wagers or receive a huge payoff that skews overall results, keeping records of those wagers over one season or year will probably not be enough. Looking at those wagers (for profit/loss) over a longer period will provide a more effective analysis.

For example, a couple of years ago I managed to cash several pick sixes in a short period. They were not huge paying but over that two-month period, they totaled $40,000. I had bet about $6,000 in pick-six tickets. At the end of that particular year, if I had looked at my wagers blindly, I would have concluded that I should concentrate on pick sixes and ignore all other types of wagering since my return on those pick six bets was significantly higher than the return on all other types of wagers I had made that year. But I might have played the pick six only seventy-five times that year — which is not enough of a sample size to make any significant conclusions.

Gambling: Dealing with Streaks and Luck

Regardless of whether you are a professional gambler or a casual gambler, you have to be able to deal with the extremes in good luck and bad luck, brutal losses, exhilarating wins, and, on occasion, tragedy when horses suffer fatal injuries. For most players, obtaining or having the ability to deal with these ups and downs will come from experience, but I have a couple of thoughts that may help.

1. A player should recognize the existence of and be prepared for both winning and losing streaks so he won't be affected by those streaks when they occur.

2. A player should have an overall view of gambling that "lessens" the impact of one result or event.

Winning and Losing Streaks

"My voucher has 90 cents on it. Does anyone have a dime so I can play a $1 trifecta and get out for the day?" — Lonnie, near the end of a bad day.

While I expect to win every day, week, month, or year, obviously I am aware that I will have losing days, weeks, months, and years. And while I don't have to like losing streaks, I have to be prepared to deal with them and so do you. Realize that no matter how successful you have been in the past and despite all the work you put into a season, you still may finish the year with losses. It is the nature of gambling!

In dealing with a losing streak, I review the results over several days and review my speed figures. If I feel my handicapping is okay, I just assume that some random events have been the cause. I may back off in my pick threes and trifectas and concentrate on playing my key horse to win and then box it in the exactas with others that I feel are contenders. I keep my bet amounts consistent, but I won't resume playing the pick threes, trifectas, superfectas, or pick fours until I have had a couple of decent winning days. It is easily said, but like anything else, you can only learn from experience in dealing with losing streaks. During a losing streak, most regulars will reduce their betting and may even stop going to the races for a time. Others will try to bet their way out of a losing streak. There is no right answer that works for every individual.

While most players are looking for a way out of a losing streak, how you deal with a winning streak can be just as important. Many players will ride a hot streak to unknown heights (in terms of their personal winnings) but immediately afterward they will ride a losing streak to significant losses, sometimes losing much more than the original winning streak provided.

Here is a common scenario: A player knows the basics of handicapping, has good and bad days, but overall isn't successful. Then he has a couple of days when he does very well. The player gets on a streak and starts cashing most every race. The player may benefit from some random events such as disqualifications, incorrectly punched tickets, or any number of other possibilities that go that player's way. Before he knows it, he is flush in cash and visiting the track more often, and his betting substantially increases.

Many players in this situation don't think, "I have been losing for several years; therefore I had better take these winnings and return to my former level of betting." Instead they think, "I always knew I could be successful at the track, but because of bad luck, bad rides, bad betting, or no bankroll, I haven't been able to win until now." They believe their sudden success has been long over-due and, of course, don't see an end to it. Because of this view, they don't see the luck that has been involved (sometimes luck to the extreme: if you flip a coin enough times, it will come up heads ten-plus times in a row at some point). When the luck disappears, their losses usually exceed anything they might have won because they increased their betting. In many cases they start to chase those losses because they only remember how well they did recently. They may continue to bet until they run out of money and may even disappear from the racetrack altogether.

The best advice I can offer to deal with streaks is to remain consistent in your wagering. If you stay consistent, you will not be susceptible to one of the more common downfalls that many players find themselves caught up in: chasing their losses with bigger and bigger bets.

A Perspective on Gambling Events

While the ability to deal with short- or long-term streaks is an important part of a successful player's skills, having a "don't care" attitude toward any one bet and the result also can be helpful.

One of my good friends at the track, after he loses a close photo or his horse is disqualified, etc. — anything that results in his horse getting beat — will say something like "I could stop a freight train going downhill on ice." When bad things happen, he deals with it by using humor. He will recognize the situation, maybe make a quick, humorous comment, and then move on to the next race. Seasoned gamblers have to be thick-skinned when it comes to the final result of any individual bet. The ability to brush off tough loss-es, incorrectly punched tickets, questionable disqualifications, etc., is another key part of the successful player's skills.

Also, don't dwell on tough losses. Everyone is going to lose (either via a head-bob, a disqualification, terrible ride, etc.) a race his horse could or should have won. Obviously, it is not easy to forget immediately a tough loss involving a significant amount of money. But look at it this way: Somewhere, sometime you were lucky to win a bet — maybe a horse that was going to beat your horse had significant trouble or some other unknown factor made you a winner. At the time you won, you may not have been aware of just how lucky you were, as the following example illustrates.

I cashed a pretty good-sized pick four at Emerald Downs one year. I had singled the second leg of that pick four, a maiden race with several first-time starters. I liked the horse I singled (I wasn't just guessing), and he won by a couple of lengths or so. But I knew going into the race that one of the first-time starters might be able to beat my choice. Later, one of those first-time starters, a horse that was getting some play in that race and appeared on the vet's list as having "bled" after that race, came back in its next start and won easily. There is no way my horse could have come close to threatening the other horse had that other horse not "bled" in his first lifetime start.

It is human nature to assume that when we are right about a race and our horse wins, it wasn't luck. Most players are aware of luck only when bad luck strikes. Players don't look back and remember the head-bobs they won or the times they were moved up via disqualification.

Summary

Remember, no matter how well you handicap, you should have your own betting strategy that fits with your style of handicapping and your goals. It is also important to be prepared with a plan (win versus exotic options) for betting the day's races before they begin. Reviewing your decisions on a daily basis and keeping records of your results will go a long way toward helping you improve your bottom line. Also, use all the available wagering options to your advantage and don't be afraid to become creative in your wagering. Finally, realize that gambling involves luck. There is a fair amount of luck involved in wagering on the horses, be it good or bad. You can boil down an individual race to a set of probabilities and some of those probabilities involve luck. Bad luck is part of playing the races so don't dwell on it.

PART III

Avoiding Common Misjudgments and Misunderstandings

The next three chapters discuss areas where I've found many players commonly make assumptions, such as about how horses think, or use information, such as various statistics, in their handicapping without completely understanding those areas. A better understanding of horse behavior, strong betting "angles," and how to use statistics can help improve a player's overall handicapping.

Do Horses Know
They Have Won?

Much of handicapping involves evaluating information. It may involve evaluating speed figures, evaluating a horse's form cycle, evaluating a horse's looks, or evaluating wagering options for value. One area in which many players include assumptions in their handicapping relates to their perception of what goes through a horse's mind before, during, and after a race.

Most players assume that horses think like we do. Trainers often reinforce this assumption. After a race you may hear them say: "Winning a race did a lot for his confidence," or "This horse thinks he is Secretariat after his last two wins." Or on the other end of the spectrum, you might hear them say: "If you get a good horse beat enough times, pretty soon it will not be able to beat slower horses, horses it would have easily defeated earlier." In addition, as a handicapper, many times you will be faced with a horse that you think is a strong contender in a race but that horse has either never won a race or lost several races in a row. Whether a horse is coming off a win, or several losses, or has never won a race, your beliefs about how horses think could be a key in how you evaluate that horse's chances.

Proving what horses know about racing may be impossible, but I do believe, from being around horses and watching thousands of races, that some conclusions can be drawn. These conclusions may be important in the way you then decide to evaluate the chances of a horse that, for example, appears to be a strong contender but has lost several races in a row.

Before discussing what I believe horses know about racing, I have to offer a disclaimer. My beliefs, for the most part, can't be proven, and there are many who would disagree with them. Also, my beliefs are about racehorses in general. Some very intelligent horses may prove me wrong.

If you are evaluating the way horses think to give yourself an edge in handicapping, there are several questions that you might want to ask. First, you and I know where the finish line is, we know the purpose of a race, but do horses know where the finish line is and do they understand the concept of being the first one there? The quick answer is that, in general, I don't believe horses understand the concept of the finish line. That doesn't mean they don't know they've won a race or that they don't want to win. It also doesn't mean that they won't improve after a win. To discuss why I believe that horses don't understand the concept of the finish line, let's start with the end of a race.

From repetition (both during morning exercise and afternoon/evening racing), the horse knows that at a certain point (near the finish line on the racetrack) the rider stops asking it to run, so the horse learns, or becomes aware, that the race or exercise is over. While I obviously don't know what goes on in a horse's mind, I don't think horses "know" exactly what the finish line is. They just know they will not be asked to run anymore once they reach a specific point. Even if they are aware the race is over, I don't think they "know" they have to be in front exactly at that finish line (which, of course, is invisible) to "win" the race. My beliefs are, in part, based on the following observations.

When something spooks a horse during the post parade, the horse may rear, throw the rider, and then run off. Does the horse then sprint to the finish line, cross it, stop, and jog back to the winner's circle? No. Most will run toward the area on the track (in most cases, the quarter chute) where they enter and exit for morning workouts in an effort to get back to their stall. Additionally, when a horse loses its rider in a race, you will see the horse:

1. stop running soon after losing the rider,

2. run with the field for a while then bolt to the outside fence near where it normally exits the track daily,

3. run with the field throughout the race but never really pass any other horses (herd instinct),

4. or continue to run, probably passing most if not all the field (since the horse doesn't have the weight of a jockey to carry) and get to the finish line first. In this case the horse probably will continue to run after passing the finish line.

So what might these observations show? In the fourth scenario, in which the horse wins the race without the rider, it shows that horses love to run, not that they necessarily want to win. The rest of those scenarios indicate that horses probably don't understand the concept of the finish line and of getting there first and that they just want to run with their friends or go home (the barn).

The second question that you might want to ask to give yourself an edge in handicapping is this: If a horse has not won a race after several tries or has lost many races in a row, does that mean the horse has no desire to win? If that same horse appears to be a strong contender in a race, some players will ignore the horse because of the horse's losing streak. What about a horse that has run second or third for several races in a row and is the favorite — do you assume the horse doesn't want to win?

When a horse first starts its career, it may not even understand the purpose of running in a race. Of course, a lot goes into training a horse before its first race, but the experience of the paddock, post parade, loading into the gate with the field, the start, and the actual race cannot be duplicated in the morning. Some horses obviously will run very well in their first start. Their mental abilities and their physical talent make up for the inexperience. Other horses don't quite know what is going on and will learn from experience. They might be physically talented enough to win, but the mental part isn't there yet. As a horse grows accustomed to race days, it will probably become more focused.

It may take several tries before a horse wins. Also, even after it first wins or even wins several races and matures, it is not immune to losing several in a row. Some players feel that once a horse has lost several consecutive races, that horse has lost its desire to win and thus can be ignored as a contender.

Since I don't believe horses understand the concept of a finish line, I also don't believe that horses on a losing streak have lost their desire to win. But, there are legitimate reasons why a horse may not seem to want to win. For example, experienced horses may cheat or protect themselves during a race (in human sports vernacular they are "mailing it in"). They are aware that pain may result from running, so they slow down; they don't try as hard, not because they have lost several races but because of pain from fatigue or injury.

I am sure you have come across horses that are zero for fifteen, zero for twenty or so lifetime, or a horse that has very few wins and several seconds and thirds. Again, if you like a horse with that type of record in a particular race, you may find yourself asking if the horse has the desire to win. I will not be stopped from playing a horse that I think looks best in a race, even if its win/loss record is very poor or if it has been beaten several times. For example, I find it hard to believe a horse that has run second several times in a row has the ability to think, I've passed all but one horse, so I better not go by that last one.

Most likely, a horse that has had several second places has been pretty consistent in its performance but seems to have been in races in which there was always one better horse. The horse may have been beaten by a combination of circumstances that added up to a long losing streak.

For example, I am not afraid to bet a horse like Rattle Bag, who has had many losses over his career, if I think he looks best, as I concluded on September 6, 2001, when he was zero for nineteen going into a one and one-sixteenth-mile maiden claimer at Emerald (Figure 7.1).

Rattle Bag was a victim of his early success. While he never won a race, he did finish fourth in a stakes as a two-year-old. Many times two-year-olds that show some promise early in their career will be overmatched when three or four years old. Their connections still remember the horse running well as a two-year-old and refuse to drop the horse down in class for several races. Also, while Rattle Bag did fail many times, none of his losing races had been at this lower level.

Since he had been overmatched and misplaced his entire career, many would say that this horse, who showed talent early, couldn't beat the slowest horses on the grounds now because it

Figure 7.1 — Field for 8th race, Emerald Downs, Sept. 6, 2001

e Bag

3EmDfst 6½f :224 :46 1:104 1:172 3↑ Md 10000(12.5-10) 53 7 8 85¾ 86¾ 65¼ 46¾ Gutierrez J M LB121 f 7.40 78- 16 Bay Morn118½ Crosscreek Road1184½ Iceskate1181 Circled, late gain 9
3EmDfst 6½f :223 :452 1:104 1:172 3↑ Md 8000 57 7 7 79¼ 67½ 44½ 43½ Cedeno O LB123 f 3.60 81- 16 AngerMngement118¾ SilvrSunst1181 MomsRcruit1191¾ 6-w, belated rally 7
7EmDfst 1 :24 :482 1:131 1:384 3↑ Md 14000(16-14) 58 8 75½ 74¾ 84¾ 67 67 McFadden D J LB121 f 12.40 65- 30 Dancinonadare118hd *Bright Stout*119nk Love a Bull113no Failed to respond 8
2EmDfst 1 :232 :464 1:113 1:381 3↑ Ⓢ Md 14000(16-14) 63 1 59½ 511 58½ 57½ 43¼ Linares M G LB121 f 8.70 72- 27 *HndsomWllDo*1182 EloqntAngl113nk SttlSnshn1181 Swung wide, mild gain 6
5EmDfst 6½f :224 :462 1:111 1:172 3↑ Md 16000(16-14) 54 3 8 74½ 86½ 77 57¾ Linares M G LB123 f 6.10 77- 15 Alfurune1131½ SkywlkerSelect1185½ SettlSunshin119½ 7-wide into stretch 9
4EmDfst 6f :223 :46 :583 1:113 3↑ Md 16000(16-14) 52 8 6 68½ 68½ 65 23 Linares M G LB123 f 11.00 78- 13 HardRockJazz1233 RattleBag123½ SettleZipper118nk Swung 6 w, late gain 8
3EmDsly 5½f :214 :451 :574 1:041 3↑ Md 16000 36 1 5 56½ 79 611 613 Conklin J LB123 f 11.40 78- 13 Sir Radar1235¾ Flying Cinder1182 *Krisco Kid*1182½ Showed little 7
3EmDfst 1 :232 :462 1:103 1:361 Clm 16000(16-14) 60 6 88½ 88½ 88½ 68 613¼ Dieguez W O LB116 f 14.60 72- 16 Nomoreskoal1185 Always C1171¼ Muscovy114nk Passed tiring rivals 8
2EmDfst 6f :22 :443 :564 1:10 3↑ Ⓢ Md 20000(20-18) 65 1 4 59 49½ 47½ 27½ Dieguez W O LB116 f 10.60 83- 12 Murdock1177½ Rattle Bag1162½ *N. Y. Sharpy*1222¾ 3-wide, up for 2nd 6
2EmDfst 6½f :23 :461 1:111 1:174 3↑ Md 16000(16-14) 64 2 7 62½ 53½ 46 35½ Dieguez W O LB116 f 13.70 78- 15 Tahoe Affair1185 *My First Lady*113nk Rattle Bag116nk Split rivals, rallied 7
3EmDfst 6½f :224 :462 1:11 1:171 3↑ Md 16000(16-14) 45 2 6 76½ 76¾ 611 613¼ Whitaker J7 LB109 f 3.90 73- 18 TaterTate1164½ *TahoeAffair*1183½ BasketofStrs1141 Checked sharply 1/4 p 7
9EmDfst 1 :232 :461 1:101 1:344 SeatlSlewH46k 59 4 75 89 811 912 818 Dieguez W O LB110 f 59.00 74- 16 ⒹShake Loose119nk Makors Mark1184½ Sou'wester116no Outrun 9
9EmDfst 1 :243 :484 1:131 1:382 Clm 32000(32-27.5)N2L 61 4 67½ 64½ 65 55½ 53½ Chaves N J LB118 f 11.60 70- 25 Aldorado1191 HitawyJy118nk Theycllmecolonel1191½ Swung 5 w, mild bid 6
7EmDfst 1 :23 :46 1:104 1:36 3↑ Md Sp Wt 15k 65 2 58 55 54½ 45½ 37 Dieguez W O LB116 f 26.90 79- 13 Salish Basket1162½ Target's Away1164¾ Rattle Bag1162 In tight 5/16 7
6EmDfst 6f :222 :454 :58 1:10 Md 25000 38 3 8 86½ 84 77½ 510 Nuesch D LB121 fb 6.10 80- 07 Aldorado1212½ Betterbegoodtome121¾ Briartic Drive1212¼ Saved ground 9
9EmDfst 6½f :222 :453 1:104 1:171 WTBALads47k 46 2 10 1010 1010 915 916¼ Jauregui L H LB116 fb 12.30 71- 16 *NoCurfew*116nk CscdeCsy1201½ FirstDownDlls116no Broke slowly, no rally 10
8EmDfst 6f :22 :45 :572 1:102 Md Sp Wt 14k 67 7 6 75¾ 75¼ 54½ 41½ Chaves N J LB118 fb 4.30 86- 13 Briartic Gold118nk *It's a Waki Fact*118½ Wishy118¾ Bobbled start, wide 8
9EmDfst 6f :221 :452 :573 1:104 EmrldExprs43k 55 1 6 65½ 66½ 65¼ 54¾ Chaves N J B120 fb 27.00 81- 14 MontanaHoofer120½ PlaneOTrick120¾ ElttaesBy1202 Late gain, no factor 7
9EmDfst 5½f :213 :45 :574 1:041 ⓈCaptnCondo35k 62 6 7 77¼ 79 77 47½ Chaves N J B119 b 24.10 83- 09 IMAdevil119nk ElttaesBay1192¼ *MontnHoofer*1195 Hopped start, bore out 7

oll

9EmDfst 6f :222 :461 :583 1:113 3↑ Md 5000(6.25-5) -0 2 9 88¾ 109¼ 1117 1122¼ Mercado V V LB116 b 71.80 59- 15 The Cats Back1233½ Laurenzo118nk Lorenzo's Gambler123nk Outrun 12
3Wts fst *5f 1:073 3↑ Md Sp Wt 1k - 2 7 76½ 66 67¼ 55 Braden D B119 b 21.60 - - BallisticBarclay1221 ToBadBrad1241¾ SkiingFree1261 4-wide into stretch 7
ously trained by Quillan Shellie
2PM fst 5½f :234 :481 1:02 1:081 Md 6500(7.5-6.5) 23 3 1 31 53½ 68 712 Braden D LB118 b 45.20 71- 19 Scaffolds Legacy1204 Iza Bullet1183 Citybassboy122½ Speed, tired 7
6PM fst 6f :231 :47 1:02 1:151 3↑ Md 3500 13 4 4 53¾ 88¼ 88½ 811½ Braden D LB117 b 57.20 64- 20 Justjzz1233 HoustonRodeo123no ⒹⒽDesertDustDvil123 Brief speed, faded 8
1PM fst 6f :232 :471 1:02 1:151 3↑ Md 3500 13 2 5 53 53¾ 66 610¾ Gutierrez J M LB121 b 14.50 65- 15 UnrulyWon1233½ PierhdJump116nk PkbooCughtU1231 Failed to respond 6
ously trained by Rogers Allen E
6GG fst 6f :22 :444 :57 1:094 Md 12500 9 4 8 108¾ 1019 1020 1023¼ Roux P LB118 b 190.90 68- 07 Readyforwaterbnk1185½ *ExpressOvernight*1182 FvoriteFriend118nk Outrun 11

pnogarnish

1EmDfst 1 :231 :472 1:131 1:394 3↑ Md 6250 23 4 67½ 64¼ 98¾ 813 818 Whitaker J5 LB113 b 11.90 49- 24 Tuff Nab1183½ Salty Lad118¾ Anna's Bouquet1182½ Showed little 10
1EmDfst 1 :234 :474 1:123 1:38 3↑ Md 12500(12.5-10) 18 4 54½ 64¾ 69½ 617 629¾ Cedeno O LB118 b 8.30 46- 24 *Point Blank*1135 *Bay Morn*1183¾ *Seattle Sunshine*1183½ Outrun 6
7EmDfst 6f :221 :453 :574 1:104 3↑ Md 20000 28 4 8 89¼ 810 811 816 Cedeno O LB118 b 31.50 69- 14 On El Bon1181 Skywalker Select118nk Bright Stout119½ Outrun 8

T Bailey

3EmDfst 1 1/16 :24 :48 1:13 1:452 3↑ Md 6250(6.25-5) 43 4 67½ 610 67¾ 68½ 58½ Cedeno A LB118 b 2.80e 62- 25 Shaman Spirit121½ *Tuff Nab*118½ Harbour Mountain1216¾ Went evenly 9
9EmDfst 1 1/16 :234 :474 1:133 1:463 3↑ Md 5000(6.25-5) 40 5 79 89½ 75 57 49 McFadden D J LB116 b 20.00 56- 31 *BasketofStars*123hd SeattleSunshine1188½ Mac'sCap119¾ 5-wide, no threat 10
5EmDfst 6½f :222 :46 1:104 1:171 3↑ Md 6250 38 1 10 119¼ 109 810 616¼ Jawny A B119 b 64.90 69- 18 Dr. Raymond1189 Mad Jazz1132¾ *Cyalator*1233 Bumped 1/8 11
10EmDfst 6½f :23 :462 1:112 1:174 3↑ Md 8000 -0 6 12 118 1111 1117 1126¾ Gonsalves F A B118 b 60.90 56- 11 Joe Holiday1181¼ Lookout Pass1185½ Basket of Stars1231 Outrun 12

y Lad

-11EmDfst 1 :231 :472 1:131 1:394 3↑ Md 6250 49 8 44 31 2hd 21½ 23¼ Radke K LB118 fb 2.70 64- 24 Tuff Nab1183¼ Salty Lad118¾ Anna's Bouquet1182½ 3-wide, drifted late 10
-9EmDfst 1 :242 :482 1:132 1:402 3↑ Md 6250(6.25-5) 49 1 32 32½ 33 2hd 2½ Lopez L C LB118 fb 5.30 63- 28 Timely Jazz113½ Salty Lad1181½ Coffee Fields1233 3-w, bid, held off 10
-2EmDfst 6f :223 :461 :584 1:122 3↑ Md 8000 41 7 4 52½ 63¾ 64½ 66 Linares M G LB118 b 7.90 71- 17 Will E Rule118½ Indian Rider118½ *Briarticat*1231¾ 5-wide, lacked rally 7
-10EmDfst 6f :221 :46 :582 1:112 3↑ Md 12500(12.5-10) 43 6 8 87 95 69 611¾ Perez M A LB118 b 11.10 70- 19 Altoad1181¾ *Dancinonadare*1181½ Lookout Pass1184¼ Angled 8w, no rally 10
-7EmDfst 6f :222 :453 :58 1:11 Md 25000(25-20) 31 5 4 2hd 21½ 46½ 612¾ Cedeno A LB118 b 9.70 72- 12 Lucky Bluff1182½ Handsome Son1182¾ OnReady1184½ Dueled inside, tired 7
-7EmDfst 5f :221 :46 :584 Md 25000 36 6 7 73¼ 74¾ 65½ 59½ Gonsalves F A LB118 b 3.70 77- 11 PrimdonnPoppy115nk *CtchthSun*1185½ SismicWv1181½ 5 wide throughout 7
-3EmDfst 5½f :222 :462 :592 1:06 Md 25000 8 1 7 54½ 55 45½ 412 Skelly R V B118 b *2.10e 70- 16 CharlieHaan1182¼ OnReady1184½ *NiteTrainSlew*1185¼ Off slowly, mild gain 7

ual Benefit

-9EmDfst 6f :222 :461 :583 1:113 3↑ Md 6250(6.25-5) 37 11 6 67½ 75¼ 65½ 65½ Russell B R LB118 *2.50 75- 15 TheCtsBck1233½ Lurenzo118nk LorenzosGmblr123nk 7-wide, no response 12
-10EmDfst 6½f :223 :46 1:114 1:182 3↑ Md 6250(6.25-5) 55 2 10 118¾ 108 41½ 21 Whitaker J LB118 6.30 79- 16 Care to Win1181 Mutual Benefit1182 Laurenzo118hd 4-w, angled out, rally 12
-3EmDfst 6f :222 :451 :584 1:121 3↑ Md 6250(6.25-5) 37 9 4 86¾ 89 69 57 Linares M G LB118 4.30 71- 17 GrnnysGun118½ *RelTrueSpirit*1163½ TommysTune1131½ 6-wide into stretch 11
-4EmDfst 5½f :222 :461 :59 1:054 3↑ Md 10000(10-8) 47 8 3 31½ 42½ 54½ 54¾ Lopez L C LB119 14.50 78- 16 Majuro Beach123¾ LookoutPass1181¼ SnowshoeFlyer118hd 4 wide, evenly 8
ualified and placed 8th

youkidding Me

-10EmDfst 1 :234 :472 1:123 1:381 3↑ Md 6250(6.25-5) 36 8 79¾ 714 815 819 719¾ Chaves N J LB118 b 21.30 55- 27 *Silver Sunset*1184¾ *Harbour Mountain*1232¾ *Y B Red*1182½ Off step slow 8
-10EmDfst 6½f :223 :46 1:114 1:182 3↑ Md 6250(6.25-5) 37 3 11 108¾ 1110 108 88½ Chaves N J LB118 b 10.30 71- 16 Care to Win1181 Mutual Benefit1182 Laurenzo118hd Off step slow, wide 12
-5EmDfst 6f :221 :461 :592 1:131 3↑ Md 6250(6.25-5) 42 3 10 1011 1011 75½ 54½ Lopez L C LB118 b 4.40 69- 20 JensFncyFce121¾ PnioloRod1191½ Redllboutm1231 Hpped start, late gain 10
-10EmDfst 6½f :223 :46 1:111 1:18 3↑ Md 6250(6.25-5) 38 11 11 86¾ 68½ 713 711¾ Lopez L C B118 19.40 70- 15 SignlService1182 CretoWin1182 AngerMngmnt1181¾ Awkward into stride 11
iously trained by Jones Brendon
-2GF fst 5f 1:04 Md Sp Wt 1k -0 2 4 42½ 33½ 35 36 Ashburn M B128 3.00 69- 17 Illmkeyousmile1241½ *NoAnticiption*1204½ AryoukiddingM1287¾ Long drive 5
-4MC fst 5½f 1:083 3↑ TBMaiden3k - 5 6 55 48½ 47½ 27 Ashburn M B125 4.20 - - Cool Memories1287 Areyoukidding Me1252 Road Class124hd Long drive 6

Figure 7.1 continued

Bravo Ragazzo

19Aug01-11EmDfst	1	:231 :472 1:1311:394	3↑ Md 6250	37	3	22	21	1hd	43½	610¼	Margrave L	LB118 b	27.80	57- 24	Tuff Nab1183½ Salty Lad118¾ Anna's Bouquet1182½	Prompted, le
3Aug01- 3EmDfst	6½f	:223 :452 1:1041:172	3↑ Md 8000	25	4	5	33	33	510	517	Lopez L C	LB118 b	15.50	68- 16	AngerMngemnt118¾ SilvrSunst1181 MomsRcruit1191¾	Gave way a
22Jly01- 6EmDfst	6½f	:222 :453 1:1031:172	3↑ Md 12500(12.5-10)	28	3	9	910	98½	1013	1017½	Lopez L C	LB118 f	22.60	67- 14	Handsome Son1184 Letmikiedoit1131¼ *Point Blank*1181½	
27Apr01- 5EmDwf	5½f	:221 :454 :5811:043	Md 12500	33	4	6	68¼	66	46½	49¾	Perez M A	B121	7.80	79- 11	Alandem1212¾ SkywlkerSelect121½ SettleZipper1216½	Passed tirin

Danzig Heights

30Aug01- 9EmDfst	6f	:222 :461 :5831:113	3↑ Md 6250(6.25-5)	21	1	12	1110	97¾	88¾	811¾	Baze G	LB119	43.50	69- 15	TheCtsBck1233½ Lurenzo118nk LorenzosGmbler123nk	Hopped star
5Aug01- 6EmDfst	6f	:222 :46 :5811:104	3↑ Md 12500(12.5-10)	–0	8	4	74	89	917	933	Gonsalves F A	LB118 b	40.30	52- 11	Lake'sLegacy1182¾ Letmikiedoit1182 CrosscreekRoad1183¾	Showe
15Jly01- 5EmDfst	6½f	:221 :442 1:0921:162	3↑ Md 25000(25-20)	–	1	5	64¼	813	822	-	Gonsalves F A	LB118 b	20.20	- 11	EsyLovin118¾ MyCousinJoy1181¾ SkywlkrSlct1181¾	Through early,

Figure 7.2

Eighth Race Emerald Downs- September 6, 2001

1 1/16 Miles. (1.39¾) MAIDEN CLAIMING. Purse $4,600 FOR MAIDENS, THREE-YEARS-OLDS AND UPWARD. Three year olds 118 lbs. Older 123 lbs. CLAIMING PRICE $6,250, if for $ allowed 2 lbs. (NWRA reserves the right to retain possession of all registration papers for any horses claimed at Emerald Downs until the conclusion of the current race meet.) UP TO $449 TO WA-BREDS.)

Value of race: $4,600. Winner $2,530; second $920; third $690; fourth $345; fifth $115. Mutuel pool $28,313.00. Exacta pool $23,147.00. Trifecta pool $31,263.00. Superfect $17,349.

Last Raced	Horse	Med/Eqp	A	Wgt	PP	St	1/4	1/2	3/4	Str	Fin	Jockey	Cl'g Pr	Odds $
18Aug01 ^{3}EmD^{4}	Rattle Bag	LBf	4	116	9	8	8^{hd}	6^{2}	$3^{1½}$	1^{hd}	$1^{4½}$	WhitakerJ	5000	2.00
19Aug01 ^{11}EmD^{2}	Salty Lad	LBb	3	116	5	3	$4^{½}$	$4^{2½}$	$2^{1½}$	2^{1}	$2^{2¼}$	RadkeK	5000	1.90
30Aug01 ^{9}EmD^{6}	Mutual Benefit	LB	3	118	6	5	$6^{1½}$	5^{hd}	4^{1}	3^{hd}	$3^{4¾}$	GnsalvesF	6250	3.10
4Aug01 ^{3}EmD^{5}	Joe T Bailey	LBb	3	118	4	4	7^{1}	8^{4}	6^{hd}	5^{1}	4^{1}	LopezL	6250	9.10
26Aug01 ^{10}EmD^{7}	Areyoukidding Me	LBb	3	116	7	9	9	7^{1}	7^{2}	6^{4}	5^{nk}	Linares M	5000	28.70
19Aug01 ^{11}EmD^{6}	Bravo Ragazzo	LBb	3	118	8	1	$1^{½}$	1^{1}	$1^{½}$	4^{2}	$6^{9¼}$	MargraveL	6250	27.20
19Aug01 ^{11}EmD^{8}	Ginuponogamish	LBb	3	120	3	7	3^{hd}	3^{hd}	$5^{½}$	7^{5}	$7^{19¾}$	VenturaH	6250	16.40
30Aug01 ^{9}EMD^{8}	Danzig Heights	LB	3	118	1	2	$2^{1½}$	2^{hd}	8^{10}	8^{10}	$8^{23¾}$	MitchellG	6250	21.60
30Aug01 ^{9}EmD^{11}	Mt Doll	LBb	3	116	2	6	5^{2}	9	9	9	9	MercadoV	5000	70.90

Off Time: 9:03 **Time Of Race:** :24⅕ :48⅕ 1:13⅗ 1:39 1:45⅘

Start: Good For All. **Track:** Fast. **Won driving.**

$2 Mutuel Payoffs:

9	Rattle Bag	6.00	2.80	2.60
5	Salty Lad		3.00	2.20
6	Mutual Benefit			2.60

$1 Exacta 9-5 Paid $7.00; $1 Trifecta 9-5-6 Paid $17.30. $1 Superfecta 9-5-6-4 Paid $32.60.

had been beaten too often. Again, since I really don't believe horses "think" like this, I won't be afraid to bet them if they are finally placed where they belong. Rattle Bag probably should have been about even money in this field. But, most likely because of his zero-for-nineteen record, he wasn't even favored, despite every Beyer speed figure in his past ten fast-track races being higher than any other horse's Beyer figure in its last race! Rattle Bag had no problem winning this race despite his win/loss record (Figure 7.2).

Also, be aware that it is pretty easy for a horse to lose several races in a row, sometimes ten or more. For example, I will get some more mileage out of one of our horses, The Novelist. After The Novelist's race on December 29, 2001, which he won, he lost twelve straight races (Figure 7.3).

Figure 7.3

Novelist

-2BM	fst	6f	:221	:444	:572	1:10	3↑ Clm 16000(16-14)	**80**	1	4	34	32	1hd	2¾	Castro J M	**LB**117 fb	11.20	88- 13	ColorsoftheWolf112¾ TheNovelist1173 Inclintor1171½	Bid 3w, led, caught 5
-2BM	fst	6f	:221	:443	:564	1:092	3↑ Clm 16000(16-14)	**81**	4	3	21	2hd	2½	53	Baze R A	**LB**117 fb	8.40	89- 09	Murdock117nk De Witt122½ Royal Irish117¾	Pressed, 2w, weakened *6*
-9BM	fst	6f	:222	:444	:564	1:09	3↑ Clm 12500(12.5-10.5)	**79**	5	1	1hd	12	2hd	22½	Baze R A	**LB**117 fb	*1.70	91- 11	*OlympicSuccss*1172½ ThNovlist1173 AlnbthGold1123	Jumpd shadows 7/16p *7*
-6BM	fst	6f	:22	:45	:572	1:101	3↑ Alw 33000N1x	**70**	2	5	2½	63½	76½	77¾	Duran F5	**LB**116 fb	7.20	80- 15	Nikawa1211½ Mining for Fun1211 Weinhard1211½	Stopped btwn foes turn 7
-6SR	fst	6f	:221	:451	:573	1:101	3↑ Alw 39316N1x	**76**	4	6	45	42¾	44	43¼	Lumpkins J	**LB**122 fb	4.50	83- 16	Synful Cajun117¾ Kick'n the Pants1221½ Weinhard1221	Broke in air 6
-10Sol	fst	6f	:213	:44	:563	1:083	3↑ Alw 12500s	**69**	7	7	73¼	33	45	68	Castanon A L	**LB**117 fb	4.90	95- 01	CourtCosts1193½ NorthrnTd112¾ CortShnngns1173½	Circled 4w, flattened *9*
-1BM	fst	6f	:221	:442	:563	1:10	3↑ Alw 39200N1x	**78**	1	4	52¾	33	33	21	•Castanon A L	**LB**123 fb	3.90	88- 11	All Access1231 DH The Novelist123 DH Zadar1232½	Shifted out,late rally 5
-2BM	fst	6f	:223	:452	:574	1:104	4↑ Alw 33920N1x	**80**	5	3	32	33	32	42½	Castanon A L	**LB**119 fb	5.20	82- 19	DmntheTorpedoes1191¼ *AllAccss*119¾ SnstionlGuy114½	4wide, outfinished 5
-6BM	fst	6f	:221	:441	:562	1:092	4↑ Alw 32000N1x	**83**	8	3	41¼	1½	11½	2hd	Castanon A L	**LB**119 fb	30.60	92- 11	GottGotoWork119hd ThNovlist1191 SnstonlGuy114½	Bid 4w, clear, tagged *9*
-4GG	fst	6f	:221	:444	:564	1:092	4↑ Clm 20000(20-18)	**78**	6	7	75¾	67½	44½	66	Schvaneveldt C P	**LB**117 fb	11.00	84- 18	*My Friend Lumpy*1192 Hot Video1172 Aclare1171½	Bmpd, shffled back *8*
-2GG	fst	6f	:22	:444	:563	1:09	4↑ Clm 22500(25-22.5)	**81**	3	5	44½	44½	23	34	Schvaneveldt C P	**LB**116 fb	13.60	88- 13	AmrilloPride1173 FirstStringer1111 TheNovelist116½	3w, no late response 6
-9GG	wf	6f	:222	:451	:571	1:094	4↑ Alw 12500s	**79**	7	1	31½	31	3nk	41½	Gonzalez R M	**LB**117 b	2.60	86- 10	Spinmeister117¾ Fancy High117¾ Steadiest117hd	Chckd 1/2, wknd late 7
-2GG	sly	6f	:214	:45	:572	1:101	3↑ Clm 10000(10-9)	**86**	3	9	43½	31½	12	12½	Gonzalez R M	**LB**117 fb	5.10	87- 19	ThNovlst1172½ FlyngDnoumnt1171½ BthBnny1171½	Rallied 3wide, driving 9

But in many of those losses he was a victim of circumstance (at least in my opinion):

December 29, 2001: Received a nice trip and won.

January 21, 2002: Raced wide on a day when the track strongly favored the inside. It had rained earlier in the morning, the track was drying out all day, and the inside increasingly became the place to be. He still ran pretty well.

February 9, 2002: Our trainer entered him "conditionally" on our approval. The trainer had another horse in the race, First Stringer, and wanted the race to go. He said he knew Amarillo Pride (a large class dropper trained by Jerry Hollendorfer, ridden by Russell Baze) was the one to beat, but both The Novelist and First Stringer were doing well. The Novelist ran well for third after a wide trip but again caught a track surface that appeared to favor horses that raced along the inside.

March 16, 2002: We couldn't get a race to fill for more than five weeks. When we finally did get into a race, The Novelist was completely eliminated at the start. He was in post #6; the #7 horse came in and the #5 horse came out, sandwiching him, and costing him several lengths. Luckily he didn't get injured.

April 5, 2002: We had planned to keep him running in claiming races, but the first condition (an allowance race: non-winners of two lifetime, claiming races not considered) came up, and I asked our trainer to enter. I had been watching the fields for the first condition and didn't think they were very strong. I thought the horse had been facing similar horses in his past two claiming races. We entered and he ran well; The Novelist (he was 30-1) just got caught at the wire by the favorite. Ouch!

April 26, 2002: Appeared to have a nice stalking trip while wide, but he was unlucky and caught another inside bias. Golden Gate and Bay Meadows are notorious for inside speed biases during the winter and spring.

May 23, 2002: Dead-heated for second after being blocked a little on the turn. Overall a good race, but here he was beaten fair and square.

July 14, 2002: Notice the short layoff before this race. It turns out we had entered him in eight different races since May 23 but none of them filled. When we finally got a race to go, he had another rough trip. He again was squeezed at the start and shuffled back to last. He then made a very strong move on the turn while four wide but expectedly tired. Bad luck.

August 3, 2002: Caused his own problems here. He broke in the air (about six lengths slow) and then ran very well for fourth, but the start eliminated him from any chance at a win.

August 30, 2002: One thing about this horse is that he does not want to be sent early and he does not run well along the inside. Unfortunately, he drew inside that day and the rider sent him early. He bailed out entering the turn and finished evenly.

September 21, 2002: We were getting desperate for a win by this time. We dropped him drastically in claiming price and secured Russell Baze as his rider. Unfortunately, the horse was sent again to the lead, where he dueled with another horse and put that horse away. He drew clear leaving the turn but was caught by a perfect tripper, Olympic Success (who also was dropping way down in claiming price). Olympic Success returned to win his next start despite being raised from $12,500 claiming to $20,000 claiming.

October 20, 2002: His eleventh straight loss. Despite the horse's not running well when forced to duel early, he again was caught in a speed duel. To me, he still ran pretty well; things just didn't go his way. Sometimes if a horse breaks sharply and wants to run off early, there isn't much the rider can do about it, no matter what instructions we gave the rider.

November 3, 2002: We wanted to drop back down in claiming price, but this race came up with a small field. Unfortunately, he drew the #1 hole (a tough post for a horse with his style). Anyway, despite getting bumped pretty good at the start, things did set up well for him because he was third off a two-horse speed duel. He took the lead leaving the turn but got caught by Colors of the Wolf; no real excuses here, just a good race without a win.

With his second-place finish at 11-1 on November 3, The Novelist had lost twelve straight races. Did he lose his "will to win"? I doubt it. In fact, at least to me, he ran several nice races and kept trying every time. In many of the twelve races, he raced against strong biases, had rough trips, or faced a pace scenario that favored others. He did lose a couple of those races fair and square, but, overall, his losing streak was a matter of circumstance. While I had some insights to his losing streak that you might not have when looking at other horses that have lost several races, just be aware that horses like him run every day. If you like a horse that hasn't won in a while, don't be afraid to back the horse if the losing streak is your only concern. By the way, if you check back (page 99, Chapter 4), you will that see The Novelist lost ten straight races prior to making his first start for us a winning one. Also, after a break, The Novelist scored back-to-back wins in September of 2003 at Bay Meadows.

One last example. Figure 7.4 shows the running lines for the last three races of Para Usted, a horse running in southern California. He won his next start (on November 1, 2002) after running third and second in his previous two starts. Nothing special about this.

Figure 7.4

Usted

SA fst 1⅛	:231 :471 1:122 1:451 3+ Md 25000(25-22.5)	67 3 88¾ 78½ 44 43 2²	Martinez F F	B122	5.90 76- 22 Ufology119² *Para Usted*122¹ Continentalcolonel119²	3wd bid,2nd best 8
Fpx fst 1⅛	:221 :461 1:121 1:451 3+ Md 20000(20-18)	71 7 711 78 54½ 44½ 31½	Martinez F F	B120	3.30 84- 09 *Breathless*120½ Vaudeville Time115¹ Para Usted120¹	Came out,rallied 8
Dmr fst 1	:23 :472 1:13 1:391 3+ Md 25000(25-22.5)	55 2 77 78 6⁵ 66½ 56	Martinez F F	B123	4.80 73- 17 DontCryforMe1181½ SuperShinknsen118¹ RreSton118²	Lugged out bit 7/8 8

Figure 7.5 (following page) shows Para Usted's entire past performances to that point; going into the November 1 race, he was zero for twenty-two. He won at 9-1, but was 9-1 reasonable for the November 1 race off twenty-two losses? If you just looked at his previous two starts (the second and third), 9-1 might appear pretty generous.

I am not saying that you should completely overlook a horse's win percentage. Just don't throw out a horse that appears to be a contender because of a low win percentage. Others will be throw-

Figure 7.5

Para Usted

```
12Oct02-10SA fst 1 1/16   :231 :471 1:122 1:451  3+ Md 25000(25-22.5)          67  3  88 1/2  78 1/2  44    43    22    Martinez F F      B122   5.90  76- 22 Ufology119 2 Para Usted122 1 Continentalcolonel119 2        3wc
22Sep02- 6F px fst 1 1/16  :221 :461 1:121 1:451  3+ Md 20000(20-18)            71  7  711    78    54 1/2  44 1/2  31 1/2  Martinez F F     B120   3.30  84- 09 Breathless120 1/2 Vaudeville Time115 1 Para Usted120 1       Cam
23Aug02- 8Dmr fst  1       :23  :472 1:13 1:391   3+ Md 25000(25-22.5)          55  2  77    78    66 1/2  56    Martinez F F              B123   4.80  73- 17 DontCryforMe118 1/2 SuperShinknsen118 1 RreSton118 2       Lugge
 9Aug02- 8Dmr fst  1 1/16  :224 :47 1:121 1:453   3+ Md 25000(25-22.5)          65  1  79 1/2 911   99    66 1/2  54 1/2  Martinez F F     B123   7.50  70- 20 Fly Me Faster118 hd Spoonman118 2 Rasty118 2              Passed
10Jly02- 8Hol fst  1 1/16  :234 :471 1:111 1:44   3+ Md 25000(25-22.5)          71  7  79 1/2 710   611   58 1/2  35    Martinez F F       B123  10.00  78- 13 MonroeDoctrine121 1 GoldenHours118 4 ParUsted123 nk      Came
19Jun02- 5Hol fst  1 1/16  :23  :47 1:12 1:452    3+ Md 25000(25-22.5)          64  6  1013   913   69 1/2  58    36    Espinoza V         B123   7.20  70- 19 Rehabilitated115 1/2 Swift Hero116 5 1/2 Para Usted123 2     4 wide
26May02- 9Hol fst  1 1/16  :231 :463 1:113 1:441  3+ Md 25000(25-22.5)          72  9  1011  69 1/2  49 1/2  310   412 1/2  Espinoza V     LB123   4.40  70- 22 CliforniLite123 10 GoldenHours117 2 WildSuccess116 nk  5wd,4w
20Apr02- 2SA fst   1 1/16  :232 :472 1:121 1:443  4+ Md 25000(25-22.5)          65  1  910   911   87 1/2  65 1/2  59 1/2  Krigger K 5     LB117   4.90  71- 17 El Nino Rial122 1 1/2 High Counselor121 2 Politarium122 3   Impro
 4Apr02- 8SA fst   1       :223 :461 1:111 1:374  4+ Md 25000(25-22.5)          77  6  610   68 1/2  65 1/2  32 1/2  22    Espinoza V      LB117   6.50  80- 20 Morning Wine122 2 Para Usted117 1 Politarium122 3        3wd m
27Feb02- 6SA fst   1 1/16  :23  :461 1:11 1:441   4+ Md 25000(25-22.5)          73  8  812   818   714   57 1/2  37 1/2  Nakatani C S     LB121  11.60  75- 17 Taormina121 4 1/2 Sir Maskalot119 3 Para Usted121 no      3wd into
10Feb02- 9SA fst   1 1/16  :472 1:121 1:514       4+ Md 25000(25-22.5)          67  6  911   913   811   36 1/2  37 1/2  Espinoza V       LB121   6.10  69- 19 Nick of Time121 5 Skeeman121 2 1/2 Para Usted121 5 1/2      3wd, 4
19Jan02- 2SA fst   1 1/16  :23  :461 1:121 1:451  4+ Md 25000(25-22.5)          69  10 912 10 11   69    35    35 1/2  Espinoza V         LB121   8.10  72- 21 Arbiter123 4 1/2 Nick of Time121 1 Para Usted121 2          La
26Dec01- 9SA fst   6 1/2f  :214 :441 1:062 1:162  3+ SMd 32000(32-28)           61  2 12  1210  1013  711   513 1/2  Nakatani C S         LB122  10.30  72- 12 Jerry's Call123 2 BSwift122 8 Passionforcashin120 1   Came out,
19Oct01- 8SA fst   1       :224 :46 1:104 1:373   3+ Md 32000(32-28)            69  5  914   812   99 1/2  78 1/2  76 1/2  Baze T C       LB119  16.70  77- 16 Saintly Act119 1 Native Colony122 2 Jive Talking119 2 1/2     Bit aw
 4Oct01- 8SA fst   1       :23  :464 1:113 1:373  3+ Md 32000(32-28)            68  3  99 1/2 810   810   67 1/2  45 1/2  Baze T C        LB119   2.50  77- 16 Milenrin119 3 1/2 Intercosproblem120 no YukonChrly117 2     4 wide
15Sep01- 5F px fst 1 1/16  :223 :461 1:124 1:451  3+ Md Sp Wt 37k               67  2  68 1/2 54 1/2  53 1/2  57    410 1/2  Stevens S A   LB115  11.20  75- 11 Potus115 2 Native Colony120 2 Truly's Teddy115 8          Came o
 6Aug01- 1Dmr fst  1 1/16  :232 :464 1:111 1:451  3+ Md 40000(40-35)            64  1  41 1/2 65 1/2  513   57    34 1/2  Baze T C          B118   8.60  72- 15 Ivegotuundermyskin118 1 1/2 Pestle118 3 PrUsted118 2     Saved gr
14Jun01- 3Hol fst  1       :23  :461 1:102 1:432  3+ Md 40000(40-35)            70  8  814   814   712   48   48 1/2  Baze T C           B116  24.00  78- 13 French Packet123 3 Audix116 nk Official Decision116 5       Imp po
20May01- 6Hol fst  6 1/2f  :221 :45 1:102 1:17    3+ Md 50000(50-45)            61  6  10    11 14  10 12  89 1/2  86 1/2  Baze T C       B117  62.20  79- 17 StrryHevn117 1/2 ActsLikWinnr123 hd SpcilMttr117 2   Bmpd strt
 1Mar01- 6SA my    1       :24  :474 1:124 1:392        SMd Sp Wt 53k           58  7  77 1/2  819   714   612   510 1/2  Valenzuela F H   B120  54.60  63- 27 Romnceishope120 nk ShipShpe120 nk ExcessiveOne120 1      Off bit,
17Feb01- 5SA fst   6 1/2f  :214 :441 1:10 1:164        SMd Sp Wt 46k            59  8  7    89 1/2  810   810   712   Jauregui L H         B120  45.30  72- 15 ExcssivNois120 2 BttorRoylty120 8 Hightndntrst120 1/2   Split foes
27Jan01- 1SA my    6f      :22  :45  :573 1:102        SMd Sp Wt 46k            63  3  7    79 1/2  79 1/2  78    56 1/2  Valenzuela F H   B120  63.20  81- 11 Stoney120 1/2 Bettor Royalty120 nk Excessive One120 1/2
```

WORKS: Nov7 Hol 4f fst :49 2 H *18/38* Sep21 BM 5f fst 1:01 2 H *8/31* Sep1 Dmr fst :49 4 H *19/29* Aug17 Dmr 5f fst 1:00 2 H *23/64*

ing the horse out, which might result in better odds.

Sometimes I can be a little leery of playing a horse that has had several losses if I know what contributed to those losses and the problem is still present.

On occasion I have noticed that the ability of horses to run well without winning is due to some minor injuries. As the horse nears completion of the race, pain from those injuries increases as fatigue increases. The horse slows down. This might be evidenced by slightly decreasing speed figures in each race. Also, the losses may be a function of hard races and stress (from being at the racetrack). After the horse is given a break and returned to the races, the horse can win.

Finally, I am sure you have heard the comment about a horse being "all racehorse." This relates to a horse's desire to run even through problems and pain. There are horses, and then there are racehorses. Horses will quit when facing any significant obstacle. Racehorses will try regardless of the situation or any minor injuries. They just want to run.

The last question you may want to ask yourself to get an edge in handicapping is this: If a horse wins a race, will the victory boost its confidence and lead to an improved performance in the next race? The quick answer, I believe, is maybe.

After a horse wins, it can be treated a bit differently.

Owners/trainers/grooms give it more attention, which can make the horse happier. Don't underestimate the possible improvement of a horse that has become happy. Being stabled on-track is very stressful for most horses. There is a lot going on around them that can cause stress. In addition, they are kept in a stall for twenty-three hours a day. In this situation, if you can get (or keep) a horse happy or feeling good and eating well, the horse will usually run its best. I also think horses become aware, through praise and the extra attention, that they have done something good. This may improve their confidence and lead to improvement on the track.

Also, some horses don't quite figure out that the goal is to get to the lead at any point in the race. They may want to race within the pack (herd instinct), as mentioned in the scenario earlier in this chapter where a horse that has lost its rider still won't pass any horses during the race. When they are young, these horses may run well several times without winning a race. It is possible that once they finally win a race, they do understand a little better the purpose of racing, their confidence increases, and, thus, they improve in their next races.

So the question follows, after a loss or several losses, do horses become unhappy? While I think a win may at least do most horses some good (for the reasons mentioned above), I don't think a loss hurts a horse's mental state. While a horse that wins probably gets a little more attention, it's not as if horses that come off a loss or several losses are ignored. The life of a losing horse isn't much different from that of a winning horse. Some horses can be happy without ever winning a race, and others can be sour no matter how many races they win.

After a loss, a trainer may say in an interview that a horse was mad because it lost. More likely, the trainer was mad; the horse just wanted dinner. I find it hard to believe that a horse becomes mad if it loses a race.

Summary

After watching thousands of races and observing horses before and afterward, I don't think they really understand the concept of a finish line. However, any individual horse can be helped out by a win. In most cases, though, win or lose, horses just want to be fed after a race. It also is hard for me to believe that horses "remember" what happened to them (in regard to winning or losing a race) two or three weeks or two or three months earlier. I just don't think they are intelligent enough to relate the results of a race today with those of previous races.

If you encounter a horse that you believe is the likely winner of a race but which has a poor win percentage and/or has lost several races in a row, I would lean on the side of playing the horse and not worry too much about that horse's previous losses.

8

Sprinter to a Route: Are You Missing an Opportunity?

Players are always looking for angles in handicapping. These are situations in which the player can expect large improvement over a horse's previous race. One of the strongest "angles" in horse racing is the ability of a horse that has been sprinting, while racing on or near the lead in those sprints, to show large improvement when going to a route.

Why is this such a powerful angle in racing? If you are using pace figures, you will know pace figures earned in sprints have no direct relationship with those earned in routes (two-turn races). Obviously, the raw times for the sprints are much quicker.

For example, at Emerald Downs the par for older $10,000 claiming males is :45⅕ and 1:10⅗ for a six-furlong sprint (half-mile and finish). The par for a mile and one-sixteenth route (half-mile, three-quarters mile, and finish) is :46⅘, 1:11⅗, 1:44⅕.

If a horse coming off a par pace and final time while sprinting meets a similar horse coming off a par pace and final time while routing, the sprinter will have a huge advantage early. After setting or pressing fractions of about :45⅕ in a sprint, the horse will think it is out for morning exercise if the first half-mile is done in :46⅘ while routing. This is the reason why this angle in racing is so successful. When a sprinter goes a route (two-turn race) and meets other horses that have already been routing, the sprinter may find itself on the lead and in control (or just off the lead) without having expended any significant energy in relation to its previous efforts.

This angle is also successful because many bettors reason that horses that tire late in a sprint will tire even more in routes. "If horse X tires in a six-furlong race, how can the horse possibly last a mile?" As a result bettors may avoid playing these sprinters in a route; thus, many times you can get great value on these types of horses.

I'm sure you have come across a deep-closing sprinter that is trying a route for the first time. You may have read comments like "stoutly bred gelding has been crying for more ground and gets it today." But these deep-closing sprinters tend to be poor bets, both in relation to their odds and the fact that most late-closing sprinters don't do well at a route. Why does the deep-closing sprinter fail when routing? The horse "flattens out" going the longer distance because its punch is gone before it reaches the stretch. At a sprint the horse probably benefited from the fast early fractions, but it is hurt by the slower early fractions in a route. It finds itself with too much to do, trying to catch horses in front of it that haven't expended as much energy by the time they reach the homestretch.

You have probably never read the comment "front runner, pace presser has tired in recent sprints; this stopping sprinter is crying for more ground" — when in fact, it has been looking for the longer distance all along. When the front runner tries the longer distance with the usually slower pace, the horse will have more energy for the finish. Thus the longer distance helps the horse that has been tiring in sprints.

Synful Hour came off two excellent pace-pressing efforts while sprinting. He next tried routing (a mile) on August 18, 2001, and figured to have complete control of the early pace; his only excuse would be if he truly couldn't get the distance (Figure 8.1).

This is not to say that you should bet against every closing sprinter and bet every front-running sprinter when each tries two turns for the first time. Just realize the big advantage that the front-running/pace-pressing sprinter has (Figure 8.2).

In Figure 8.3, Right Angle shows typical improvement when trying a route. He has been pressing the early leaders while sprinting, then moves to a route, takes command early, and wins easily, earning the biggest Beyer speed figure of his career to that point (75). Many horses will run their best route effort with this scenario.

Figure 8.1 — Field for 7th race, Emerald Downs, Aug. 18, 2001

ıl Hour

8EmDfst	6f	:214 :443 :57 1:10	Clm 16000(16-14)N2X	80 1 6 2½ 2hd 12 11½	Russell B R	LB118 b	6.70	89-20	*Synful Hour*1181½ Joe Holiday1182 Proud Native1183	Dueled, shook clear	10
6EmDfst	6½f	:221 :45 1:1031:17	Clm 16000N2X	68 8 1 2hd 21 3½ 22	Perez M A	LB118 b	8.60	85-11	Sage Road1182 *SynfulHour*118hd *AlnaabtheGold*1191¼	Dueled, game for 2nd	9
8EmDfst	6f	:222 :454 :58 1:104	[S]Clm 25000(25-22.5)N2X	53 5 7 72¾ 41¼ 64½ 57½	Whitaker J5	LB113	7.40	77-13	*DukesTune*118nk Winterstrr118nk ImYerHucklebry1183½	5 wide turn, tired	7
2EmDsly	5½f	:22 :453 :5731:04	[S]Clm 25000(25-22.5)N2L	23 1 2 42¼ 45 49 417½	Whitaker J5	LB113	*1.40	74-14	GmeIM1182¼ *DukesTune*1183½ Feelinlikemckee11811¾	Chased inside, tired	5
7EmDfst	6f	:22 :45 :5731:11	Clm 32000(32-25)N2L	45 1 2 1½ 1hd 54½ 58¾	Nuesch D	LB118	5.00	76-13	From Venus1153¼ Road Afleet118nk Slew Stew118nk	Dueled inside, tired	7
7EmDfst	6½f	:22 :441 1:0931:162	WTBALads51k	46 8 5 52½ 86¾ 76¾ 712	Baze G	LB118	13.20	78-08	Dr. Slew1163¾ Diglett116nk *Jumron Won*120nk	Outrun	8
3EmDfst	5½f	:221 :46 :5821:043	Md 20000	63 9 5 21 1hd 11½ 13½	Jawny A	LB118	36.30	89-12	SynfulHour1183½ *HoodooPek*1183¼ [D]ChiliRehno1181	Increased advantage	10

Holiday

8EmDfst	6f	:214 :443 :57 1:10	Clm 16000(16-14)N2X	76 9 5 85¾ 74¾ 22 21½	Matias J	LB118	7.90	87-20	*SynfulHour*1181½ JoeHoliday1182 ProudNative1183	Swung 6 w, closed fast	10
5EmDfst	1	:233 :461 1:1041:373	Clm 16000(16-14)N2X	67 4 64 54 23 23 35¼	Ventura H Jr	LB119	4.20	73-28	*HndsomeWillDo*1174¼ FlyBuddyFly1201 JoeHolidy1192½	Inside, evenly late	7
3EmDfst	6f	:221 :451 :5721:102	Clm 14000(16-14)N2X	72 5 2 52½ 41¾ 42 32¾	Russell B R	LB116	3.90	84-16	FrostyCndin1182½ ImYerHucklebery118nk JoHolidy1162½	Closed willingly	6
5EmDfst	6½f	:221 :45 1:1031:171	[S]Clm 16000(16-14)N2X	62 2 3 42½ 32½ 32½ 34	Ventura H Jr	LB119	9.20	82-15	AlnbtheGold119nk BritishAssult1183¾ JoHolidy1192	Lacked late response	8
10EmDfst	6½f	:23 :462 1:1121:174 3↑	Md 8000	62 12 2 2hd 31 1½ 11¼	Russell B R	B118	*1.20	83-11	JoeHoliday1181¼ LookoutPss1185½ BsketofStrs1231	Prompted, led, clear	12
4EmDfst	5½f	:22 :453 :5741:041	Md 8000(8-7)	64 8 2 62¼ 62 21½ 24	Russell B R	B121	3.80	87-15	Washington Moon1194 *JoeHoliday*1213 MadJazz1214½	5 wide, finished well	8

: Oct20 TuP 4f fst :471 H *3/27* Oct12 TuP 3f fst :391 B *23/27*

erkind

9EmDfst	1	:241 :48 1:1211:372	Clm 25000(25-20)N2X	79 2 11 1½ 1hd 1½ 2hd	Gonsalves F A	LB118 b	*2.90	79-24	Swim Away118hd Colterkind1184 Winterstarr121¾	Bore out late, caught	8
7EmDfst	6f	:221 :453 :5741:103	Clm 25000(25-20)N2X	73 5 3 31½ 31 11½ 21¾	Cedeno A	LB118 b	4.00	84-16	Right Return1181¾ Colterkind1183 Charlie Haan118hd	3-w, drifted, caught	6
6EmDfst	6f	:22 :451 :5741:104	Clm 25000(25-20)N2X	72 2 5 2hd 1hd 1hd 33¼	Cedeno A	LB119 b	*1.80	82-18	Winterstarr1181¼ Sea Victory1182 Colterkind119no	Dueled inside	6
3EmDfst	6f	:221 :452 :58 1:111 3↑	Md 12500	75 10 6 51¾ 11½ 15 13½	Cedeno A	LB118 b	*3.00e	83-16	Colterkind1183½ Sweetsness1183½ *D' Casper*1182½	Bold bid, drew clear	10

cinonadare

9EmDfst	1	:241 :48 1:1211:372	Clm 25000(25-20)N2X	70 6 810 89¾ 88¼ 75½ 44¾	Cedeno O	LB118 fb	11.90	74-24	Swim Away118hd Colterkind1184 Winterstarr121¾	3-wide, no threat	8
7EmDfst	1	:24 :482 1:1311:384 3↑	Md 16000(16-14)	71 3 87¼ 86¾ 73¾ 43½ 1hd	Cedeno O	LB118 fb	3.30	72-30	Dancinonadare118hd *Bright Stout*119nk Love a Bull113no	Up in final strides	8
10EmDfst	6f	:221 :46 :5821:112 3↑	Md 12500(12.5-10)	69 2 10 1011 84 34½ 21¾	Cedeno O	LB118 fb	6.80	80-19	Altoad1181¾ *Dancinonadare*1181½ Lookout Pass1184¼	Full of run	10

ously trained by McAnally Ronald

8Hol fst	7f	:231 :464 1:1241:264	[S]Md 32000(32-28)	44 7 3 3½ 41½ 43½ 64¼	Pedroza M A	LB120 b	9.20	61-26	ItstheRelthing1201 *RmmbringJck*120½ ClifomiPoppy120nk	Shuffled bit 3/8	9
2SA fst	1 1/16	:23 :47 1:1141:452	Md 32000(32-28)	30 4 1013 1019 1018 1020 1022½	McCarron C J	B120	8.80	53-18	TruePssion1204½ *GoOnOrnge*1205 WordlssMonrch120nk	Inside trip, outrun	10
6SA fst	5½f	:213 :45 :5711:033	[S]Md Sp Wt 40k	38 6 8 1110 1214 1115 1115¾	Puglisi I	B120	60.50	74-07	Tit for Tat1204 B Swift120nk Ron Cherry120hd	Angled in, no threat	12
4Dmr fst	5f	:22 :454 :582	[S]Md Sp Wt 47k	43 1 6 911 914 912 810¼	McCarron C J	B118	19.40	86-08	SomewhtChilly1184 RonChrry1181 GoodMting1181	Saved ground, outrun	9

iral's Cap

-8EmDfst	6½f	:221 :45 1:0921:154	[S]OClm 40000	73 6 7 77 65¼ 64½ 44½	Conklin J	LB116	37.60	88-11	*Sullivanitis*1182¼ WgonWheel116½ RightReturn1161¾	Swung 6 w, mild gain	7
-9EmDfst	1 1/16	:233 :463 1:1021:422	TacomaH40k	64 3 22 35 711 814 816	Conklin J	LB111 f	75.90	70-24	Jade Green1151½ Sabertooth1163 *Diglett*120hd	Gave way after 5/8	8

iously trained by Howard Rhonda J

-2EmDfst	6f	:222 :453 :5731:10 3↑	Md 25000	73 5 3 32½ 32½ 11 12¾	Ventura H Jr	LB119	7.20	89-10	AdmirlsCp1192¾ *FoolAround*1181½ MyFinlAnswr118½	Stalked, kicked clear	6
-8EmDfst	6f	:213 :451 :5741:111 3↑	Md 32000	51 3 7 42½ 62½ 65½ 68¾	Ventura H Jr	LB119	19.60	74-17	*Right Return*1181 Only PoeKnows119nk HezaPappySlew1182¼	Went evenly	8

iously trained by Smith Larry D

)-4EmDfst	5f	:22 :451 :58	Md 20000(25-20)	66 5 2 1hd 1hd 2hd 2hd	Mitchell G V	LB116 b	3.70	91-12	CatchtheSun118hd AdmiralsCap1163½ JdeGreen1186	Grudgingly gave way	8
)-7EmDfst	5f	:221 :46 :584	Md 25000	43 5 5 3nk 5¾ 43 47¼	Mitchell G V	B118 b	7.80	80-11	PrmdonnPoppy115nk *CtchthSn*1185½ SsmcWv1181½	Shuffled back 1/4 pole	7

ony Park

-9EmDfst	1	:241 :48 1:1211:372	Clm 20000(25-20)N2X	67 3 42 3½ 42½ 53½ 66¼	Linares M G	LB116 f	26.30	73-24	Swim Away118hd Colterkind1184 Winterstarr121¾	Saved ground	8
-5EmDfst	6½f	:223 :46 1:11 1:174	Clm 8000(8-7)N2X	64 8 5 51¼ 4¾ 12 12¼	Matias J	LB121 f	*2.60	83-15	Colony Park1212¼ *Nite Train Slew*1182¼ Kid Grady119nk	5-wide, led, held	8
-6EmDfst	6½f	:221 :45 1:1031:17	Clm 16000N2X	48 6 9 85¾ 76½ 810 810½	Russell B R	LB118 f	*3.10	76-11	Sage Road1182 *Synful Hour*118hd *Alnaab the Gold*1191¼	6-wide into stretch	9
-8EmDfst	6f	:223 :454 :5811:111	Clm c-10000N2L	68 8 7 62¾ 41¾ 1½ 11	Matias J	LB118 f	*1.60	83-15	Colony Park1181 Pazhalsta121hd Alnaab the Gold1191½	4-w final 1/4, held	9

med from K and J Farm for $10,000, Coffey Junior Trainer 2001(as of 5/25): (33 9 6 4 0.27)

1-1EmDfst	6f	:214 :451 :5731:10	Md 6250	80 5 2 26 23½ 11 17	Matias J	LB121 f	*1.30	89-12	*Colony Park*1217 Y B Red1213¾ *Knight Trick*12110¾	As rider pleased	6
1-3EmDfst	5f	:22 :453 :582	Md 8000	42 6 6 63¼ 44 32 22½	Matias J	LB121 f	5.90	82-10	Arctic Comet1212½ *ColonyPark*1212 Toad'sBoy121½	Bumped early, late bid	10
1-3GG fst	6f	:22 :45 :5731:11	Md 8000	36 8 1 2½ 21 34 58	Cedeno O7	LB111 fb	16.10	75-11	ProdofPrsdnt1182½ OCtonllyWndy1182 ShpCnyon1182½	Gave out stretch	8
0-1EmDfst	6f	:224 :47 :5941:13	Md 12500	22 1 4 1½ 1hd 45 413¼	Gonsalves F A	LB117 fb	11.50	62-22	Seattle Reign117¾ D' Casper1175 *Gabe*1177½	Set pressured pace	6
0-1EmDfst	5f	:222 :453 :582	Md 16000	2 1 5 74¾ 78¼ 711 820¾	Nuesch D	B118 fb	17.60	68-16	Smokin Cigar119no *Frosty Canadian*1189¼ D' Casper118nk	In tight 7/16	8

im Away

01-9EmDfst	1	:241 :48 1:1211:372	Clm 25000(25-20)N2X	79 7 52½ 51¼ 31 2½ 1hd	Cedeno A	LB118	3.00	79-24	Swim Away118hd Colterkind1184 Winterstarr121¾	Bumped late, just up	8
01-8EmDfst	6½f	:22 :443 1:10 1:163	Clm 25000(25-22.5)N2X	65 8 7 83¼ 51¾ 63½ 57	Cedeno A	LB118	10.10	82-11	Wagon Wheel1182¾ Frosty Canadian118½ Sage Road1183	Wide, mild rally	9
01-3EmDfst	1	:233 :471 1:1241:374	Clm 20000(20-16)N2X	73 4 42½ 32 1hd 2½ 1hd	Cedeno A	LB122	3.00	77-27	SwimAway122hd *WgonWheel*1181¾ FlyBuddyFly1184¼	Led, bumped, lasted	6
01-7EmDwf	1	:241 :473 1:1241:382	Clm 16000(16-14)N2X	62 2 42 31½ 3nk 1½ 11¼	Cedeno A	LB118	4.80	74-25	*Swim Away*1181¼ Proud Native1111½ Fly Buddy Fly121hd	3-wide, drew out	7
01-8EmDfst	6f	:222 :454 :58 1:104	[S]Clm 25000(25-22.5)N2X	62 3 4 42 31 43 44	Cedeno A	LB118	11.00	81-13	*Duke's Tune*118nk Winterstarr118nk I'm Yer Hucklebery1183½	Bid,hung	7
01-3EmDwf	5½f	:221 :454 :5821:05	Md 12500	54 4 5 3½ 2hd 1½ 11½	Cedeno A	LB121	*2.00	87-11	SwimAway1211½ LloydofSynastry121½ DCasper1211¼	Stalked, edged clear	7
00-3EmDfst	5f	:222 :46 :59	[S]Md 10000	55 9 7 53¾ 42½ 22½ 22	Mawing M A	B118	*3.70	84-16	Pazhalsta1112 *SwimAway*1184¼ *Mamsdieselpusher*1181	Inside move, rallied	10
00-2EmDfst	4½f	:22 :46 :523	Md 16000	41 6 9 77¾ 77½ 54¾	Mawing M A	B118	42.70	85-14	BritishAssault1182 Cartright1181¾ ChiliRehno1181	Swung 6 w, belated bid	9

Figure 8.2

Seventh Race Emerald Downs- August 18, 2001

1 Mile. (1.33%) CLAIMING. Purse $11,400 FOR THREE-YEARS-OLDS WHICH HAVE NEVER WON TWO RACES. Weight 121 lbs. Non-winners of arace in 2001 allowed 3 lbs. CLAIM PRICE $25,000, if for $20,000 allowed 3 lbs. (Maiden races, claiming and starter races for $20,000 or less not considered.) (NWRA reserves the right to retain possession of a registration papers for any horses claimed at Emerald Downs until the conclusion of the current race meet.) (PLUS UP TO $1,112 TO WA-BREDS.)

Value of race: $11,400. Winner $6,720; second $2,280; third $1,710; fourth $855; fifth $285. Mutuel pool $50,138.00. Exacta pool $34,042.00. Trifecta pool $36,558.00.

Last Raced	Horse	Med/Eqp	A	Wgt	PP	St	1/4	1/2	3/4	Str	Fin	Jockey	Cl'g Pr	Odds
2Aug01 ⁸EmD¹	Synful Hour	LBb	3	119	1	2	1¹ˣ	1¹	1ʰᵈ	1ʰᵈ	1¹	Baze G	25000	3.6
5Aug01 ⁸EmD⁴	Admiral's Cap	LB	3	119	5	4	3ʰᵈ	3ˣ	3²	2²	2⁶	Ventura H	25000	5.7
29Jly01 ⁹EmD²	Colterkind	LBb	3	118	3	3	2²	2²	2¹	3⁴	3⁶ˣ	GnsalvesF	25000	2.7
29Jly01 ⁹EmD¹	Swim Away	LB	3	121	7	6	6⁴	4¹ˣ	5⁵	4²	4⁵	Cedeno A	25000	2.3
29Jly01 ⁹EmD⁴	Dancinonadare	LBbf	3	115	4	7	7	7	6²	6⁶	5ˣ	Cedeno O	20000	8.1
2Aug01 ⁸EmD²	Joe Holiday	LB	3	118	2	1	4ˣ	5²	4ˣ	5²ˣ	6²¹	Matias J	25000	6.5
29Jly01 ⁹EmD⁶	Colony Park	LBf	3	115	6	5	5¹ˣ	6³ˣ	7	7	7	Linares M	20000	43.6

Off Time: 4:16   **Time Of Race:** :23%   :46%   1:10%   1:23   1:36%

Start: Good For All But Dancinonadare.   **Track:** Fast.   **Won driving.**

©EQUIBASE

Be the Bunny is another sprinter with early speed going a route. The only difference between him and other sprinters is that he is seven years old and trying this distance for the first time. Many players will assume that since he has yet to attempt routing by this age, he probably can't route. Had a horse with similar form (let's say a three-year-old) been trying a route, it probably would have been bet down much lower than Be the Bunny was on September 8, 2002 (Figure 8.4). Be the Bunny quickly opened up a lead and was able to hold on late at 11-1.

A horse doesn't have to be on the lead or close to the lead; just being within four or five lengths of the fractions of a sprint will give the horse an advantage when going to a route. As a two-year-old, Four Checker showed two successful sprint-to-route efforts (Figure 8.5). His first route effort on October 4, 2001, was a winning one and came after three sprints. Although he was not on the lead in his previous start, in which he finished second while sprinting at Fairplex Park on September 15, he wasn't that far off either. Notice the significant improvement in his Beyer speed figure in that first route try (from 64 to 73). Then he won again on November 18, at Golden Gate Fields, in a similar scenario: coming off two runner-up finishes in sprints, even a bit farther off the half-mile in each. Again, his Beyer speed figure improved substantially in that route (70 to 82).

One word of warning: Just because a horse raced on or near the lead in its sprints and should easily have the lead in today's route doesn't mean the connections (owner/trainer/jockey) want to

Figure 8.3

Right Angle

13Dec01- 1GG fst 1 :222 :46 1:11 1:37 Clm c-(25-22.5) **75** 1 11½ 11 11 12 12 Russell B R **LB**117 b 2.20 87- 17 Right Angle1172 Easter Halo117nk Mountain Flag117½ Well rated, drvng 6

Claimed from Hoffman Lathrop G. for $25,000, Shoemaker Leonard Trainer 2001(as of 12/13): (171 28 22 30 0.16)

28Nov01- 6GG fst 6f :22 :443 :5711:103 Clm 25000(25-22.5) **72** 5 5 32 32 21½ 21 Russell B R **LB**117 b 5.30 84- 12 *Sharp Park*1191 *Right Angle*1173 Red Reigning117¾ Stlkd 3w, even late 8

26Oct01- 5BM fst 6f :22 :444 :5631:09 Str 32000 **58** 4 1 44 44½ 67½ 711 Russell B R **LB**118 b 2.60 85- 07 HurricneSmoke1186 FourChecker118nk *ShrpPrk*118hd Well placed, empty 9

4Oct01- 6BM fst 6f :223 :454 :5811:112 Clm c-(25-22.5) **69** 8 2 32 1hd 12 21 Gonzalez R M **LB**117 b 2.60 83- 14 VacationDy1191 RightAngle1173½ ReveltheStr1193 Bid 3w, led, outdueled 9

Claimed from Avery, Greg, Franco, Richard and Goldstein, Sy for $25,000, Sherman Art Trainer 2001(as of 10/4): (300 60 45 47 0.20)

13Sep01- 7BM fst 5½f :221 :451 :5711:032 Alw 33376N1X **55** 6 6 41½ 54 59¼ 611 Alvarado F T **LB**118 b 3.50 83- 13 Cappuchino118¾ Almudin1181 Green Team1182 Bobbled start 6

Figure 8.4

Be the Bunny

8Sep02- 7EmDfst 1 :223 :451 1:1021:362 3↑ Clm 20000(25-20) **81** 7 13 13 1hd 11 1nk Chaves N J **LB**119 fb 11.70 84- 15 BetheBunny119nk ItsWkiFct1192½ HmiltonIslnd123¾ Set pace, just lasted 7

25Aug02- 7EmDfst 5f :212 :441 :561 3↑ Alw 25000N$Y **67** 1 4 62¼ 62¾ 74¾ 77 Kenny J **LB**104 fb 26.90 89- 04 Makors Mark1021¼ Only Poe Knows116no April Surprise1102½ No factor 7

10Aug02- 6EmDfst 6½f :214 :441 1:0911:154 3↑ Clm 12500(12.5-10) **81** 3 1 2hd 11 1½ 31 Kenny J7 **LB**112 fb 10.50 92- 11 CscdeCsey119hd WgonWheel1201 BethBunny1121¾ Dueled, drifted, game 7

13Jly02- 6EmDfst 6½f :22 :444 1:0921:16 3↑ Clm c-12500 **53** 4 1 1hd 31 88¼ 812¾ Whitaker J **LB**119 fb 3.80 79- 12 *Bashi*120nk Alnaab the Gold123nk Better Than That1191¼ Dueled, stopped 8

Claimed from Potter Vicki for $12,500, Belvoir Howard Trainer 2002(as of 7/13): (245 27 39 38 0.11)

Figure 8.5

Four Checker

18Nov01- 2GG fst 1 :22 :45 1:0921:353 Str 32000 **82** 2 2½ 3½ 31½ 11 12½ Castro J M **LB**118 b *1.80 94- 08 Four Checker1182½ Cody Steele1182½ Easter Halo118½ Bid 3w, driving 7

9Nov01- 1GG fst 6f :221 :451 :5721:104 Str 32000 **70** 1 5 57 56 45 2½ Castro J M **LB**118 b 3.50 83- 13 *SharpPark*118½ *FourChecker*118½ GameWellPlnned1187 Angled out, rallied 5

26Oct01- 5BM fst 6f :22 :444 :5631:09 Str 32000 **70** 6 6 55½ 67½ 56½ 26 Castro J M **LB**118 b 7.30 90- 07 HurricaneSmoke1186 FourChecker118nk *SharpPrk*118hd 5w 1/4p, no threat 9

4Oct01- 5BM fst 1 :232 :473 1:1221:382 Md 25000(25-22.5) **73** 7 63 43½ 31½ 1hd 12½ Castro J M **LB**118 b 3.50 82- 20 FourChecker1182½ SilverBrite1182½ GretAlrm1185½ 3w trip, dueled, drvng 8

15Sep01- 9Fpx fst 6½f :222 :46 1:1121:174 Md 32000 **64** 1 4 63¼ 43½ 33½ 23 Castro J M **LB**118 b 4.10 86- 11 FairVictory1183 *FourChecker*1182 FtWshington1181 Saved ground to lane 9

16Aug01- 6Bmf fst 5½f :22 :46 :5831:051 Md 20000(20-18) **42** 6 6 910 99¾ 89 45 Packer B R **LB**118 7.20 80- 12 FirstPlcDncr1181½ Thmoonshnr1221½ LudcrousSpd1182 3w turn, late rally 11

26Jly01- 6SR fst 5f :222 :454 :583 Md 12500 **52** 6 2 3nk 1hd 2½ 2nk Packer B R **LB**118 24.10 89- 09 JohnndRyn118nk FourChckr1182½ FuturArticl1181 Dueled, waited, missed 8

WORKS: Nov4 **BM** 4f gd :492 H *6/16* Oct27 **BM** 4f fst :493 H *7/10* Oct20 **BM** 3f fst :373 H *2/2*

go to the lead when routing. Sometimes, if the horse has questionable breeding for a longer race or has never routed before, the connections decide the prudent thing is to restrain (take back) the horse early and let it make one late run. They reason the horse has a better chance of getting the distance if it saves energy early. The thought is that the horse will have something left for the finish. In most cases they are wrong and have thrown away their best chance of winning (sprinting clear early) by eliminating the advantage their horse had going into the race.

Summary

Clearly, there are horses that can't get a distance. However, if I think the situation is right, I am not afraid to bet even the most poorly distance-bred horse or the most faint-hearted/stopping sprinter when either of these types is going a route after pace-setting/pressing sprints just because of the significant early advantage the horse may then have. I know I will be betting horses that end up not being able to get the distance, but I have found this to be one of the best angles to play and sometimes will get big prices on these types of horses.

For example, Super Script tired badly after pressing the pace in sprints, but when going a route for the first time that season on June 30, 2001, she was able to get clear early and win at 25-1 odds

(Figure 8.6). She repeated a similar pattern when going from a sprint to a route on May 16, 2002.

Super Script

Figure 8.6

16May02-3EmDfst	1	:24	:47^{2}	1:11^{4}	1:37	4↑(F)Clm 7000(8-7)	**71**	3	1^{2}	1^{2}	1$^{1\frac{1}{2}}$	1^{1}	1$^{1\frac{1}{2}}$	Rivera J M^{7}	**LB**113	7.20	81- 19	SuperScript113$^{1\frac{1}{2}}$ JdeBeuty118^{hd} CpblofGold120$^{12\frac{3}{4}}$	Drifted, came in, h
28Apr02-4EmDfst	5f	:22^{1}	:45^{1}		:57^{3}	4↑(F)Clm 6250	**45**	2	4	6^{5}	6$^{5\frac{1}{2}}$	6$^{5\frac{1}{2}}$	6$^{8\frac{3}{4}}$	Mancilla O G	**LB**118	14.00	80- 08	*Something Classy*118$^{3\frac{1}{2}}$ Run ZRoad120$^{2\frac{1}{4}}$ Barmara118^{nk}	Trailed througho
14Sep01-7EmDfst	6½f	:22^{3}	:46^{1}	1:12	1:18^{4}	3↑(F)[S]Clm 6250(6.25-5)	**36**	3	2	2^{hd}	2^{hd}	7$^{5\frac{1}{2}}$	7^{13}	Cedeno O	**LB**122	7.80	65- 20	*Lefa Theda*122^{hd} Gaiter Girl119^{3} Ragtime Ruthie120$^{1\frac{3}{4}}$	Dueled, stopp
25Aug01-8EmDfst	1¼	:46^{4}	1:12^{2}	1:39	2:04^{1}	3↑(F)Str 12500	**31**	2	1^{5}	1$^{\frac{1}{2}}$	5$^{2\frac{1}{4}}$	9^{20}	9$^{32\frac{1}{4}}$	Cedeno O	**LB**123	7.80	56- 21	WatershedPark118$^{5\frac{1}{2}}$ *RedcliffBay*123^{3} JadeBeauty116$^{3\frac{3}{4}}$	Set pace, stopp
28Jly01-6EmDwf	1	:23^{2}	:46^{2}	1:11^{3}	1:40	4↑(F)Clm 12500(12.5-10)	**–**	6	2$^{\frac{1}{2}}$	2$^{1\frac{1}{2}}$	4^{7}	8^{22}	-	Cedeno O	**LB**122	4.00	- 26	ClerlytheBest117$^{2\frac{1}{4}}$ RedcliffBy122^{nk} MiklsStrr119$^{3\frac{1}{2}}$	Vied, stopped, eas
14Jly01-8EmDfst	1	:23^{2}	:46^{3}	1:11^{3}	1:38^{4}	4↑(F)Clm 12500	**70**	3	1^{2}	1^{2}	1^{2}	1$^{1\frac{1}{2}}$	2$^{\frac{3}{4}}$	Cedeno O	**LB**122	6.60	71- 28	RedcliffBy118$^{\frac{3}{4}}$ SuperScript122$^{1\frac{1}{2}}$ *ClerlytheBest*122^{1}	Grudgingly gave w
30Jun01-6EmDfst	1	:24	:47^{3}	1:12^{3}	1:39	4↑(F)Clm 12500(12.5-10)	**71**	6	1^{2}	1^{2}	1^{1}	1$^{1\frac{1}{2}}$	1^{hd}	Cedeno O	**LB**118	25.20	71- 27	SprScrpt118^{hd} YongContryStr118$^{1\frac{1}{4}}$ ClrlythBst122^{1}	Inside, fully extend
3Jun01-7EmDfst	6½f	:22^{3}	:45^{3}	1:10^{3}	1:17^{1}	4↑(F)[S]Clm 16000	**39**	6	1	2$^{\frac{1}{2}}$	2$^{1\frac{1}{2}}$	7^{10}	7$^{13\frac{1}{2}}$	Mitchell G V	**LB**118	17.50	72- 11	Asummrforwindy118$^{\frac{3}{4}}$ DontIgnorHr119$^{1\frac{1}{4}}$ MornnMst118^{3}	Dueled, stopp
6May01-8EmDfst	6½f	:22^{2}	:45^{4}	1:10^{3}	1:17	4↑(F)Clm 16000(16-14)	**19**	4	2	2^{hd}	7$^{7\frac{1}{4}}$	7^{11}	7$^{23\frac{3}{4}}$	Mitchell G V	**LB**118	13.50	63- 15	DancingGoose111^{hd} MornnMist118$^{1\frac{3}{4}}$ AlaskSlew120^{no}	Brief foot, stopp

Don't be afraid to back horses with double-digit losses after they have pressed the pace while sprinting and then go to a route. At least consider the horse a contender.

Can Statistics Lie?

Much of this book discusses the more common areas of handicapping such as speed figures, trouble/biases, form cycle analysis, body language, etc., that players look at regularly. Of course, players use other information to help evaluate a horse's chances in a race. This includes historical statistical information on horses, post positions, trainers, and jockeys. In addition, another piece of information that players look for is a "key race." The key race concept has become very popular and led the *Daily Racing Form* to italicize next out winners in the past performances of each horse several years ago. However, using either statistical information or the key race concept has drawbacks. Those drawbacks are discussed in this chapter along with a couple of comments about track biases and other pieces of information some handicappers use.

Statistics

In attempting to gain an edge, some players use all sorts of statistical information published in the *Daily Racing Form* or sold through other publications such as *Thoro-Graph* or *Today's Racing Digest.*

However, many players are not aware of the potential drawbacks of using statistics to handicap, such as whether the "sample size" was large enough to draw conclusions. One of the first things taught in a statistical analysis class is the value (significance) of sample size. For example, prior to Fusaichi Pegasus' victory in the Kentucky Derby, the favorite had lost in the previous seventeen years. Some players were using this statistic to predict why Fusaichi Pegasus, a heavy favorite, would not win. Seventeen or so races is nowhere near enough of a sample size to determine anything regarding horse, trainer, or jockey statistics. Having a sample of one hundred races might not even be enough in some situations.

Another consideration is the value of those statistics, which we'll cover in the rest of this section by examining some of the more common statistics handicappers use.

Trainer Statistics

The most common statistics used by players are trainer statistics, such as win percentage with first-time starters, first starts off claims, or first time trying a route, etc. A specific example might be "trainer X is three for seventeen with horses that have not raced in 180 days or more."

This statistical information can be misleading for two reasons. The first is that, in most cases, many of the statistics are derived from limited data. For example, let's say you are looking at a horse that is receiving Lasix for the first time. In the *Daily Racing Form*'s past performances, the trainer of this particular horse is shown to be three for eighteen (17 percent) when giving a horse Lasix for the first time. However, as mentioned earlier, a sample size of eighteen races is not enough to form a significant conclusion. To take this a step further, let's say the trainer's overall record is twenty-two for 122 (18 percent) this year. If the trainer wins at an 18 percent rate overall, and 17 percent of the time when adding Lasix for the first time, you could reasonably conclude that adding Lasix has no effect on the potential for this horse winning today with this trainer.

The second potential problem is that most of this statistical information is based on several years of data, and the trainer may be facing different circumstances now than when those results were tabulated.

For example, the type of horses in a particular trainer's barn is going to affect his season statistics significantly. If the barn is full of well-bred unraced two-year-olds, that trainer's statistics will be very different than if the same trainer had previously operated a claiming stable of older horses. Also, note that some trainers do well with two-year-old first-time starters but do poorly with three-year-old and up first-timers, yet published statistics usually combine the two age groups.

Also, be aware that trainers can get better over the years. Using statistics that combine their results over the previous few years may have no relevance for this year if the trainer has improved.

Trainer statistics also can be misleading for other reasons. A few years ago a certain trainer (I'll call him "Zeke") started the meet at Emerald Downs by winning with several horses returning from a layoff. Zeke won with the first five or six horses he started that year. When asked about his success, Zeke said that he normally left town to train at another track when Emerald Downs was closed, but this year he had stayed home. Since he was home, he started his horses back at a private training facility earlier than in previous years, and they were pretty fit once Emerald Downs' backstretch opened for training. Other trainers had only seventy-five to eighty days to prepare their returning horses (Emerald's backstretch opens about eighty days prior to the first racing day).

The next year bettors backed Zeke's horses in their seasonal debut, yet all lost. It turns out that Zeke had left town for the winter break and worked at another track. When he returned to Emerald Downs, he was in the same boat as most of the other trainers; he had seventy-five to eighty days to get his horses ready, and this time they were not as fit as they had been the previous year.

Players also must take into account that a trainer's claiming statistics can be misleading. For example, sometimes an owner wants a horse his trainer doesn't think much of and ordinarily wouldn't claim. The resulting claiming statistics are then more attributable to the owner's decision to claim rather than the trainer's regimen. Or, an owner might want a horse for breeding and isn't really interested in how the horse runs after the claim, also skewing the trainer's claiming statistics.

Some trainers may claim a horse for a friend who is unlicensed or for a trainer at a different track or for any number of possibilities. These types of claims occur more than you might think, yet statistics don't and can't distinguish among such claims.

Post Position Statistics

The inside posts tend to have much higher win percentages than the outside posts; for example, the #1 hole may win at 15 percent of the time and the #10 hole at 8 percent. But part of the reason may be field size rather than post position. For example, if there is a five-horse field, the #1 hole, from a random point of view, has a 20 percent chance to get a winner from that post (one out of five). If there is a ten-horse field, the #10 (and #1) hole has only (again from a random point of view) a 10 percent chance of getting a winner from those respective posts (one out of ten). The larger the field size, the smaller probability any one post has in getting a winner. Couple this with the fact that most tracks offer small fields of horses rather than large fields, and it creates the inaccurate impression that winning from posts #10, #11, and #12 is impossible.

Another problem with post position statistics is that in small fields or in fields with late scratches, the #1 and sometimes #2 holes are left open. This is done to give those horses breaking from inside posts more room. When tracks do shift these horses out, the #1 horse may actually start in post position #3 and all others are shifted out, yet the statistics are kept as if the horses were loaded, starting in the #1 hole.

Jockey Statistics

In looking at jockey statistics, there would be many of the same potential problems associated with those statistics as with trainer statistics. These potential problems include lack of a significant sample size. Another potential problem is that the quality of the horses the rider is receiving would have to be included in those statistics in order for them to have any real value, which is very hard to incorporate in a statistic.

Summary

At the beginning of this section when discussing statistics and talking about trainer statistics, I was addressing specific situations such as a trainer's win percentage with horses returning off layoffs of 180 days or longer. I don't want to give the wrong impression that keeping records of trainers and trainer patterns, which many players use for their home tracks, isn't profitable. In fact, having information on trainers and trainer patterns (not strict statistical information) at the tracks you are playing can be very valuable. Also, I am not saying that statistical information on trainers, post positions, etc., is not useful, but I strongly recommend that you use that information with caution. Obviously statistical information can at times be valuable. For example, if a trainer is zero for forty-eight with first-time two-year-old starters, I might stay away from horses of his in this category. However, in many cases the sample size of those statistics is small, which may invalidate the usefulness of any particular statistic. Other times, the statistic may have no real value in evaluating a horse's performance in today's race as there are other elements at work that are more important.

Track Biases

Determining track biases is also subject to a lack of sample size. On any given day most racetracks offer eight or nine live races of varying types. For example, two of them might be on the turf, two might be short sprints, two might be longer sprints, and the last two might be routes. Concluding a bias existed could be tough because of the limited number of races on varying surfaces and at varying distances. Just be aware of the limited sample size when analyzing results for the existence of a track bias.

Key Race

One of the more popular angles that many handicappers look for is a key race, a race from which several horses run well in their next starts. On a rare occasion there will be a race from which most every runner returns to win in its next start, but most key races are defined as having two or three horses return to win, with others running well without winning (running second or third).

I believe that true key races are very rare and the reasons horses win while exiting any particular race are really the result of other factors, not because of a key race. Of course, many players believe in the key race concept and will actively keep track of how each horse does when exiting any particular race in hopes of determining a key race.

I have come across all sorts of theories about how key races occur, ranging from the bizarre (one guy told me that horses transferred energy to each other during the race which was then used in their next starts) to the most plausible and simple (a strong field for the level). Handicappers who are trying to identify a key race before it becomes well known may look for a race in which several horses contested a faster than normal half-mile fraction, or one in which the final time was well above par — or a combination of both. Other handicappers may look for different things in trying to identify a key race, such as a race in which several horses were making significant drops in class.

Many key races are not readily identifiable because there was nothing special about the pace or the final time, and the horses in that race had no real reason to improve in their next start — but several did. Anyway, most key races are identified after a horse or two have returned and done well in their next starts. Players who think they have identified a key race will tend to bet every horse out of that race. They may ignore all other aspects and play the horse only because that horse was in the key race. They mistakenly believe that the "key race" angle will supersede all other handicapping factors.

Handicappers also look for the opposite of a key race, the "negative key race." This is a race in which the better-placing horses return to run poorly. Then players may downgrade the remaining horses out of that particular race. I do recognize that there are races in which several horses come back and run well and there are also races in which several horses come back and run poorly. However, I approach the key race concept just as I approach the use of statistics in my handicapping — with caution. The main reason for this caution is there may be other reasons horses run well while exiting any race.

For example, one reason is that some horse has to win every race. No matter how bad the horses in any particular race are, there will be a winner, a second-place finisher, a third-place finisher, etc. Unless they are first-time starters, those horses will have exited a race in which a horse or two has run well.

Another reason is that horses will often improve regardless of the race they last ran in. For example, let's say there was a maiden claiming sprint that was run in decent (slightly above par) time. The winner of the race comes back to beat non-winners of two lifetime while favored (nothing surprising about that). The second-place finisher comes back to break its maiden in its next start when favored (nothing surprising about that). The third-place finisher also comes back to win its next start (dropping a level in claiming price when favored). The horse that raced fourth after setting the pace in the original maiden race, instead of sprinting again, goes to a route and wins wire to wire. Now the top four finishers out of that maiden race have come back to win, and many will conclude the race was a key race. However, the results were not surprising at all and probably had nothing to do with a key race.

Take the opposite scenario — let's say a three-year-old claiming sprint is run and produces decent speed figures; the half-mile and final times are slightly above par. The winner of the race ran big, so its connections jump the horse up in class and try routing (while not favored, the horse is decently bet) and the horse runs a close fourth. The second-place finisher comes back at the same level but catches a wet track when favored and runs out of the money. The third-place finisher drops in class and runs poorly; later the horse pops up on the vet's list as having bled. Many players, taking the three results together, assume the race was weak, yet each horse had a legitimate excuse for its next start.

My final scenario is for a race that comes back with pace and final speed figures well above par. Handicappers who are looking to identify a key race immediately look at this race as having the potential to be a key race. But then the first few horses exiting the race all run poorly in their next start. Many players will conclude the race was not strong and may adjust those good speed figures down. But, what if the first few horses out of that particular fast race all bounced in their next start? That's something that is reasonable, isn't it?

In each of these scenarios (and there are many others), the resulting finishes, either good or bad, of each individual horse were not a function of that race being a key race (or a negative key race) but were normal results you would expect in horse racing. Trying to predict the performance of one horse based on the performance of another horse or other horses just because those horses exited the same race seems a bit of a reach.

Other Information

You have to evaluate many pieces of information when looking at any one race. And sometimes knowing just a little more than other bettors can work strongly in your favor.

For example, a fairly popular horse raced at Emerald Downs three or four years ago. One of the reasons he was popular was that it became known he had only one eye. He competed in the higher-class races at Emerald Downs before leaving Emerald Downs and racing in southern California for a couple of years. As he became older, he moved to the fair circuit of northern California. While he moved from track to track in northern California during the summer, the general public at those tracks was probably unaware that the horse had one eye. Because the horse was missing his right eye he needed an outside post to run well. Drawing an inside post left him unable to see the rest of the field.

One afternoon I was skimming through the *Daily Racing Form* before Emerald's live card was scheduled to start, and I ran across the horse; he was running at Solano. The horse had not done well at all in his previous couple of starts but in each case he had drawn an inside post. This particular day, he drew outside. I knew (or at least thought I knew) why he had run poorly in his last two starts, and I took a shot on him only because of that piece of information from a few years earlier. While he won easily as the longest shot on the board, I knew there was a lot of luck involved in this bet — first, even to notice that he was running, especially with all the tracks being offered on a daily basis, and also to have the "setup" that occurred on the day I saw him entered. But it did remind me that any piece of information — while at the time you note it, may not seem too important — can be very valuable later on, sometimes years later.

Conclusion

I have a few additional observations I would like to leave with you that may help you improve your handicapping. Avoid playing these types of horses in these cases:

1. Any heavily bet horse that comes off a significantly improved effort over its previous efforts without an obvious reason is unlikely to repeat that effort. Some of the obvious reasons for significant improvement when you can expect a repeat performance may be a change in equipment, medication, trainer, distance, track surface, etc., but always be leery of a horse that jumps up and runs a big race for no apparent reason.

2. While I feel one of the strongest angles in predicting improvement is a front-running sprinter going to a route, there is one scenario when this angle tends to be a bad play: playing a two- or three-year-old maiden sprint winner that is going to a route and meeting winners for the first time. Many horses that break their maiden impressively sprinting while earning big figures will be heavily bet even when trying two turns and facing winners for the first time. While they can win, their prices can be too low to justify playing them.

3. Heavily favored deep closers that benefited from an extreme (fast) pace scenario in their last start. These types of horses are dependent on what happens in the race (pace), and since they come from behind, they must also overcome more potential trouble.

4. Any heavy favorite that is suspiciously being dropped in class. Remember, no one gives anything away. Again, this type of horse may win, but there is usually a good reason for a big drop and you will be better off avoiding this type of horse or skipping the race.

5. Any heavy favorite in a race with several unknowns. In a race in which there is one horse that has run at the track recently and most of the rest of the field includes several first-time starters, several horses trying a different distance/surface for the first time, several shipping in from another track, or several coming off lay-offs the public tends to ignore these unknowns and goes with the known quantity. Thus, that horse becomes way overbet.

6. A heavy favorite that draws a poor post for its style.

7. Last year's champions in their first starts after a layoff. This can be either nationally known horses or local horses. In many cases the objective of the trainer/owner is future races, and whether these horses win their first start back isn't the most important thing. Some will win, but many will fail at short prices only because players assume they are pointing for that first start back when they are not. Most players are aware of this angle, but it can become more useful when the heavily favored horse is running at a distance that is probably not its best. For example, if a marathon turf horse (such as a top horse that was very successful at distances of a mile and a quarter or longer) is making its first start at a shorter distance, such as a mile and one-eighth or less.

8. The horse that always seems to find trouble. It acts up in the gate, won't change leads in the stretch, and/or won't relax early in a race (rank). There are all sorts of bad habits horses develop and will repeat from race to race. In all of these scenarios, playing the horse is okay, but reconsider playing the horse when it is heavily bet.

9. Don't accept as fact what everyone else may believe. For example, a lot of players when encountering a horse that is returning from a rest will look to see how the horse did in its first lifetime race. Let's say this horse won its first lifetime start, raced several more times, and then was rested. Some players, looking at the fact that the horse won its first race, will say, "He is proven to run well fresh." Breaking its maiden in its first start does not offer proof that the horse will run well after a layoff.

10. As discussed in the value and wagering chapters, it will help to have enough money to last the day and also have some sort of plan on how you are going to play selected races in advance. I am always amazed when I get behind someone at a SAM machine

who has, for example $12 on his or her voucher. This person starts punching a tri-box that costs more than the $12, then cancels, tries a part-wheel, which again ends up costing more than he or she has. The person's next step is to punch some individual straight trifectas, and as he gets down to the last dollars, the decisions become excruciating. This type of player doesn't want to be forced to make those final choices, knowing he may be leaving out the winning combo. The lack of money to last the entire card has done this person in.

In this book, I do not offer a specific method to approach handicapping and wagering. While the book covers many of the more important areas of handicapping, it is still up to you to decide the areas of handicapping you would like to focus on. Those areas should be ones you enjoy, understand, and, because of your individual skills, are able use to an advantage. Many players concentrate on one area of handicapping, but most successful players are still aware of all other areas. You need this diversity to give yourself more opportunity when coming across any individual race.

Some players, instead of trying to be aware of many, if not all, areas of handicapping, want to simplify handicapping. They either look for certain angles or try to boil racing down to a single variable. For example, you may hear comments like "The #6 won because he was first-time Lasix" or "The #2 won because he had the highest Beyer" or "The #7 won because she was the only speed in the race." Horses do not win because of one and only one factor. Obviously, it doesn't hurt any horse to be clear on the lead early or have the highest Beyer speed figure or be first time Lasix — but that doesn't guarantee victory. Only after the fact does it become so "obvious" to some players. Horse racing is complicated, and it is not easy to select winners and bet properly, but therein lies the challenge.

One of the more common mistakes I see others make is refusing to learn from their experiences. They complain after losing, yet go right back and repeat the same handicapping and betting approach that led them to those losses in the first place. They don't keep records. They only remember the winning days that reinforce their methods. When they lose, rather than fault their methods (of either handicapping or betting), they blame other things such as a bad ride. Evaluating your handicapping and betting on a regular basis is a must to learn and to keep improving. One of the strongest "angles" in playing the races is your own experience and the knowledge you gain over the years. Another mistake I see players make is many become influenced by others' opinions. Have the confidence in your picks to ignore what others are touting.

Finally, realize that horses are horses. It doesn't matter if they are Breeders' Cup starters or $2,500 claiming horses. Many players are afraid to bet cheap claimers, fearing those horses' form is inconsistent or those horses are all hurt. Some players won't play maiden races and other players shy away from the best races such as Breeders' Cup races, assuming that all the horses are very good. Again, in my experience, this is not true. You can be just as successful playing $2,500 claimers as playing top stakes horses. The same handicapping principles apply.

Appendix A:
Pars and Variants

Pars (Historical Pars)

Pars are a historical average of winning times for a certain group of horses. Most pars are broken down among class levels, age groups (two-year-olds, three-year-olds, and four-year-olds and up), sex (male vs. female), and distance. Beyer Associates and other figure makers commonly use the older $10,000 claiming horses as a base figure. Here would be an example of establishing a par for that class level.

You would find all the fast-track older $10,000 claiming horse races, write the winning times (also fractional times, if you are interested in pace figures) for as far back as necessary to obtain a decent sample size, and then average those times out. The result would be the pars for that particular class level/age/sex/distance. You would try to do this for as many different class levels, ages, sexes, and distances offered at your track.

Many find it easy to come up with accurate pars for the more commonly run races, but it can be difficult to come up with accurate pars for every class level, age, sex, and distance due to a limited number of races in each of those categories.

Another problem facing handicappers who are trying to establish pars is the maturation of two- and three-year-olds. For example, a three-year-old filly in February is a much different horse from a three-year-old filly in November. As I have mentioned several times, if you have additional interest in speed figures and calculating pars, please refer to those books listed in Chapter 1.

Variants

A variant is a figure resulting from measuring the effect of the track surface on the final times of the races for that day. A track variant may be determined by comparing the actual times of any particular day's races with the historical pars. Or, the variant may be determined by comparing the actual times of any particular day's races with the expected (projected) times.

For example purposes, I will use historical pars: Let's say a racetrack had an eight-race card with all the races being six-furlong sprints for older $10,000 claiming horses. The historical par for this race is 1:10 flat. Here are the mythical result times for each race:

Race 1: 1:10⁴⁄₅
Race 2: 1:10³⁄₅
Race 3: 1:10
Race 4: 1:11
Race 5: 1:09⁴⁄₅
Race 6: 1:10¹⁄₅
Race 7: 1:10²⁄₅
Race 8: 1:10²⁄₅

You would average the amount that each race differs from the historical par for this race, which is 1 minute, 10 seconds flat to determine the variant for that day. In this case:

Race 1: ⁴⁄₅ of a second slower than average
Race 2: ³⁄₅ of a second slower than average
Race 3: 0 (same as par)
Race 4: ⁵⁄₅ of a second slower than average
Race 5: ¹⁄₅ of a second faster than average
Race 6: ¹⁄₅ of a second slower than average
Race 7: ²⁄₅ of a second slower than average
Race 8: ²⁄₅ of a second slower than average

The variant is determined by adding up the differences for the eight races; in this case, you would get a total of ¹⁶⁄₅ slower than par and dividing this figure by the number of races (eight). The result for this day would be a track variant of +2 (slow by ²⁄₅ of a second). You would then adjust all horses' times that day by ²⁄₅ of a second, as the surface "slowed" those horses down.

Appendix B

The Thoro-Graph Sheet for The Novelist (shown on page 188) starts with his five-year-old season and goes through the beginning of his eight-year-old season. How to interpret a Thoro-Graph sheet is listed below. For more information regarding Thoro-Graph, please visit its web site (thorograph.com). The staff at Thoro-Graph is very responsive to any questions regarding their products.

Thoro-Graph — The Basics

The lower the number the faster the race. On our scale 1 point = ~ 1 length at five furlongs increasing to two lengths at 1¼ miles. Each sheet has four calendar years going back from right to left. The last race a horse ran would be the uppermost number in the rightmost column corresponding to the horse's age.

Five pounds in weight = 1 point all distances. The figures are adjusted for weight carried in previous races. If two horses run a TG figure of 10, a horse in at 115 will beat a horse in at 120 by one point, or one length at five furlongs.

Each path out from the rail (1 path) = 1 length of ground loss. Considering all else equal, in a one-turn race a horse in the third path runs two lengths better than a horse on the rail. The figures are not adjusted for horses that are off poorly or stumble from the gate. Appropriate notations are made next to the figure.

Dirt Figures: 25^1 = 25¼; 25^2 = 25½; 25^3 = 25¾.

Turf races are denoted by "–", e.g., –25 is 25 on the turf.

Typeface key

Races 5½ furlongs and less are in *italic light face* e.g. 25^2
Races 6 furlongs to less than 1 mile are in light face, e.g. 25^2
Races 1 mile to 1⅛ miles are in **bold face,** e.g. $\mathbf{25}^2$
Races more than 1⅛ miles are in *italic bold face,* e.g. 25^2

Race summary key

Up to eight running lines are provided for each horse. From left to right, the running line denotes race, date, track, race number, track condition, distance, race condition, finish position, beaten lengths, weight, odds, Thoro-Graph figure, path, and equipment/medication information. All trainer changes, not just claims, are listed.

Summary code key

BAR	Barshoe or aluminum pad worn
bl	Blinkers
f	Front bandages
FC	Front caulks
BC	Back caulks
FBC	Front and back caulks
L	Lasix
B	Bute
N	Nasal strip

Track condition key

gd	Good (dirt or turf)
my	Muddy
sy	Sloppy
wf	Wet-fast
sf	Soft
yl	Yielding

Graph code key

st	Stumbled start or during race
gate	Fractious gate or ran off
op-	Off poorly less than 2 lengths
op	Off poorly ~2 lengths
op+	Off poorly 4 or more
rank	Erratic, buck jumped, jumped shadows
bled	Bled during race
bi bo	Bore in, bore out
T	Big trouble during race
tu	Taken up, steadied, or checked
X	Ran on a dead rail

$	Heavily bet for no obvious reason
!	Buried race faster than appears to public
h?	Horse may not have been extended
h_pace	Unusually fast pace
s_pace	Unusually slow pace
time?	Time of race is in question
•	Change of equipment, trainer, medication, etc. (See race summaries for exact change)
Quit	Stopped — final figure not representative

THE NOVELIST

95 (Mar-12) dk b/ g Old Stories - Piratical (Pirateer)

2iJun03	EMD1	ft	6	1:09:00 CLM10k	5	18	121	23	25³	1w	BL bl1
01Jun03	EMD7	ft	6	1:09:00 CLM12.5k	5	6¾	119	24	14²	1w	BL bl1
				broke slowly, advanced inside, lacked late response							
				trainer change from Feeny, Chuck							
03Nov02	BM2	ft	6	1:11:06 CLM6k	2	¾	117	11.2	7¹	1w	BL bl1
				tracked pace, shifted out 1/4p, came 3wide, led, overhauled							
20Oct02	BM2	ft	6	1:10:48 CLM6k	5	3	117	8.4	9³	2w	BL bl1
				pressed pace, bid 2wide, weakened stretch							
21Sep02	BM9	ft	6	1:09:06 CLM12.5k	2	2½	117	1.7	10¹	2w	BL bl1
				dueled early, jumped stakes into turn, clear, weakened							
30Aug02	BM6	ft	6	1:10:30 ALW30kNW1	7	7¾	116	7.2	15²	2w	BL bl1
				pressed pace between horses, stopped							
14Jul02	SR6	ft	6	1:10:77 STR12.5k	4	3½	122	4.5	10¹	4w	BL bl1
				broke in air, 4 wide turn, rallied belatedly							
09Jun02	SOL10	ft	6	1:10:01 ALW32kNW1	6	8	117	4.9	8¹	2w	BL bl1
				allowed to settle, circled 4wide turn, flattened out							
23May02	BM1	ft	6	1:11:01 ALW32kNW1	2	1	123	3.9	6	4w	BL bl1
				unhurried, saved ground, shifted out upper stretch, came late							
26Apr02	BM2	ft	6	1:10:94 ALW32kNW1	4	2½	119	5.2	6	4w	BL bl1
				stalked leaders, 4wide turn, outfinished							

Trainer Profile

WENZEL, TOM.

Category	Starts	Wins	Win%	ITM	ITM%	ROI
Overall	79	18.2		190	43.9	1.69
4-1 or less	203	56	27.6	114	56.2	1.74
over 4-1 to 10-1	150	18	12.0	96	37.3	1.65
over 10-1	80	5	6.3	20	25.0	1.00
Last 90 days	57	7	13.5	15	28.8	1.35
Sprints	366	63	17.2	160	43.7	1.66
Routes	67	16	23.9	30	44.8	1.84
Dirt (inc off tracks)	424	78	18.4	189	44.6	1.84
Turf	9	1	11.1	1	11.1	1.57
Off tracks (Dirt)	35	4	11.4	17	48.6	1.15
Colts/Geldings	206	35	17.0	81	39.3	1.57
MSW	30	4	16.7	13	43.3	1.25
MCL	212	44	20.8	102	48.1	2.13
CLM	122	12	9.8	51	41.7	1.32
STK	18	2	11.1	5	27.8	0.60
ALW	46	9	19.6	25	54.3	1.32
2-y-o	67	7	10.4	26	38.9	1.89
3-y-o	216	44	20.4	98	45.4	1.51
4-y-o+	17	5	29.4	13	52.9	3.31
Last race 7 days and under	274	47	17.2	122	44.5	1.89
Last race 30-89 days	33	4	12.1	13	39.4	2.18
Last race 90+ days	42	6	14.3	15	35.7	1.59
2nd race off layoff	34	4	11.8	13	38.2	0.57
1st time out of 3-y-o+ (MSW)	9	1	11.1	3	33.3	1.70
1st time out of 3-y-o+ (MCL)	25	4	16.0	9	36.0	1.80
1st race after trainer change	36	9	25.0	17	47.2	2.59

Sire Profile

Category	Horses	Starts	Wins	Win%	ITM	ITM%	SW	TQ
Overall	95	1735	199	11.5	599	34.5	21	21¹
2-y-o	45	187	21	11.2	68	36.4	0	25¹
3-y-o	82	605	72	11.9	210	34.7	0	25²
4-y-o	64	480	52	10.8	163	31.9	0	19²
5-y-o+	51	463	54	11.7	158	36.3	1	16
Dirt	95	1378	166	12.1	474	34.4	0	21²
Off tracks	70	346	32	9.3	120	35.5	1	22²
Turf	8	11	1	9.1	2	18.2	1	15²
1st time turf	8	8	1	12.5	1	12.5	0	16
Over 1M out	34	1451	170	11.7	623	42.9	0	21¹
Less than 1M	58	284	29	10.2	76	26.8	1	23
1st time out	56	95	9	9.4	28	29.5	1	31¹
Fillies/Mares	41	724	68	9.4	238	32.9	1	23
Colts/Geldings	50	1011	131	13.0	361	35.7	20	20

THE NOVELIST

95 (Mar-12) dk b/ g Old Stories - Piratical (Pirateer)

	5-YEAR-OLD	6-YEAR-OLD	7-YEAR-OLD	8-YEAR-OLD
JAN				
FEB				
MAR		GG 12y	GG• 8¹w tu	
APR		GG 9³ wf tu	GG 7	
MAY	EMD 18²	GG 8	BM• 5¹	
JUN		BM 10²	GG• 9² op+	
JUL	EMD 20³	GG 6	GG• vet scratch Mairo□ay	14² op
AUG	EMD 12²wf		GG 8¹	EMD•
			GGG•	
SEP	EMD 23³		BM 6	25²
OCT	EMD 12²		SOL 10	EMD
NOV	EMD 12 tu	SA -12³	SR -10	
	GG• 12y op	BM -7¹	BM 15²⁻	
DEC	GG• 10³	BM• 10²	BM 10¹	
	GG 14²	GG 10²	BM 9³ T	
		GG 6sy op		

Thoro-Graph figures © 2004 by Thoro-Graph, Inc.

Bibliography

Ainslie, Tom, and Bonnie Ledbetter. *The Body Language of Horses.* New York: William Morrow & Co., 1980.

Beyer, Andrew. *Beyer on Speed.* Boston: Houghton Mifflin Co., 1993.
———. *Picking Winners: A Horseplayer's Guide.* Boston: Mariner Books, 1994.
———. *The Winning Horseplayer.* Boston: Houghton Mifflin Co., 1994.

Brohamer, Tom. *Modern Pace Handicapping.* New York: DRF Press, 2000.

Parker, Trillis. *Horses Talk: It Pays to Listen.* Parker Productions, 1989.

Quirin, William. *Winning At The Races: Computer Discoveries in Thoroughbred Racing.* New York: William Morrow & Co., 1978.

Ragozin, Len. *The Odds Must Be Crazy.* New York: Little Brown & Co., 1997.

Acknowledgments

I would like to thank the *Daily Racing Form* for granting permission to use Past Performances and Result Charts, and George Cottrell of the *Daily Racing Form* for his assistance in obtaining those past performances and charts. Also thanks to Thoro-Graph, especially Alan Benewitz, for granting permission to use a Thoro-Graph sheet and offering examples.

Without the significant contribution of others, this book would not exist. I am indebted to Susy So and Kris Fulsas for their suggestions on cuts, additions and/or revisions to an early draft of this book. Thanks to Gary Shore as I borrowed one of his many one-liners in the first sentence of this book. Vital and important contributions were made in editing every page of this book and completion of this book by the staff at Eclipse Press, including Jackie Duke, Judy Marchman, Tom Hall, Rena Baer, Brian Turner, and Russell Johnson. Finally, thanks to my wife Lisa and her father Bob who offered critical assistance in the organization and writing of this book.

The only way I know to thank the horses who give us so much enjoyment is to say, if you also enjoy horse racing and have the ability, please donate to a Thoroughbred retirement fund to insure these animals have a long and happy life after their racing days are over.

About the Author

John Lindley prepares Parker's selection sheet, which has been sold at Emerald Downs in Washington State since 1985. He also provides daily trip and trouble notes to Emerald Downs for distribution around the track and on its website. To help newcomers to the track, he created a pamphlet, *Exotic Wagering Guide.*

Lindley appears regularly on Emerald Downs' weekend radio show, *Win Place and Show,* broadcast on a Seattle sports-talk radio station, and has been a frequent guest on Emerald Downs' daily in-house television show, *Handicapper's Corner.*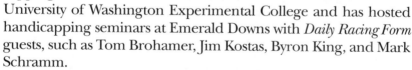

Every year he educates the track's customer service staff on the basics of racing, handicapping, and wagering.

He has taught basic and advanced handicapping classes at Emerald Downs and at the University of Washington Experimental College and has hosted handicapping seminars at Emerald Downs with *Daily Racing Form* guests, such as Tom Brohamer, Jim Kostas, Byron King, and Mark Schramm.

An active owner since 1988, Lindley also manages a partnership that races and breeds Thoroughbreds.

Other Titles from
Eclipse Press

THOROUGHBRED
Legends
SERIES

To order these titles and to subscribe to *The Blood-Horse* magazine visit
ExclusivelyEquine.com or call 800-866-2361.